I0796049

THE COSTUME HOUSE

The Inside Story of Cosprop

'We entered Cosprop as ourselves and walked out as the person we were playing.' – Helena Bonham Carter

THE COSTUME HOUSE

The Inside Story of Cosprop

From *A Room With A View* to *Game of Thrones*

KEITH LODWICK

Yale University Press, New Haven and London
in association with Cosprop

CONTENTS

Preface Dame Judi Dench 6
Foreword Chris Garlick 8

Introduction
HISTORY OF A COSTUME HOUSE 10
60 Years of Cosprop

CHRISTOPHER PRINS 1949–2005 18
An Appreciation by Tom Rand

Chapter One
THE REDESIGN OF THE COSTUME DRAMA 22
1965–1999

Chapter Two
MERCHANT IVORY 54
The Renaissance of the Costume Drama

Chapter Three
THE WORLD OF JANE AUSTEN 86
Designing for the Regency Era

Chapter Four
INSIDE THE COSTUME HOUSE 106
The Workrooms

Chapter Five
MAKING A GOLDEN AGE 142
Television Costume Drama

Chapter Six
RAISING THE CURTAIN 178
Costume for Stage

Chapter Seven
NEW FRONTIERS 190
Cosprop in the Twenty-First Century

Cosprop: Influence and Legacy 222
The Bright Foundation 223
Epilogue 223
Notes 224
Select Productions by John Bright 229
Biographies 230
Acknowledgements 231
Image Credits 232
Index 234

PREFACE

For the many decades I have known John Bright and have been visiting Cosprop for costume fittings, I have always known that I am going to be cared for and nurtured in the most talented way. John is Cosprop and Cosprop is John, everything about the place is touched by his accomplished hand.

And John is the actor's costumier. Through his own training as an actor, he understands how important it is to feel completely comfortable in the clothes you are given to wear in front of the camera or on the stage. He effortlessly knows how to help in the search for the truth in the character that is about to be played and, by some sixth sense, understands how to make the actor relax into the costumes. What's more, the quality of the garments that he and Cosprop produce are exquisite and never fail to delight.

Cosprop is a magical place that is an important part of the nation's rich cultural heritage. It is central to the thriving period costume industry. I believe it must be treasured and celebrated while it is still in the full flush of its success. This book should be essential reading for lovers of costume drama and for aspiring costume designers and makers. The industry as a whole should value this document as a glimpse into what excellence can be achieved in one lifetime, with the right balance of vision and modest ambition.

Dame Judi Dench

(opposite) Eleanor Lavish (Judi Dench) and Charlotte Bartlett (Maggie Smith) in *A Room with a View* (1985)

FOREWORD

To walk into a costume house full to the brim with period clothes is a magical experience. It seems as if every actor who has been dressed there has left their indelible mark and there is a palpable sense of this rich history as you walk through the building. Cosprop is such a place. Entering its elegant reception, you are taken into the plant-filled entrance hall, past the principal actors' fitting rooms, where hundreds of famous bodies have been fitted into corsets, breeches and many layers of finery. Next you encounter the Accessories Room, which resembles a glittering black cave of necklaces, rings, tiaras, handbags and silver-handled canes. From here, you pass cases of costumes on mannequins on the way to the vast warehouse. Every inch of the cavernous space is filled, not only with suits and dresses, but also with every element of clothing and trims required to create period outfits dating from the Middle Ages to the Swinging Sixties. The dozens of rails of costumes housed here are a 60-year labour of love, made by generations of Cospropians under the watchful eye of John Bright or acquired as original pieces.

In the pumping heart of the building are Millinery and Dye Rooms and an Alterations Workroom, all vital parts of the business. In the largest workroom, costume makers and tailors produce a steady stream of garments; one moment making an 1860s' crinoline ball gown, the next a 1920s' flapper dress. By design, there is little evidence of the back-office business activities in the building, and so the overwhelming impression to the visitor is that of creativity and artistry.

John Bright established Cosprop in 1965 as an ambitious 25 year old. Right from the word go, he set the tone of the company with an informal approach to costuming quality period pieces inspired by actual historic clothing. In the years that followed, he hired a number of young costume makers and costumiers who grew their knowledge and practical expertise together. The informality came from youthful enthusiasm and the excitement of working on increasingly prestigious productions. At the same time, a generation of British costume designers were benefiting from a first-class apprenticeship in the large costume departments of the BBC and ITV, tackling projects as diverse as a variety show one week to a 26-part adaptation of a novel by Charles Dickens the next. Many of these designers were of a similar generation to the Cosprop team and working relationships between them flourished and continued for decades.

Cosprop evolved and grew over the decades, never outstripping itself and measuring its growth with the expansion of the stock (costume items that can be used in a number of performances), which is the beating heart of the business. As the company's reputation spread, more costumes were being commissioned by productions, so that most of the new pieces that were added to the stock were paid for by these projects. This financial model gave the company a firm foundation, allowing for the rapid expansion of stock in the 1970s and 1980s.

For John Bright and the Cosprop team, it is important to keep the quality of the garments in the stock at a high level and true to their period. One of the most important aspects of this quality control is to ensure that the best fabrics are chosen: wools, silks, cottons and satins are not replaced by artificial textiles unless there is a very good creative reason to do so. The Cosprop team have been encouraged to become experts at period clothing across the 250 years from 1700 to the 1950s, so that they can expertly advise and support designers to achieve an authentic look. The costumiers are able to dress an actor from head to toe in ensembles truly evocative of their time, using the large collection of historic garments that have been amassed as reference. The costume makers, using these garments, are able to produce work that reflects the different dates of the productions. The techniques used to achieve the effect of historical veracity involves some of the same methods that would have been utilised by seamstresses and tailors in their day, but with a pragmatic use of modern practices.

During the 1980s and 1990s, Bright's career as a costume designer took off and was recognised when he won an Oscar and a BAFTA in 1987 for the Merchant Ivory film adaption of E.M. Forster's novel, *A Room with a View*. This production sparked an interest in Victorian and Edwardian costume more widely, bleeding into the fashion world and everyday culture. The respected association with Merchant Ivory, who produced a splendid series of highly regarded period dramas over a 30-year span, also proved to be a calling card for the company. It effectively represented Cosprop's aim to provide stellar costumes, which had truth and realism, in the recreation of the past in film, television and the theatre.

As the company entered the twenty-first century, a changing world of film and TV production in turn impacted its suppliers and costumiers. With the advent of widespread streaming services, the industry map became more complex. The potential for more series to be made across the ever-expanding platforms was an exciting opportunity, but there was also concern that the high standards led by BBC period dramas, for example, would not be maintained or would be diluted. Likewise, the film industry had to compete or merge into the rich world of the streaming services. With increasing global access to the internet, the tastes of audiences has both diversified and polarised. The range of period productions has grown, with more traditional dramas, such as *Downton Abbey*, being as popular as such shows as *Peaky Blinders* and *Bridgerton*, which introduce contemporary twists. In the film industry, an increasing trend of costume designers setting up their own workrooms – rather than using costumes houses to dress their star principal actors and to help to build up the stock – poses issues for the longevity of all costume houses. The houses are also impacted by the retirement of many of the designers that Cosprop grew up with, who respected and understood the value of what Cosprop has to offer.

Despite these challenges, Cosprop remains at the forefront of the industry, with an authoritative reputation that precedes it. New generations of designers and actors are ever keen to work with John Bright and the skilled Cosprop team, as well as to use the rich bank of stock for their principal cast and crowd scenes. Bright's expertise and unassuming strength of purpose are still a beacon of professionalism, recognised across the media industries. His achievement of balancing the development and creative management of Cosprop as the sole Director, with a successful designing career, is unprecedented. His efforts also extend to lifelong philanthropy and The Bright Foundation, a charity established and funded by him to promote access to and enjoyment of the arts by children and young people, continues to grow with his support and guidance. Bright's remarkable career will be celebrated as long as Cosprop, his spiritual home, flourishes – as it surely will for many years to come.

Chris Garlick
Company Manager, Cosprop

1. The Workroom, Cosprop

KD DAY

HISTORY OF A COSTUME HOUSE

60 Years of Cosprop

'Actors walk in with just a script and the name of their character. They walk out with that character fully formed in their mind, having brought him or her to life through the angle of a hat, the fabric of a coat or the feel of a pair of shoes.'[1] – John Bright

Located on London's Holloway Road, the sign above the entrance to Cosprop reveals little of what lies behind the former garage. Once you enter, the atmosphere is one of calm and serenity. It could be the reception of a spa hotel with its potted plants and classic white Lloyd Loom furniture. The building then becomes a revelatory experience, as it expands further and further to reveal three centuries of dress history.

Cosprop is a place for transformation, for study and research, underpinned by the authority of a museum; it is a home and store for clothing that not only informs us about the past but also has the potential to create something for the future. Characters created at Cosprop have won major awards for costume design, acting and directing; a costume may ignite a global fashion trend, or create a beloved character that is adored worldwide, revisited in film festivals, and even analysed in scholarly appraisal. For 60 years, Cosprop has been managed, organised and curated by John Bright. Through his work as a costume designer, a costumier,[2] maker, advisor, collector and historian, Bright's intelligence and eye for detail is in thousands of film, television and stage productions.

John Bright's interest in acting and the theatre-making process was rooted in childhood. Whilst at school, his mother hired some costumes for a school play from Winifred Hoyle in Brighton, which he recalls 'were basic but nice. I remember an Elizabethan costume and tunic, breeches, cape, hat with feathers, stockings but no shoes, just buckles and bows on elastic to be pulled over one's own lace-ups'.[3] Always curious, he noticed that another boy had a much more resplendent costume, 'I looked inside the costume, the label inside was B.J. Simmons & Co., one of the leading theatrical costumiers in London and it was at this moment that a fascination for costume was born.'[4]

2. (opposite) Rail of costumes in the Stock Room, Cosprop

To further his development, he was sent for elocution lessons and his tutor, after putting him through several acting grades at RADA, introduced Bright to her Amateur Dramatics Society, which performed in Cripplegate Theatre in London. His first play was Dodie Smith's *Dear Octopus*, where he played the young son. He worked on the costumes for other productions including *A Woman of No Importance*, setting up a workroom in the family dining room, which in time housed the beginnings of Cosprop while the conservatory that led off it became a puppet theatre.

After secondary school, Bright's father enrolled him at Southwest Essex Technical College and School of Art (now Waltham Forest College), where he began a fashion course because no theatre course existed near home. 'I was never interested in fashion. It was really an appeasement of my father who was very Victorian. I wanted to be an actor but he wouldn't hear of it. I had to do something that he considered a trade so I enrolled on a four-year course in fashion.'[5] In 1957 he began his course following in the footsteps of former students Ken Russell, film director, and his wife Shirley, a costume designer. He worked alongside Marion Foale and Sally Tuffin, who became important fashion designers in the

1960s and 1970s, and James Wedge, who became a milliner. This specialism in fashion taught Bright the key skills of life drawing and pattern cutting, and the most important thing he learned from the Head of Art School Stuart Ray, who taught life drawing, was to 'look and really see, don't start with the outline, start at the centre.'[6]

Bright's course tutor, Daphne Brooker, was very interested in theatre and took him to see the mainly original collection of music hall clothing at The Players' Theatre in London. Bright used the collection to take patterns and to learn about period clothes. In 1958 Brooker took her students to Paris to see the spring fashion shows; they saw shows at Dior, Givenchy and Chanel against the stunning mirror staircase on the Rue Cambon. The Paris experience, however, put Bright off high-end fashion.

***Apart from the shows, which were quite theatrical, I decided fashion would never work for me in that all the clients seemed ancient and it was all about pandering to rich people which was not that interesting. We visited Clignancourt Market in the north of Paris where I bought some very good period clothes, some still in use today.*[7] – John Bright**

These Parisian purchases formed the genesis of what would become Cosprop.

In 1961 he was introduced to the fashion historian and collector Doris Langley Moore, who was starting a fashion museum in Bath, and he was invited to make some jewellery to display with the clothes. Langley Moore's response to Bright's efforts was that they weren't constructed as they would have been but they gave a good idea of how period jewellery looked. At that same meeting, one of Langley Moore's guests came in and was introduced as the actor Montgomery Clift.

[Clift] *asked about the jewellery – as I handed him the box he said, 'John, this opens up new worlds for me!' This was the first film star I had ever met. He had just finished the filming of Freud, which Doris had designed and now he was staying with her and she said he was drinking her out of house and home.*[8] – John Bright

When Bright's course came to an end, he chose repertory theatre, and the first production of the new season was *Jane Eyre* with Annette Crosbie. Jane Howells, the Director, visited his parents' house and together they designed the costumes, hiring some costumes from Oldham Repertory Theatre to complete the play's design. In 1962 Bright applied for a grant to go to an acting school to learn about costume design from an actor's point of view and he joined a new school, which was an offshoot of the Theatre Workshop at the Theatre Royal Stratford East. There, he found himself involved with several productions including *A Christmas Carol, The Servant of Two Masters* and *Bartholomew Fair*.

During the summer, Bright worked at Regent's Park Theatre to make men's clothes for a production of *Love's Labour's Lost*, designed by David Walker. This led to work at the Chichester Festival Theatre. Bright recalls the privilege of being 'a witness to Laurence Olivier directing his wife Joan Plowright and actors such as John Neville, whose old-school acting style went against the grain for Olivier'.[9] Opportunities continued to present themselves and a spell at the National Youth Theatre at a time when 'Helen Mirren playing Cleopatra left a big impression'.[10] In 1964 John returned to Hornchurch Theatre, this time as the Director's Assistant and Costume Designer. He managed to combine this with some acting with Edward Fox in *Chips with Everything, The Happiest Days of Your Life* and *Henry V*.

In 1965 John Bright was at a crossroads and so, with his savings, he decided to start a costume house with the items he had already accumulated, filling his parents' dining room, along with others he then acquired. He found premises at 77 Gloucester Avenue, Primrose Hill, London and set up shop as a costumier, calling the company Cosprop.

On reflection, it was a risky move perhaps at a time when many of the older costume houses were closing – Samuel's, Fox's and B.J. Simmons had closed in 1964. My vision was for a costume house that was less formal and more flexible in dealing with the ever-increasing demands of television and theatre.[11] – **John Bright**

Bright heard through the grapevine that some collectors had acquired items from the costume houses that had closed but had decided to sell them rather than begin a new costume house of their own. He bought a selection of costumes for £40 at 5 shillings each. His family also donated clothes from the 1920s and 1930s to the growing stock.

On 6 August 1965 Bright took possession of the building, which would be the first home of Cosprop. He lived on the top floor, the shop area became the costume store, workroom and reception, with a second workroom downstairs. Cosprop opened on 18 September 1965. Once Cosprop was open for business, friends and relatives lent support by commissioning Bright to make clothes for them. As work started to come in from theatres such as the Swan Theatre, Worcester, The Queens Theatre, Hornchurch Theatre and Colchester Repertory Theatre, he became self-sufficient within a short period. Every production was an opportunity to obtain more items for the stock, either by purchasing originals, still available in London antique and market places, or by making them in the workroom.

This period of Swinging-Sixties London, which was experiencing a counter-culture revolution in art, film and theatre, contributed to the creative zeitgeist. The work of John Bright and the staff at Cosprop also fuelled a revolution in the design and recreation of historical dress – a revolution that went on to set a new standard and approach to clothes on film. Cosprop developed quickly and a new generation of designers, who were emerging in the 1960s, began to come to Cosprop for research, costume making and advice.

What John Bright created is something of a miracle for costume designers. The museum is an absolute treasure trove and always inspiring, I used Cosprop throughout my career, no matter what period I was working in.[12] – **Anthony Powell, Costume Designer**

In 1966 Cosprop created its inaugural costume for television, Miss Havisham's wedding dress for a BBC adaptation of *Great Expectations* (1967; fig.4), designed by Joyce Hammond. Distinguished stage actor Maxine Audley portrayed Miss Havisham and Estella was played by Francesca Annis, who would continue to have her costumes fitted at Cosprop over her 60-year career.

3. (opposite) John Bright photographed by Christine Hill for *The Stage* magazine, 1975

4. (right) Miss Havisham (Maxine Audley) and Pip (Christopher Guard) in *Great Expectations* (1967; Costume Designer Joyce Hammond)

5. (above) John Bright working on designs for *A Room with a View* (1985)

6. (left) John Bright painting puppets for *The Puppet Maker* (1977)

7. (opposite) Chris Prins and John Bright in a costume fitting with Robert Hardy for *Sense and Sensibility* (1995)

I bought the fabric, a damask material in Camden Town, it was a straightforward construction and we broke it down in rather a crude way, but it was filmed in black and white so it really worked when you saw it on screen.[13] – John Bright

Around 1966 Costume Designer Joan Ellacott, whose career began at the Gainsborough Studios in the 1940s went to Cosprop for help costuming the television series *The Forsyte Saga* (1967), not only a landmark in television programming but the template for the BBC's costume drama format.

Costume Designer David Walker chose to come to Cosprop when he started working on Director Tony Richardson's *The Charge of the Light Brigade* (1968; p.26). The film turned out to be a pivotal moment for the company, 'and it is extraordinary to think that our initiation should have been on such a landmark production'.[14] Cosprop was also growing at a time when television was about to expand in scope and scale. Similar to Hollywood in the 1940s and 1950s when Technicolor begin to surpass black and white, British television in the early 1970s experienced the same process. Cosprop's contribution to the 1970s' costume dramas has also been central to their success and legacy, which paved the way for the first golden age of television.

Once Cosprop was established, the collection expanded rapidly. Bright begin to acquire props to add to costumes for hire and he began to make his own films, including a film about the process of costume design. 'I have always been interested in puppets (fig.6); this has to do with a fascination with scale. The ability to create and control a complete environment, and a way of acting without having to be on stage oneself.'[15] Bright's film *The Puppet Maker* (1977) is a fairytale, filmed in North London and at Castle Neuschwanstein (the castle that inspired Disney) in Germany. Actors included Jan Francis, known for her work in *Secret Army* (1977) and *Dracula* (1979), and Jo Kendall, who also appeared in *Howards End* (1992; p.75) and *The Remains of the Day* (1993; p.80). Christine Hill, former Company Manager, recalls making and filming Bright's puppet films:

John has always been remarkably intuitive at being able to discover talents in people, encouraging them to develop their strengths and generously allowing them to make mistakes along the way. I was Cosprop's first Company Manager in 1975, and having had a photo exhibition at the Pentax Gallery in London, John asked me to help him make his films. He had many stories in his head, from writing the scripts to designing the sets and costumes. We made three films:* Costume, The Puppet Maker *and* Say Beau, *which was screened at the Belfast Film Festival. John's legendary attention to detail was applied to making the puppets, their costumes and the sets.[16]

For more than 30 years, Christopher Prins was the Head of Men's Wardrobe at Cosprop and he organised and supervised the men's stock, fitted actors and found the perfect clothing to create each new character to the designer's concept. Company Manager Chris Garlick notes that Prins worked alongside Bright building up the men's costumes: 'Together they

developed a stock of genuine and reproduction costumes into a stylistically consistent collection of outfits.'[17]

Prins's contribution has never left the Cosprop DNA, as many costume designers reflect,

Chris was more than a master of his craft, he was a magician. His knowledge of Cosprop's stock and his sense of the period was outstanding. His ability to understand not just the character we were creating but the actors wearing the clothes and the designer whose work he was interpreting set him apart. He was an excellent psychologist with an extraordinary gift for reading people. It was like spending an afternoon with friends in a great big dressing-up box.[18] – Elizabeth Waller, Costume Designer

Over its history, Cosprop has witnessed the shift from film production to television programming in the 1970s; the renaissance of the costume drama in the 1980s; a revival of film production in the 2000s and a second golden age of television in the twenty-first century. Cosprop has also experienced the transition from analogue to digital filmmaking, which had a major impact on costume design. Through all these changes in technology and audience taste, Cosprop has continued its creative momentum whilst remaining true to its core purpose: to develop a more authentic style of costume based upon genuine historic clothing. Costume Designer Jacqueline Durran has said, 'It's important to think about what John instigated in 1965. What John gave his name to is the idea of authenticity and he has been one of the main protagonists in this movement, he is a pioneer.'[19]

We owe a great debt to John Bright, who revolutionised the whole world of period design. The tradition had been to make

clothes from new materials but John went back to the source and collected original pieces and used them to recreate a true sense of the period.[20] – **James Acheson, Costume Designer**

Cosprop has continued to grow and expand in numerous creative directions: it holds a vast stock of costumes and accessories; it is a museum and an archive for researchers; and it is a workshop that cultivates artisanal craft of the highest calibre. Cosprop's original remit was to specialise in costumes covering 1700 to 1945, but the business has developed to cover any time in history including fantasy, such as *Game of Thrones* (2011–19; Costume Designer Michele Clapton; p.164). The Elizabethan era has become a particular strength of the company, with work on major films including *Elizabeth* (1998; Costume Designer Alexandra Byrne; p.46), *The Other Boleyn Girl* (2008; Costume Designer Sandy Powell) and *Anonymous* (2011; Costume Designer Lisy Christl).

Costume houses exist all over the globe serving the film, television and theatre industries, and Cosprop holds a special place in the heart of costume designers and makers. Similar to an atelier or a fashion house, Cosprop has developed a 'house style'. Under the expert eye of Bright and his superb team of costumiers, makers, dyers and milliners, the different rooms in the costume house collaborate to create each new character to the costume designer's vision.

With Bright at the heart of the organisation, he has had input, at some level, into every production that has passed through the company's history. In the costume workflow, there is not one element that Bright has not advised on – research, recreation, fabric choice, dyeing, stock, trim, fitting and finishing. This work has been in parallel with his career as an Oscar- and BAFTA-winning costume designer. As both a costume designer and a costumier, John Bright occupies an extraordinary and unique place in the history of British stage and screen.

Every day, the staff at Cosprop weave in and out of the different workrooms, each with their own unique specialities, working together in the creation of new clothing narratives. This process is largely verbal, with thoughts and ideas expressed and exchanged between design and realisation. Whilst makers maintain a workbook capturing the design brief, measurements and other essential information, the practice of creating costume is a handcrafted method.

Cosprop offers a complete look to a film. Most films are costumed and made by different costume houses – some productions are so large, it's the nature of the industry, but the Merchant Ivory films and projects such as **The Portrait of a Lady** ***were all done by us, and that's what gives a film a very strong, unified visual look.***[21] – **Nancy Knapp, Head of the Workroom**

Up until the mid-1960s, period films tended to reflect the era in which they were designed. Bright's vision for Cosprop was to move costume design away from the fashion of the period it was created, and towards a more truthful recreation of the past, while observing a focus on storytelling and character. Susie de Broë-Ferguson-Hanbury, Womenswear

8. (left) John Bright, May Koenraads and Cosprop staff celebrating the Oscar win for *A Room with a View* (1985)

9. (opposite, above) John Bright in conversation with Keith Lodwick, 22 February 2024, Victoria and Albert Museum, London

10. (opposite, below) John Bright at the Victoria and Albert Museum, London, 2024

Costumier from 1971 to 1981, has said 'Cosprop's reputation was built on social realism, the main reason why I wanted to go and work with John.'[22]

The reality of period and of character, that is Cosprop's strength. They have been hugely responsible for period clothing being so much more real than it was before.[23] – **Tom Rand, Costume Designer**

Actors also relished the opportunity to work with a more authentic approach to the creation of their characters' clothing.

John and Jenny [Beavan] created wardrobes for people, they didn't create costumes as we might think of them. There was history in every item of clothing and this design process really helped us as actors.[24] – **Helena Bonham Carter**

Characters and their clothes – the two are intertwined – have the power to live on in the audience's imagination, and some of the most indelible images of cinema and television from the past 60 years have been designed and created at Cosprop. Lucy Honeychurch (Helena Bonham Carter) being kissed on a hill overlooking Florence in *A Room with a View*; Ruth Wilcox (Vanessa Redgrave) strolling through her country garden in *Howards End*; Mr Darcy (Colin Firth) emerging from a lake in *Pride and Prejudice*; Captain Jack Sparrow (Johnny Depp) swaggering on his ship in *Pirates of the Caribbean*; the imperious Dowager Countess (Maggie Smith) in *Downton Abbey* and streetwise Tommy Shelby (Cillian Murphy) in *Peaky Blinders*, all exemplify costume design that has inspired high-street fashion and a million imitations. These characters have influenced

generations of costume designers, filmmakers, dress historians and fans of film and television around the world.

In the twenty-first century, Cosprop thrives because of its exceptional quality and authenticity. Ultra-high-definition cameras used in filmmaking and televisions in most homes scrutinise the visual image like never before; we can see every single stitch of Cosprop's creations. From its beginnings in 1965 in a tiny flat in London to a flourishing business today, containing more than a million items, Cosprop continues to create characters for future narratives, beloved the world over.

CHRISTOPHER PRINS 1949–2005

An Appreciation by Tom Rand

'The best of all costumiers.' – *John Gielgud*

'He was matchless. A master artist' – *Edward Fox*

For 34 years the lead costumier of the Men's Costume Department was Christopher Prins. For many of those years he was the man in charge, except of course for John Bright. In those early years of the company, everyone did something of everything. It was in the very best meaning of the words 'homemade'. It was impossible to tell where one person's work began and someone else had taken over. Costume makers would trim hats if time was short, milliners would make petticoats, and everyone would pack boxes. At the centre of it was Chris, he was never shy of hard work and long hours.

When Chris joined Cosprop in 1971, aged 22, the company had only been going for six years, but John Bright had already built up a remarkable collection of original clothes and worked tirelessly interpreting them. At that time, it was possible, if you looked carefully and as hard as John Bright did, to find special clothes from collectors or antique dealers. In some respects, it was a more innocent time and before the age of terms such as 'vintage' and 'retro', words we didn't use.

At that time, there were many other costume houses in London, mostly in London's West End, all had dressmaking and tailoring departments and most had huge stock built up over decades. Some were beautifully organised and the stock was well cared for, some were not.

Cosprop was not only new, but it was also radically different. The emphasis was not just on quality, right from the beginning, the aim was for authentic clothes of whichever period, not for generalised 'costumes'. Chris, as young as he was, fitted into this philosophy and work ethic. He found his professional home and for those often long hours, it was home.

The year that Chris joined Cosprop saw the release of one of the most significant films made for lovers of perfect costume design, Luciano Visconti's *Death in Venice*, designed by Piero Tosi. The film became a template for many designers and had a huge influence on the characterisation of all the clothes. The beauty and poetry of the work was something very new and visionary for many of us, the film was a huge inspiration for Chris.

Throughout the 1970s, the work that Cosprop did was on television productions of classic serials, adaptations of Dickens, Austen, Thackeray and Trollope. Using a lot of original clothes and faithfully made reproductions to detailed and well-researched designs, enabled Cosprop to build up an excellent and authentic-looking stock of both men's and women's costumes.

There were a number of excellent costumiers in the Womenswear Department, including Susie de Broë-Ferguson-Hanbury and Jane Smith, whose expertise and professionalism and sense of humour were valued by Chris. In the Men's Department, Chris was aided by Kevin Lawley. All members of the workrooms hugely respected and admired Chris, however exacting he could be.

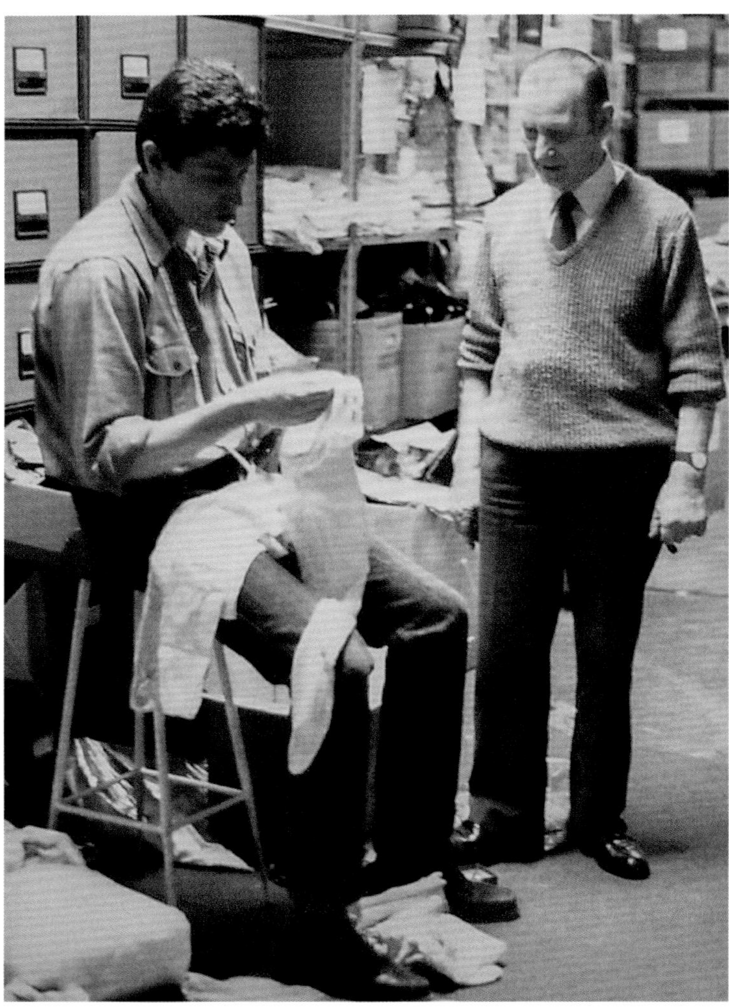

11. Christopher Prins and George Wright, Caretaker, Cosprop, mid-1970s

Chris was central to the build up of the men's stock. One of the tailors in the early years had little patience with indecisive actors or designers. His work was excellent but it was Chris who smoothed the pathway. Eddie Mogil wasn't interested in the storyline, his concern was in the fit of the suit and the length of the sleeve. He wasn't impressed if the actor was a knight and had fifty years' experience or had just won an Oscar, what was his inside leg measurement and had he got a dropped shoulder?

Chris's skill in fitting was finessed and honed during those early years and he learned a lot from John. To watch Chris fitting a suit or a jacket onto an actor was fascinating as he almost hypnotised the fabric to mould naturally around a shoulder and hug the contours of a body.

A large proportion of the stock at Cosprop is from the years between 1840 and 1940. During those 100 years most men's civilian clothing of all classes was in a very limited colour palette: black, grey, navy and dark brown. There were specific summer weight and light-coloured clothes for the wealthy but otherwise dark and sombre was the norm. Chris had an extraordinary visual memory for items in his stock.

In 1995 I was asked to design the costumes for a new play by Ronald Harwood called *Taking Sides*, directed by Harold Pinter. Set just after the end of the Second World War in occupied ruined Berlin, it concerned the accusations of being a Nazi collaborator against the orchestral conductor Wilhelm Furtwängler. The play was a character study of mostly men and about the role of the artist in war. It was a perfect job for Chris, especially as I knew of his love of classical music. When I discussed the project with him, he asked who was to be playing Furtwängler and when I told him Daniel Massey, his face fell.

Years earlier, Cosprop had dressed a West End revival of a play set in the 1890s in which Daniel had a leading part. In those days, West End theatres had 'dress parades' in which the actors walked onto a bare stage with unhelpful lighting, and whoever felt they had something to contribute would say what they thought about 'the dresses'. As Daniel walked forward, he made the comment 'when I bend my knee the trousers crease', Chris, sitting in the stalls, called out 'well, don't bend your knee'. After that, Chris was banished and hadn't fitted Daniel since.

I talked to Daniel about the play *Taking Sides* and he agreed to come to Cosprop. Daniel, Chris and I spoke amicably about Furtwängler and I showed them my research. The play was set in a cold Berlin winter, so a coat was needed. Chris and I looked through the rails of 1930s' coats and he pulled one out, a rather sad, long, faded black, almost navy, and almost green with age with a droopy Astrakhan collar, which had seen better days. In the fitting room, Daniel put it on, looked in the mirror and started to cry, we all did. In the mirror, staring back at us, was Wilhelm Furtwängler. It was perfect and Chris had known the exact coat.

The play started in Chichester and transferred to the West End and then, in another production without my involvement and a different cast apart from Daniel, had success on Broadway. Daniel had the coat written into his contract.

12. Christopher Prins in a costume fitting with Toby Stephens for *Onegin* (1999)

The feature films of Merchant Ivory played a significant part in the Cosprop story from *The Europeans* (1979; p.38) to *The White Countess* (2005; p.202). For more than a dozen of those films, Chris was central to the costuming of the actors. Most of the films were set during the nineteenth century and up to the start of the Second World War. The partnership of Jenny Beavan and John Bright designed most of these films to great acclaim. Chris loved working on those films and frequently with the same group of actors each time.

Many of those actors started out as young unknowns and became major film stars, always perfectly dressed by Chris. He watched their development with huge interest and pride. As young actors became used to the costuming process with Chris, they began to realise that getting the externals right at an early stage meant that the character could develop and become more real once filming begins. So often a costume fitting is the first time that an actor thinks about who it is they are going to play.

Chris was the perfect, kind, understanding guide to an actor. He was a modest man and had a remarkable way of fading into the background in a fitting room; considering he was 6 foot 4" tall, it wasn't easy when a fitting room isn't big. He never wanted to be the star of the show, but he knew his worth which was immense and unique. He loved that magical moment when, after a lot of work and coaxing, the character appears in the mirror, steps through the glass, into the fitting room and into life.

What made Chris special? Most certainly his experience of working on so many productions over such a long career and with so many different designers and being able to switch from one job to another. He had an understanding and love of actors, designers and costume itself and the perfect combination of what all those elements could achieve, with himself a hidden master of ceremonies. He loved the combination of character, period cut and fabric and he loved people. He will always be a valued part of the history of Cosprop and will continue to be missed by all who had the privilege and pleasure of working with him. As one designer so aptly said, he really was, 'Chris Prins, Prince of Costumes'.

I can clearly remember my first ever fitting with Chris Prins [who] set the bar of care and excellence so high it was impossible for others to reach. He fitted me for so many roles, including **Poirot*****, and I recall his absolute dedication to detail. He would put an article of clothing on me and before I could respond, it had disappeared – 'Rubbish!' he would say. He would listen intently to me talking about the character I was being fitted for and at the end of our session I would leave Cosprop knowing that my clothes expressed the character perfectly, with his input and his addition of little extras, such as a tie pin. Every time I enter Cosprop I remember him with my heart full of gratitude and great affection.***
– David Suchet

Tom Rand is an Oscar- and BAFTA-nominated costume designer for stage and screen

13. (opposite, from left) Mackenzie Crook, Kevin McNally, Johnny Depp, Jack Davenport, Tom Hollander

The cast of *The Pirates of the Caribbean* hope to 'make the wall' of Christopher Prins's photographs. The sign and photograph was instigated by Tom Hollander

14. (right) Many actors appreciated Christopher Prins's work, including from top left: Tom Cruise (for *Far and Away*), Sean Connery (for *The League of Extraordinary Gentlemen*), Hugh Bonneville (for *Daniel Deronda*), Christopher Reeve (for *The Bostonians*), Albert Finney (for *The Gathering Storm*) and Ralph Fiennes (for many projects, including *Onegin*)

CHAPTER ONE

THE REDESIGN OF THE COSTUME DRAMA

1965–1999

As the British film industry developed in the 1960s, a new design aesthetic was being established. The dominance of the Hollywood studio system was coming to an end and as global film markets had opened up, especially from Europe, a new realism was emerging in all aspects of film design.

The British kitchen-sink dramas of the 1950s and 1960s had seen a seismic shift from the post-war comedies of manners and with that movement, costume designers began to strive for authenticity. Whilst the contemporary dramas continued to reflect a post-war Britain in transition, the period films being produced in Europe began a new era led by directors such as Luchino Visconti and designers Lila De Nobili and Piero Tosi.

This movement was partially influenced by one of the most significant films of the 1960s, *The Leopard* (1963). Set in 1860s' Sicily, *The Leopard* was a landmark for costume and period production design.

Piero Tosi is regularly acclaimed as the most influential designer of his time. His work was not only visually alluring but historically accurate. *The Leopard* was followed by the haunting *Death in Venice* (1971), set on the Venetian Lido in 1912 and the opulent *Ludwig* (1973) set in 1860s' Germany, all making an indelible impression on the way that design was conceived in period film. Tosi was one of the first designers to use original clothing in his work, period narratives were not treated as 'window dressing'[1] but costume was designed to 'mirror personality and enable the actor to bring someone to life.'[2] This approach appealed to the new generation of 1960s' designers.

In 1965 John Bright was at the centre of this shift and his work and practice would move costume design into a new direction, which created a quiet revolution in the process.

'The 1960s were a new era for costume. We were all inspired by *The Leopard,* it opened in London around 1964, and it was so fresh in our minds. We were all talking about it. It still holds together in an extraordinary way. It is one of my favourite films.'[3] – John Bright

15. (opposite) Tess Durbeyfield (Nastassja Kinski) in *Tess* (1979)

16. (right) *The Leopard* (1963; Costume Designer Piero Tosi)

The Charge of the Light Brigade (1968)

Director Tony Richardson | Costume Designer David Walker, Design Consultant Lila De Nobili
Starring David Hemmings, Vanessa Redgrave, John Gielgud, Trevor Howard, Jill Bennett

The Charge of the Light Brigade brought together a distinguished group of filmmakers to realise 1850s' Victorian London and one of the most infamous battles in British military history. Bright recalls 'it was one of our first major film projects with an amazing group of designers'.[4]

Theatre and film director Tony Richardson approached *The Charge of the Light Brigade* with the same social realism that he had applied to *Look Back in Anger* (1959) and *A Taste of Honey* (1961), which had established the New Wave dramas that had dominated British film and theatre since the late 1950s. His film version of *Tom Jones* won the 1964 Oscar for Best Picture.

Bright had worked with Richardson at the Royal Court Theatre on *Luther* (1961) starring Albert Finney.

Richardson recognised the importance of designers in the creative process, 'designers are the great unsung and underpaid heroes of the theatre. They work longer and more conscientiously, need more background and have more responsibility than anyone else'.[5] For *The Charge of the Light Brigade*, he assembled an eminent production and costume design team to recreate the different hierarchies of military and societal clothing of the early 1850s.

Leading the design team was Lila De Nobili (art direction) and David Walker (costumes). De Nobili's painterly skill was applied across the film's colour palette and was especially evocative in the scenes set in the East End, when military recruitment takes place in the squalid back streets of Victorian London.

Julia Trevelyan Oman, one of the most respected designers of the era was brought on as Associate Art Director and John Mollo, in his first film credit, acted as military uniform advisor. Mollo spent two years building an image library of paintings, early photographs, *Punch* cartoons and lithographs that were fed into the creation of 3,500 military costumes, which were all created by the London costume house Nathan's.

David Walker was assigned the civilian scenes capturing the textures and silhouettes of pre-Crimean War London society, and he asked John Bright to provide some of the period clothes. A major wedding and ballroom scene required early 1850s' gowns for the principals and for more than 200 extras. Bright understood Walker's approach:

David was strongly influenced by Lila de Nobili, as many designers of that generation were. Lila had designed for Franco Zeffirelli. David's drawings are works of art; whilst he was at college, one of his teachers was Doris Zinkeisen, another brilliant stage designer. David was hugely influenced by her work as a sketch artist, designer and painter.[6]

Working from Walker's sketches (fig.17), Bright created clothes for Helen Cherry and Rachel Kempson, and her two granddaughters making their film debuts: Natasha and Joely Richardson (daughters of Tony Richardson). The scale of the production required an intense period of making for Bright and his small team at Cosprop.

There was so much to do that I had to make a dress in an extended day. I created the bodice in the morning when I was most awake, the skirt in the afternoon and the trimmings and finishing in the evening so it was a 12- to 16-hour day. The petticoats, the way that David thought we should do them, took ages to create, they each had five frills. There were only a couple of people at Cosprop in those days, so we did everything.[7] – **John Bright**

Richardson insisted on realism for every aspect of the film's production and the actors playing the soldiers were requested to grow beards and moustaches. They were given images of illustrations, paintings and fashion plates of the period to match their facial hair exactly to the period. These details, along with the scholarship and accuracy in the period clothing, were part of a new movement in filmmaking, which did not go unnoticed by film critics when the film was released in 1968. Vincent Canby wrote in *The New York Times*, 'the costumes look like clothes washed and worn in a pre-detergent era (fig.18)'.[8]

For John Bright and his developing costume house, the film was a vision of things to come: recreating historically accurate clothing for the film's characters. David Walker received a BAFTA nomination for Best Costume Design for his work. His approach, alongside Bright's contribution, was to begin the shift towards realism in clothing to enable actors not only to become the people they were portraying but also to authentically ground the narrative in a correct time and place.

Throughout the 1960s, Bright and the Cosprop workforce continued to work on a range of film, theatre and television projects. In 1969 the BBC began transitioning from black-and-white to colour broadcasting. There was also improvement in technical equipment, camera mobility and lighting. Costume designers responded to these visual changes with skill and adaptability. Whilst testing costumes before filming begins is standard in the industry, colour balance is part of the costume design process as Bright reflects, 'there were certain colours you just couldn't use, like cerise and certain blues, you still can't use them actually. Those challenges have resurged in the digital era'.[9]

While television became a growing new creative medium for designers, by the beginning of the 1970s, the British film industry was in decline. Producers turned to successful television sitcoms and adapted them into feature films to lure audiences back into cinemas. Film directors such as Ken Russell and Nicolas Roeg emerged during this period, as did directors of television commercials who wanted to transition into film, one of the first being Ridley Scott.

17. (opposite) Costume design by David Walker for *The Charge of the Light Brigade* (1968)

18. (below) Scene from *The Charge of the Light Brigade* (1968)

The Duellists (1977)

Director by Ridley Scott | Costume Designer Tom Rand
Starring Harvey Keitel, Keith Carradine, Diana Quick, Edward Fox, Jenny Runacre

Tom Rand's first major film as a costume designer was Ridley Scott's debut film *The Duellists* (1977). Rand began working with Cosprop in 1969, 'after working in theatre, I went to the BBC but I disliked it. I started designing commercials and began to visit Cosprop. I did a commercial for Babycham and it was set in a ball in the 1830s. Lots of money was spent on commercials then!'[10]

The duellists of the title were played by Harvey Keitel and Keith Carradine. Tom Rand's research process was based on the drawings of Jean-Auguste-Dominique Ingres, 'which told you everything about the period.'[11] Colour differentiation was also a signifier for the two title roles (fig.20).

Because the two main characters are rivals, it was important that the colouring was immediately clear to the audience ... costume is a way of helping the actor to become this other person, that's what the costume designer does, find characteristics in clothes that express to the audience and to the actor who this other person is.[12] – Tom Rand

Cosprop provided him with a rich palette of historic clothing to draw from: 'A huge portion of the Cosprop stock is real period clothing, some has become reference now but back in the 1970s we used that stock. I would talk to John and Chris really early on when I was beginning a project to ensure they were involved and to sound out what stock was available from the period I was working in.'[13]

The Napoleonic timeframe required specific uniforms that were created at costume house Costumi d'Arte (founded in 1815 by former soldier Angelo Pignotti, in Rome).

For the uniforms, I did all my own research from books, not difficult as there are so many about Napoleon's Army and because they are uniforms, there are rules to follow. The main help I got was from Ruggero Peruzzi in Rome [owner of Costumi d'Arte and a descendent of founder Angelo Pignotti] *who made all the uniforms. They were brilliant and taught me everything I needed to know.*[14] – Tom Rand

When the film was released, it won the Best Debut Award at the Cannes Film Festival and Tom Rand was widely lauded for his historically authentic costumes, which earned him a BAFTA nomination.

19. (left) Publicity poster for *The Duellists* (1977)

20. (opposite) Armand d'Hubert (Keith Carradine), Mme de Lionne (Jenny Runacre) and Gabriel Feraud (Harvey Keitel) in *The Duellists* (1977)

'I chose a silver-grey colour for Keith Carradine because it seemed more refined and more inherently elegant. Carradine is tall and slim and carries clothes well. Harvey Keitel is more pugnacious, a much more aggressive human being. I chose a green and a very hot cerise colour, it had a more animal quality to it.'[15] – Tom Rand

Tess (1979)

Director Roman Polanski | Costume Designer Anthony Powell, Costume Design Assistant Joanna Johnston
Starring Nastassja Kinski, Peter Firth, Leigh Lawson, John Collin

Anthony Powell began his career working in theatre and assisted two of the most important costume designers of the twentieth century: Oliver Messel and Cecil Beaton. In the mid-1960s, Powell emerged as one of the leading designers of his generation and won his first Oscar for his costumes for *Travels with My Aunt* (1972) starring Maggie Smith. Powell began working on *Tess* in 1978 when producer Timothy Burrill introduced him to director Roman Polanski. Powell's research was meticulous although challenging as the designer recalled:

***At that time in the 1970s, practically no research material had been published on nineteenth-century English rural life. I assembled an enormous collection of pictorial research, from junk shops, of original sepia photographs of the period, especially the carte de visite pictures that everyone had taken, which depict with absolute accuracy the way that real people actually dressed and looked and held themselves as opposed to the idealised images in fashion magazines* (fig.21).**[16] – **Anthony Powell**

Costume Designer Joanna Johnston recalls, 'Anthony and I visited a museum on rural life and we discovered in this period that some female farm workers wore pattens over their shoes, which raised them above the mud. Anthony was inspired by this and we recreated them.'[17]

21 & 22. (below, left and right) Costume designs by Anthony Powell for *Tess* (1979)

23. (opposite) Costume for Tess (Nastassja Kinski) in *Tess* (1979)

Powell approached John Bright to work on the film having known him since the late 1950s. Bright recalls Powell spending research time in the museum collection at Cosprop, 'We had an original 1870s' pale blue silk dress with a diagonal rib, he was really fixed on that and it became the wedding dress. Anthony liked this costume so much, that he used it again later on when he designed *Miss Potter* (2006) because it was a similar period.'[18]

Tess was one of the productions that brought out the best in what we could do. Anthony researched every detail of a historical period to ensure accuracy. We discussed the spacing of the buttons on the bodices, and the scale of where they were set, because in the 1870s they were large. When you go into the 1880s, they become smaller and in greater quantity.[19] – **John Bright**

Inspired by the sepia-tone photographs he had collated and the Cosprop historic collection, Powell drew all the costume designs for this production on brown paper and card (figs 21, 22, 24). He also assembled a collection of images of men's and women's hairstyles from the era. Powell's theatre training meant he knew how to create the whole character – from clothing to hair – to form an entirely authentic 1880s' person.

All of Powell's extensive research and design material was presented to Roman Polanski in France, where the film was going to be made. In an early scene depicting May Day, the women in the village dance in their best clothing. Knowing this would span all generations, Powell dressed each woman in the correct period for their age, spanning 50 years of costuming.

Throughout the film I used only the paler tones – ones that registered as whites and off-whites or tones of browns, greys and greens that one finds in nature, so that the characters became an intrinsic part of the landscape. I saved the only use of strong colour until the very end of the film, when Tess has murdered her lover, and suddenly she appears in a travelling outfit that is the colour of dried dark blood red. It comes as a visual shock and that is the dress that most people remember.[20] – **Anthony Powell**

At Cosprop, Jill Harbutt worked on Tess's costumes, while the hats were made by milliner Lil Scott.

When Tess is living with Alec d'Urberville, she moved from country clothes into a higher standard of living. I made a costume for the moment when Angel Clare comes to try and reconcile with her. It was a peignoir with a beautifully embroidered finish and had a peach collar and was very delicate. Anthony added a swansdown collar to give her an aristocratic edge.[21] – **Jill Harbutt, Costume Maker**

Anthony Powell won his third Oscar for Best Costume Design for *Tess* and the film was internationally acclaimed.

'The clothes that Anthony designed for *Tess* were anchored in authenticity. He did the most incredible research on rural life and clothing during later nineteenth-century England. But, as ever, he knew exactly how and where to give clothing cinematic value and elevation and this was his trump card.'[22] – Joanna Johnston

24. (left) Costume for Tess (Nastassja Kinski) in *Tess* (1979)

25. (opposite) Costume for Tess (Nastassja Kinski) in *Tess* (1979)

The French Lieutenant's Woman (1981)

Director Karel Reisz | Costume Designer Tom Rand
Starring Meryl Streep, Jeremy Irons, Lynsey Baxter, David Warner, Leo McKern, Hilton McRae, Penelope Wilton

Tom Rand continued a long association with Cosprop when he began working on *The French Lieutenant's Woman*, starring Meryl Streep and Jeremy Irons. 'When the director of the film – Karel Reisz – and I would meet to talk about the costumes, which we did during pre-production at least once a week, Karel would never ever speak about how a character should look. I believe that costume design is not about designing costumes – it is about telling stories and helping to create characters.'[23]

The film's title character was Sarah Woodruff (Meryl Streep). Interpreting John Fowles's text was also crucial to the designer, as he recalls,

***In the book, Sarah is described as wearing 'a black, male, military coat'. Karel described Sarah as a woman who aimed to make herself more interesting and mysterious than she actually is. From those words grew the idea of a garment that she could hide or partially hide her face and her body* (fig.27)*, that would move and had a feeling of drama, of self-dramatisation. Not solid, not male, not severe, not black. The cloak is dark green with some brown in the dye and some ombré, the colour of nature.*[24] – Tom Rand**

Another influence for the film were the paintings of the Pre-Raphaelites, 'Meryl revealed to us that her own mother had been a redhead. During fittings Meryl never looked in the mirror, she only felt the fabric and tested the movement of the costumes'. Rand reflects that in films, the costume designer is often the first person that the actor meets, because of the lack of rehearsal. The costume designer often 'helps tell the actor what sort of character they are playing'.[25]

The fitting process at Cosprop was an essential part of the costume design process as Rand recalls, 'John has this amazing ability; you could say to John something about a collar from some dress that you seen decades ago and John would know exactly what you meant. He has an index system in his head unlike anyone else I've ever known. At the end of the fitting with John and Chris, when you'd done really well and the actor was standing wearing something that everyone felt was good, John would say "this is you", and he'd leave the fitting

26. (above) Publicity poster for *The French Lieutenant's Woman* (1981)

27. (opposite) Costume for Sarah Woodruff (Meryl Streep) in *The French Lieutenant's Woman* (1981)

'This woman was constrained in every way, physically, emotionally, artistically, in terms of her gender, in terms of the time in which she lived, her poverty, her class, everything. Tom decided that she would have one dress, pretty much. Like people did, I think, much more than now. You had one very good dress, it was very well-made and could stand up.'[26] – Meryl Streep

'I remember one afternoon at about 4pm, John presenting me with a length of still damp moss green wool (it had just been dyed) and asked me to cut a three-quarter circle cape for a fitting the next morning. It turned out it was for Meryl Streep.'[27] – Susan Hardy, Costume Maker

and I always liked that, he summed it up in a few words ... John Bright, Chris Prins and the staff at Cosprop have been in the forefront of a movement ... period costume being so much better than before.'[28]

***Chris [Prins] was a brilliant man. I knew him at another costume house Bermans, which no longer exists. On any film, there are usually more men than women to dress so his involvement was absolutely crucial. During a fitting with an actor you could say something to Chris, and he would disappear and come back with something that fulfilled the words that you had said.*[29] – Tom Rand**

Jeremy Irons's suits for the film were cut by Eddie Mogil and Streep's woollen dress and cape were dyed by Mathilde Sandberg. The dress was made by Mary Wing, the cape by Susan Hardy. The material for Lynsey Baxter's vividly checked dress, worn whilst she is practising her archery, came from Murray Arbeid, the couturier and fashion designer who made clothes for Princess Diana. For the clothes for the modern-day story, Rand and Streep shopped together for Anna's wardrobe and Irons wore some of Rand's own Missoni jumpers.

The image of Sarah on the Lyme Regis cobb, wearing a deep green billowing cape and hood, buffeted by the wind, became not only the key marketing image of the film but one of the most enduring images in British 1980s' cinema. The film established Streep's position as one of the leading actors of her generation.

28. Sarah Woodruff (Meryl Streep) in *The French Lieutenant's Woman* (1981)

Out of Africa (1985)

Director Sydney Pollack | Costume Designer Milena Canonero
Starring Meryl Streep, Robert Redford, Klaus Maria Brandauer

The romantic epic *Out of Africa* reunited Meryl Streep with Cosprop. The film, costumed by Italian designer Milena Canonero, charts a 20-year narrative span for writer Karen Blixen (who wrote under the nom de plume Isak Dinesen), and encompasses costumes worn by the film's African tribes, safari hunters and European aristocrats. The brief was to create a wardrobe for Karen Blixen's life, which stretched from Denmark to Kenya.

Canonero went to Denmark where Blixen's archive is held, and met with her nieces and nephews, who supplied photographs for her to study. The designer was given an item from Blixen's own wardrobe, which she used for the film – a gold pin that Blixen wore with a riding habit.

Blixen's archive and letters assisted the designer in creating the wardrobe.

She makes reference to clothes she had shipped from Paris. She said in one letter she wore a white suit to her wedding. I'm sure she had a very simple suit, but I wanted to make a little more of it. I decided to make it very French, à la mode'.[30] – **Milena Canonero**

I created the wedding suit for Out of Africa, *it was based on an illustration which Milena provided. It evolved in an organic way to the finished costume.*[31] – **Susan Hardy, Costume Maker**

Once Streep's wardrobe was created at Cosprop, the fitting process involved Bright travelling to the United States:

I went to New York with Milena and we stayed at the Mayflower Hotel, no longer a hotel today. I took 65 costumes and over two days, we fitted 45. Meryl worked from 10am until 6pm, then she went to say goodnight to her children. The Mayflower Hotel was marvellous for fittings, because you had lots of space and lots of mirrors.[32] – **John Bright**

The impact of the film's costume design was almost immediate on the fashion industry. Designers like Ralph Lauren, Donna Karan, Michael Kors, Yves Saint Laurent and Thierry Mugler all used the costume design as inspiration for their collections after the film's release. Canonero reflected, 'it was as though the fashion world was ready for the styles of the film; the costumes just caught something that was in the air'.[33]

Canonero discovered Blixen often referred to a love of hats. 'The haberdashery in *Out of Africa* was spectacular. It does something to you, wearing a hat. There were working clothes and clothes of high style, she [Karen] thought of herself in a certain way and [this] manifested [itself] in the clothes.'[34]
– Meryl Streep

29. Karen Blixen (Meryl Streep) in *Out of Africa* (1985)

Dangerous Liaisons (1988)

Director Stephen Frears | Costume Designer James Acheson
Starring Glenn Close, John Malkovich, Michelle Pfeiffer, Mildred Natwick, Swoosie Kurtz, Uma Thurman

As the 1980s progressed, the range of Cosprop productions continued to grow and the company accordingly expanded the period collection of the costume house. The major film version of the Royal Shakespeare Company play *Les Liaisons Dangereuses*, set in the late eighteenth century, gave Cosprop an opportunity to create aristocratic clothes from a fashionably sumptuous period in history.

Costume Designer James Acheson was commissioned to design the costumes. Acheson began his career at the BBC in the 1970s, designing episodes of the long-running cult series *Doctor Who*. He made the transition into feature films designing costumes for Terry Gilliam's *Time Bandits* (1981), Monty Python's *The Meaning of Life* (1983) and *Brazil* (1985). In 1988 he won an Oscar and a BAFTA for Best Costume Design for Bernardo Bertolucci's epic *The Last Emperor* (1987).

For research for *Dangerous Liaisons*, Acheson immersed himself in pre-revolutionary France and examined real clothing of the period. He studied paintings to understand how the fabric, and in particular its weight, were crucial in the construction of the clothing in the 1780s. The scale and scope of the production required a large team of expert makers, 'it struck me that it was important to find the right fabrics. Nothing I looked at had that buttery sculptural quality[35] ... The tradition had been to make clothes from new materials. John [Bright] went back to the source and collected original pieces and used them to recreate a true sense of period (fig.31)'.[36]

The clothes for *Dangerous Liaisons* were central to the film's opening title sequence. The film begins with the Marquise de Merteuil (Glenn Close) and Vicomte de Valmont (John Malkovich) being dressed by their servants.

It's an attempt to show two people dressing for battle. This is a ritual of dressing, as if they were putting on armour like a samurai warrior. It's the whole idea of protection and presentation, as they present themselves in an extraordinarily controlled image. It's the only time we see them with their servants. After that, they are left alone with each other.[37] – **James Acheson**

Acheson created a workroom in London, gathering leading costume makers. He assigned different characters to different makers and commissioned Cosprop to create costumes for Swoosie Kurtz and Mildred Natwick (fig.30). Makers at Cosprop have had a strong impact into the construction of the costumes, sometimes influencing the design process.

I was given some drawings for the costume designs, but the finished dress isn't always the same as the drawing. It is influenced by John, the actress or the designer and sometimes by the maker. Each designer has a different way of working, but they all start by spending time with John going through fabrics, character and design, considering things like whether multiples of costumes are required.[38] – **Susan Hardy, Costume Maker**

Acheson strived for period authenticity through fabric and accessories and Cosprop was central to his process, acknowledging that Bright and Cosprop 'revolutionised the whole world of period design in this country.'[39]

This attention to detail in the design of *Dangerous Liaisons* was critically acclaimed on release and the film won several awards, including an Oscar and a BAFTA for Best Costume Design.

'You made the clothes as they would have been sewn during that time period. It was all hand done, you don't want to see any machine work on camera.'[40]
– Susan Hardy, Costume Maker

30. (left) Helen Rosemonde (Mildred Natwick) in *Dangerous Liaisons* (1988)

31. (opposite) Costume for Madame de Volanges (Swoosie Kurtz) in *Dangerous Liaisons* (1988)

The Portrait of a Lady (1996)

Director Jane Campion | Costume Designer Janet Patterson
Starring Nicole Kidman, John Malkovich, Barbara Hershey, Christian Bale

A Henry James novel was the inspiration for one of the most ravishing films of the 1990s, which established Nicole Kidman as one of the leading actors of her generation in the role of Isabel Archer. The brief for Costume Designer Janet Patterson was to create an American heroine out of place in the 'glittering but cold European environment'.[41] Isabel's metamorphosis – emotional, moral and spiritual – is told beautifully through the costume design.

Patterson worked regularly with Director Jane Campion, as Sally Turner, Assistant Costume Designer on the film, reflected, 'Janet and Jane were both creative people, they worked really well together, they had made *The Piano*, which was an international hit and Janet won the BAFTA for best costume design. They both liked extraordinary and beautiful objects and places, which contributed to the film's design. Janet was also the Production Designer – which was unusual in film for someone to do both jobs.'[42]

Jane Campion's design brief for Patterson was to 'present Isabel as a portrait rather than as a complete subject, the film traces her social development and its effects on her outer person through costume and hair changes'.[43] Campion was heavily involved in the costume design process.

Jane Campion came into the workroom to look at the clothes under construction, it's unusual for a director to take so much interest. Nicole would try on original pieces to see what suited her – the dressing up session which John organises with the designer. Nicole hadn't appeared in period films before this one, except **Far and Away*****, so it was a learning curve for her, wearing period clothing.***[44] – **Jill Harbutt, Costume Maker**

The entire workroom team at Cosprop worked on the costumes, supervised by Bright and Patterson, and the costume design reflected the highly sculptural and tightly constrained fashions of the 1880s (fig.33).

Sewing can be quite mathematical; the costumes were very structural, Janet had trained as an architect and this was reflected in the designs and the period recreation, we needed mathematical drawings to work from.[45] – **Diana Thomas, Womenswear Maker**

Janet knew what she was doing, she had a very strong vision. She gave me drawings of the clothes she wanted to recreate, she was really good at sketching, she had been an architect so they were very detailed and accurate in their construction **(fig.34).** ***We had a long time to prepare for the film, which was more usual then, so we had time as the dresses were very complicated to construct.***[46] – **Jill Harbutt**

We had a long lead in time for **Portrait*****, around six months, we had time to create these beautiful costumes. Everything was made at Cosprop. Janet went through the archives with John and was meticulous with her design ideas. Because everything came from Cosprop, it gives the film a very strong visual identity.***[47] – **Nancy Knapp, Head of the Workroom**

32. (left) Publicity poster for *The Portrait of a Lady* (1996)

33. (opposite) Isabel Archer (Nicole Kidman) in *The Portrait of a Lady* (1996)

A recurring motif in the film is Isabel's 1880s' clothing with a train. In a pivotal scene, Gilbert Osmond (John Malkovich) steps on Isabel's train to entrap her and accuse her of coming between Pansy, his daughter, and a wealthy suitor. 'We made some of the trains slightly longer – because they were a plot point. Janet was very creative with her choices and pushed at the boundaries and she really appreciated our input to the design process.'[48] – Jill Harbutt

As the narrative develops, Isabel's wardrobe becomes increasingly dark and sculptural, her hair also becomes elaborate in form and appears to overpower her (fig.32). These subtle design decisions aided the film narrative's undertones of control and coercive behaviour from her husband Gilbert (John Malkovich) and Madame Serena Merle (Barbara Hershey).

Cosprop's extensive collection of accessories was utilised for dramatic effect. Isabel's black-and-white striped parasol became the instrument with which Osmond teases and hypnotises her into their marriage. The resources of a range of Italian costume houses were called on during the shoot in Italy, which Turner recalls Patterson enjoying as they 'have a different feel to the costume houses in the UK, they are much more theatrical'.[49]

Christopher Prins worked with Malkovich on his clothes,

John [Malkovich] was a costume designer himself and so he had lots of ideas about his clothes. He didn't wear a tie in the film, he wore an engraved stud, which for a period film of this time was unusual; he also wore patterned and floral shirts, rather than a white shirt which give his character a contemporary edge.[50]
– Sally Turner

34. (above, left and right) Costume design sketches for *The Portrait of a Lady* (1996)

35. (opposite) Costume for Isabel Archer (Nicole Kidman) in *The Portrait of a Lady* (1996)

Twelfth Night (1996)

Director Trevor Nunn | Costume Designer John Bright
Starring Helena Bonham Carter, Imogen Stubbs, Toby Stephens, Imelda Staunton

John Bright and Trevor Nunn have collaborated on several theatre projects including *The Life and Adventures of Nicholas Nickleby* for the Royal Shakespeare Company (RSC) in 1980. When Nunn began to develop a film version of *Twelfth Night*, Bright was his first choice of designer, saying: 'John combines an encyclopaedic knowledge of the history of costume with a daring instinct for design.'[51]

Trevor's brief to me was, this is your period – the Edwardian period. But that also presents a problem as the language of Shakespeare was not the language of the Edwardian period when you consider 'cross-gartering' for example ... I sourced Eastern European uniforms, and if you turned collars up, you could get a good effect.[52] – **John Bright**

For actor Imogen Stubbs playing Viola, 'knowing you have John Bright costuming is very good news, his approach is never abstract, always character-based'.[53]

Returning to Cosprop was frequent collaborator Helena Bonham Carter, who relishes working with Bright and what he brings to the creative process:

... a lot of the rehearsal, of which there is very little in film, happens with the costume designer, you are so grateful that someone else is showing interest in your character, because you are doing all the exploration on your own. You have the chance to express the idea and make it concrete. I love clothes and that's not a given with actors They transport me and they transform. It changes the idiom of how you move. Anything that gives me something authentic, I have a chance to suspend my own disbelief and the audience's disbelief, costume designers give us armour to go on and do the impossible, to convince the audience something is happening that's not real.[54] – **Helena Bonham Carter**

36. (opposite) Costume for Olivia (Helena Bonham Carter), *Twelfth Night* (1996)

37. (left) Viola (Imogen Stubbs) and Olivia (Helena Bonham Carter) in *Twelfth Night* (1996)

38. Costume detail for Viola (Imogen Stubbs) in *Twelfth Night* (1996)

Elizabeth (1998)

Director Shekhar Kapur | Costume Designer Alexandra Byrne
Starring Cate Blanchett, Joseph Fiennes, Geoffrey Rush, Christopher Eccleston

Film projects such as *Elizabeth* (1998) and *Anonymous* (2011) extended Cosprop's collection to include the Tudor period. *Elizabeth* was the first major feature film to depict Elizabeth I since Glenda Jackson's era-defining 1971 BBC series.

***When we began making Tudor clothes, we referred to the Janet Arnold books,* Patterns of Fashion, *they really helped build up our ideas of how to construct the clothes. Lucy Barton's* Historic Costume for the Stage *was also very helpful.*[55] – John Bright**

***If we hadn't covered the period before, we would make a mock-up and we learnt from that, dressing the actor in the fitting room at Cosprop, we were always learning.*[56] – Susan Hardy, Costume Maker**

The narrative spans 22 years covering Elizabeth I's life from princess under house arrest to Queen of England. Alexandra Byrne's design brief was to anchor the film in period but not to be restrained by historical accuracy. 'The director Shekhar Kapur was less concerned with the historical period, he was

much more interested in the storytelling. I had seen the Glenda Jackson version, I looked at portraits, I had an instinct of what I wanted to do and I created mood boards (fig.39). I took them to show him and we got on.'[57]

Byrne's theatre training 'told the truth of the story'[58] and her colour palette was crucial in communicating Elizabeth's turbulent journey to the throne via imprisonment in the Tower of London.

Historically she went to the tower in a white dress, so we made three. She steps out of the boat and the dress had to reflect the filthy water of the Thames, unfortunately these scenes ended up on the cutting room floor. Once in the Tower, I asked Shekhar, what is she wearing, she hasn't brought a suitcase with her – and he said she belongs to the tower. So she had become part of the tower and her dress had taken on the stone of the walls.[59] – **Alexandra Byrne**

One Cosprop costume echoed an emotional narrative point in the scene where Elizabeth and Robert Dudley confess their feelings for one another before she is crowned Queen of England.

I wanted Elizabeth to blend with her environment, with the oak panelled walls. Cate [Blanchett] has an innate strength which counters the silk gauze ... she is contained but holds power.[60] – **Alexandra Byrne**

Byrne won the Golden Satellite Award for Elizabeth and also received nominations for both Oscar and BAFTA awards for Best Costume design.

39. (opposite) Moodboards of Tudor clothing and jewellery for *Elizabeth* (1998)

40. (below) Elizabeth I (Cate Blanchett) in *Elizabeth* (1998)

Topsy-Turvy (1999)

Director Mike Leigh | Costume Designer Lindy Hemming
Starring Jim Broadbent, Allan Corduner, Lesley Manville, Timothy Spall, Ron Cook, Shirley Henderson, Alison Steadman, Eleanor David, Katrin Cartlidge

British director Mike Leigh was known for contemporary narratives, which mixed realism and humour often using a loyal group of actors and designers. *Topsy-Turvy* explored the creative partnership of William S. Gilbert (Jim Broadbent) and Sir Arthur Sullivan (Allan Corduner) and was set in the 1880s, exploring the creation of several of their operettas including *The Mikado* (1885). Lindy Hemming had worked with Leigh on all his films after the landmark stage and television production *Abigail's Party* (1977) and was assigned the ambitious period costume design. She had mainly designed contemporary films – *My Beautiful Laundrette* (1985), *Four Weddings and a Funeral* (1994) and the Bond films from *Goldeneye* (1995) to the later *Casino Royale* (2006).

The screenplay is created by Mike and the actors during the improvisation process. It's a complicated process and can take many weeks. We – the costume and set designers – are expected to be in the rehearsal room and provide rehearsal costumes and sets. We have ongoing discussions with the actors and this experience makes you hyper-aware of the creation of the character.[61] – **Lindy Hemming**

Whereas previous Leigh collaborations created fictional characters developed by him and the actors, *Topsy-Turvy* predominantly depicted real people in their everyday lives.

Research is my bedrock, my starting point was the Theatre and Performance Collections [at the Victoria and Albert Museum], who have an important Gilbert and Sullivan archive, so I spent long periods researching the people and their world. The actors were also conducting their own research. We were examining these people's lives and how they really lived and behaved and looking for interesting things they had done. You could read and see, in photographs, that someone had actually dyed their moustache or that someone had inherited a beautiful piece of jewellery, or you could find out that someone perhaps had an obsession with wearing the colour purple.[62] – **Lindy Hemming**

Alongside the costuming of characters off-stage, there were several scenes of the rehearsal process and staged recreations of Gilbert and Sullivan's work. With its large stock of Victorian costumes and period theatrical expertise, Cosprop was one of the houses central to this process.

I had been using Cosprop since the 1970s and their reputation as a fountain of historical costume knowledge and their enormous contribution to beautiful cinema costume was already solid among the designers that I respected.[63] – **Lindy Hemming**

With a huge number of costumes to be designed and produced, Hemming was ably assisted by future award-winning designers including Michael O'Connor, Jacqueline Durran, David Crossman and Andrea Cripps. Hemming 'immersed herself in this world'[64] with the creative team including Eve Stewart's production design, and Christine Blundell and Trefor Proud's hair and make-up design. Alongside the Japanese influenced *The Mikado* (1885), the design team meticulously recreated *Princess Ida* (1884) and *The Sorcerer* (1884).

Christopher Prins's historical knowledge was invaluable in the fitting room; working with the design team, he dressed many of the men, working with the research of the period to help show the strata of Victorian society. Important figures in the narrative included Richard D'Oyly-Carte (Ron Cook)

41. (left) Fanny Ronalds (Eleanor David) in *Topsy-Turvy* (1999)

42. (opposite) Madam (Katrin Cartlidge) and Arthur Sullivan (Allan Corduner) in *Topsy-Turvy* (1999)

'the man who put electric lighting into the Savoy Theatre';[65] and costume designer Wilhelm (Jonathan Aris). He is shown designing 'his' costumes and convincing the actors to dispense with their corsets to enable the silhouette of the kimonos required for *The Mikado*. With so many stock items required for the audience members dressed in their best finery, interspersed with busy backstage scenes, Cosprop's extensive collection was a treasure trove for the design team.

One day during her fitting, we were discussing Eleanor David's character and suddenly John appears with the precious original bodice of an 1880s' dress, which was ideal. A skirt was created to match* (fig.41)*, and it was all brought beautifully together for the moment when she sings at the piano.[66] **– Lindy Hemming**

Topsy-Turvy won several international awards, including two Oscars, for Hemming's costume design, and Blundell and Proud's hair and make-up. 'On the (painted, powdered) face of it, *Topsy-Turvy* heralds a radical departure for Leigh. A flamboyant costume drama buttressed with period songs and buttoned up in theatrical finery, it's worlds away from the film-maker's usual stomping ground of chintzy suburban angst.'[67]

'John's life of tireless collecting, and the making team at his atelier, have raised the standard of period costumes and how we view and perceive them from the distance of our times.'[68] – Lindy Hemming

Onegin (1999)

Director Martha Fiennes | Costume Designers John Bright, Chloé Obolensky
Starring Ralph Fiennes, Liv Tyler, Toby Stephens

Martha Fiennes's film version of Alexander Pushkin's novel *Eugene Onegin* united John Bright and Chloé Obolensky as costume co-designers. Obolensky had begun her career assisting Lila De Nobili and had been recommended to Cosprop and Bright by David Walker. Of the collaboration Obolensky says, 'John understands costume, because he has the sensitivity of an actor and he understands it not as the outside envelope, but what is coming from within and therefore all the possibilities that are there. I find that extremely rare, in people who design and make costumes.'[69]

For Director Martha Fiennes, the period setting presented a challenge and an opportunity.

People hardly ever touch the 1830s because it is so ugly. That leg of mutton sleeve and that waist which is dropping from Empire line, we thought how can we make this look good? ... Once we picked the year, we were then very clear about everything, the sense of that period from costume to jewellery, and then there's a next stage, to create a world of your own. So you sift from the hard reality of fact into creative interpretation and you make the reality work for you.[70] – **Martha Fiennes**

The recurring challenge for filmmakers is the interpretation of a moment in history; as Fiennes describes, 'We are not making a documentary and you can't escape the era you are working in. If you look at *Doctor Zhivago*, you notice that Julie Christie's hair is backcombed because of the time [1960s], you're always a bit influenced by your time I think, unknowingly, it's inescapable.'[71] Bright equally acknowledges this challenge, 'I'm not sure that one does get around it. I think the only thing you can do is look for something within the period that suits the moment and the person.'[72]

Bright and Obolensky's approach for Onegin was to create the correct silhouette for the period and establish character,

43. (below) Yevgeny Onegin (Ralph Fiennes) in *Onegin* (1999)
44. (opposite) Tatyana Larina (Liv Tyler) in *Onegin* (1999)

with Obolensky clarifying that, 'nobody is ever dressed from top to toe in the latest fashions. If you don't want to come out with a cliché of the period, you have to understand that people, individually according to their temperament, wear certain things that are not necessarily what one understands to be the mode of the day'.[73]

After a six-year break in the narrative, Onegin returns to society and sees Tatyana for the first time wearing a stunning red dress, made by Costume Maker Janet Ingafield (fig.46). Of the costume, Bright lined the sleeves with feather duvets to give it bounce, a trick that he discovered when he was looking through a batch of nineteenth-century clothes that had recently been offered to Cosprop.

Obolensky recalled their design of one of the ballrooms that captured the winter environment of St Petersburg: 'we opted for a mother-of-pearl frozen look for the textiles. They came simply from the landscape. When you're in St Petersburg and you look out of the window, it's all iced over, and you see that it did actually influence their choice of ornament and stone.'[74] The creation of Yevgeny Onegin was developed carefully with Christopher Prins. Through his research, knowledge of the Cosprop stock and after an extensive fitting process, Onegin began to emerge in the fitting room as Ralph Fiennes recalled,

Each ritual of preparation for the film was heavy with meaning for me; the wardrobe was like pieces of a jigsaw puzzle and in the mirror, they finally came together to form Onegin.[75] – **Ralph Fiennes**

Fiennes commented on this attention to authenticity: 'Chloé and John would always want to be sure the person was historically believable, which was absolutely right. An eccentric scarf would be described as an old friend. Something the character might have brought from his country estate.'[76]

Creating the correct period shape for Onegin involved Fiennes wearing a corset, which was accurate for the period. Ralph Fiennes's Onegin created a stunning silhouette on the screen (fig.43), which was evident from the critical response to the film as critic Derek Malcolm wrote, 'Onegin threads his way across the snowy landscape, discernible by his rakish hat, Martha Fiennes is able to portray something of his loneliness and absurdity'.[77]

When *Onegin* was released on the final day of the twentieth century, audiences and critics responded to its richly textured visual landscape. Bright and Obolensky's costumes, together with the production design by Jim Clay, created 'a rich palette of deep blacks, snowy whites and warm ochres and has a physical feel for the textures of clothing, fabrics and furniture'.[78]

45. (left) Publicity poster for *Onegin* (1999)

46. (opposite) Costume for Tatyana Larina (Liv Tyler) in *Onegin* (1999)

'To a certain extent, Liv being tall is quite useful. Things that almost form a square shape, like the red ball dress, you sort of get away with it on her. She is slim and tall and that goes against the overall shape of the dress. I think because we saw her shoulders and there was enough room from chin to the bust, it works.'[79] – John Bright

CHAPTER TWO

MERCHANT IVORY

The Renaissance of the Costume Drama

'What I know about period costume has been entirely learnt from John and Jenny, of making all those films with them, I've learned so much from them, I am totally their student.'[1] – James Ivory

'With John, we were hooked mentally and spiritually, he has a special sensibility which enhances the director's vision. Nothing looks made-up or theatrical.'[2] – Ismail Merchant

John Bright's design partnership with Jenny Beavan and the Merchant Ivory team transformed the realisation of period clothing on the screen. *A Room with a View, Maurice, Howards End* and *The Remains of the Day* are regarded as modern classics that continue to resonate with audiences in the twenty-first century.

The design contribution of Bright and Beavan not only enhanced these films but added to their longevity by creating a level of authenticity that has influenced modern practice. Bright's historic costume collection, built over a period of years, has become the principal source of historically accurate and character-based costume design. As Helena Bonham Carter remarked, 'we entered Cosprop as ourselves and walked out as the person we were playing.'[3] Bright and Beavan's work anchored the Merchant Ivory films with a strong visual identity.

The independent film company Merchant Ivory (Producer Ismail Merchant; Director James Ivory; Screenwriter Ruth Prawer Jhabvala) was established in 1961. Their early work produced acclaimed low-profile films largely based in either India or the United States, such as *Shakespeare Wallah* (1965) and *Bombay Talkie* (1970). In the early days of the company, they became known as an observer of Indian society for a western audience rather than the literary adaptations for which they later became famous.

In 1978 Merchant Ivory acquired British funding for their first adaptation of a Henry James novel *The Europeans* (1979), proving to be a pivotal moment for the company and which propelled them into a new artistic future.

'I had a wardrobe for Lucy and it reflected Lucy's position in society at that time. If we needed hats, John would go off into the deepest recesses of Cosprop and find a bit of ribbon which was perfect. I always have great admiration for the way they did period clothing.'[4] – Helena Bonham Carter

47. (opposite) Lucy Honeychurch (Helena Bonham Carter) in *A Room with a View* (1985)

The Europeans (1979)

Director James Ivory | Costume Designer Judy Moorcroft
Starring Lee Remick, Lisa Eichhorn, Tim Woodward, Wesley Addy, Robin Ellis

The Europeans (1979) aligned Merchant Ivory with literary adaptations and with superb production values. The story, adapted from a Henry James novel by Ruth Prawer Jhabvala, is an encounter between a family of pre-Civil War New Englanders and their European relations whose alien, sophisticated ways dazzle some family members and scandalise others.

Merchant Ivory had established a good working relationship with Costume Designer Judy Moorcroft, and Jenny Beavan was asked to assist on the production. 'Judy and I went to Cosprop for research and that was my first real experience of watching someone develop costumes for a film and witnessing how a costume house works. It was during this time that John and I became friends. I came to consider [Bright] my mentor as well as my constant collaborator.'[5] John Bright recalled Moorcroft's approach, 'Judy was keen on using as many real things as possible and a lot of the clothes that are now in the historic costume collection were on the rails at that time. Being a Merchant Ivory film, there wasn't much money, so we had to use stock and adapt'.[6]

For the design team, Bright and the Cosprop costumiers including Christopher Prins, Head of Men's Wardrobe, one of the challenges was adapting and fitting period clothing onto actors in the late twentieth century, as bodies have changed and developed since the original clothing was created. Bright remembers, 'Most of Lisa Eichhorn's clothes were real and adapted, we made some pieces for Lee Remick and we adapted real clothes (fig.49). Judy found some clothes in the Portobello Market, there's one striped dress she found, we dyed it then lengthened it by adding some fringing.'[7]

Through Bright's expert advice and the inspiration generated by the Cosprop stock, Moorcroft was able to supply the film's costumes virtually from one source. James Ivory recognised that the film's identity was being enhanced by its high production values and the Cosprop collection was central to this new visual vocabulary:

The Europeans ***was the first of the Merchant Ivory period adaptations to have a state-of-the-art approach to the film's look and it was characteristic of all the rest to come. Most of the extremely knowledgeable crew who were in wardrobe and hairdressing and makeup departments were English. These artists were steeped in the Victorian past by way of old photographs, paintings and extant evidence – they had taken almost an archaeological or a scientifically detached approach to the film's design which made it stand out.***[8] – **James Ivory**

The film premiered at the Cannes Film Festival in 1979 and Judy Moorcroft was nominated for an Oscar and BAFTA for her costume design work.

48. (left) Eugenia Münster (Lee Remick) and Robert Action (Robin Ellis) in *The Europeans* (1979)

49. (opposite) Costume for Eugenia Münster (Lee Remick) in *The Europeans* (1979)

The Bostonians (1984)

Director James Ivory | Costume Designers Jenny Beavan, John Bright
Starring Vanessa Redgrave, Christopher Reeve, Nancy Marchand, Madeleine Potter

The Bostonians was the second Henry James adaptation for the Merchant Ivory team. Set in 1870s Boston and New York, the narrative explores reformers and feminists after the period of the American Civil War and examines the 'Boston Marriage' – relationships that were formed between women who were financially independent. The designer Judy Moorcroft was initially offered the film but proved unavailable as she was working on *A Passage to India* (1984) directed by David Lean. Instead, Ivory offered the costume design to Jenny Beavan, who began her research at Cosprop with Bright.

Ruth Prawer Jhabvala's screenplay skilfully adapted the story into a coherent script and created a different ending to the novel. At the centre of the narrative is Verena Tarrant (Madeleine Potter) who is torn between her feelings for Olive (Vanessa Redgrave), a feminist reformer and suffragist, and Basil Ransom (Christopher Reeve), who is in love with Verena but wants her to live a life of domestic servitude. The casting of the three leads was crucial in representing this intense triangular relationship (fig.50).

Glenn Close was initially cast in the role of Olive, the main antagonist for Verena's affections. A last-minute scheduling clash resulted in Close leaving the production to star opposite Robert Redford in *The Natural* (1984). The solution was Vanessa Redgrave, an actor Ivory had long admired and always wanted to work with. Redgrave was known for her political activism and the role was ideal for her. The final part of the triangle was the role of Verena; Ivory considered several actors, including Jodie Foster, before finally casting Madeleine Potter, who made her film debut. The scheduling proved challenging for Bright and his team at Cosprop.

***Because of the sudden change in casting, we just had to get on with it. We only had three weeks to fit Vanessa, who is much taller than Glenn so a major refit had to be organised ... but I was told emphatically there was no more money for costumes. I had worked with Vanessa before which was good. I spent ages looking through stock. I found one costume in the museum, an evening dress, green and gold and if I pulled it apart it could work, but* [*there was*] *not much time for making. Vanessa is very statuesque and looks wonderful in period clothes* (fig.51).**[9] – **John Bright**

The Bostonians featured several large party scenes, which involved numerous extras dressed in 1870s' clothing. With Bright's expert eye and the use of Cosprop's collection, his role grew from costumier to designer. As the production developed, Beavan recognised Bright's design contribution and requested he received a co-design credit. 'This was the beginning of our partnership, which has been one of the most amazing things.'[10]

Ivory cast Christopher Reeve as the male lead: 'We had to wait for him to finish *Superman*. I required no audition for Chris, I knew he was the perfect person and he prepared for the role very carefully and studied the Mississippi accent in detail.'[11] The casting of Reeve was considered essential in bringing an internationally recognised Hollywood star into what financiers regarded as an art-house film. Reeve was delighted with the change of pace from the superhero role that had brought him worldwide fame and he also had his eye on the future, aware that superheroes have a shelf life.

Christopher Prins was responsible for costuming Reeve and the other male leads. Reeve had developed his body to play Superman, a very different silhouette, so expert fitting was essential to fit him into 1870s' suits.

The Bostonians built on the success of *The Europeans*, with its superb production values. The film's use of authentic period interiors, rather than artificially built sets, also enhanced the visual realism. When the film was released in summer 1984, it was a hugely popular success with *The New York Times* declaring, 'The Bostonians is, from its opening shot to last, a rare delight, a high comedy with tragic undertones, acted to passionate perfection by a cast of the best actors ever assembled by the Merchant-Ivory-Jhabvala team.'[12]

For their combined costume design work, Bright and Beavan were nominated for an Oscar and a BAFTA for Best Costume Design. Redgrave was also nominated for an Oscar and the film brought her the National Society of Film Critics award for her performance as Olive.

The Bostonians firmly established the creative relationship between Bright and Beavan with the Merchant Ivory team. It was the beginning of one of the most significant design partnerships in British cinema and the film paved the way for a series of period adaptations that not only fuelled the reinvigoration of the British film industry but had huge international appeal and success.

50. (opposite) Publicity booklet pages for *The Bostonians* (1984)

Costumes for *The Bostonians* (1984)

51. (left) Olive Chancellor (Vanessa Redgrave)

52. (opposite) Mrs Burrage (Nancy Marchand)

A Room with a View (1985)

Director James Ivory | Costume Designers Jenny Beavan, John Bright
Starring Helena Bonham Carter, Simon Callow, Daniel Day-Lewis, Judi Dench, Maggie Smith, Denholm Elliott, Rupert Graves, Rosemary Leach, Julian Sands, Patrick Godfrey

After the success of the Henry James films, Merchant Ivory turned their attention to the work of E.M. Forster, and it was these adaptations that cemented the reputation of Merchant Ivory as one of the most celebrated independent production companies in the film industry. Ivory recalls the initial approach to Forster's estate: 'They thought we wanted to make *A Passage to India*. We explained we had just made a film about this subject, *Heat and Dust*, which was still playing in London. We wanted to make *A Room with a View*, which they regarded as an inconsequential little comedy.'[13]

A Room with a View follows a young Englishwoman Lucy Honeychurch (Helena Bonham Carter), who arrives in Florence on a grand tour with her aunt Charlotte Bartlett (Maggie Smith). Through a series of events involving English expatriates, Lucy's life is changed forever. When she returns to England, she must choose between a conventional life with her bookish fiancé (Daniel Day-Lewis) or the modern young man who kissed her in the Tuscan hills (Julian Sands).

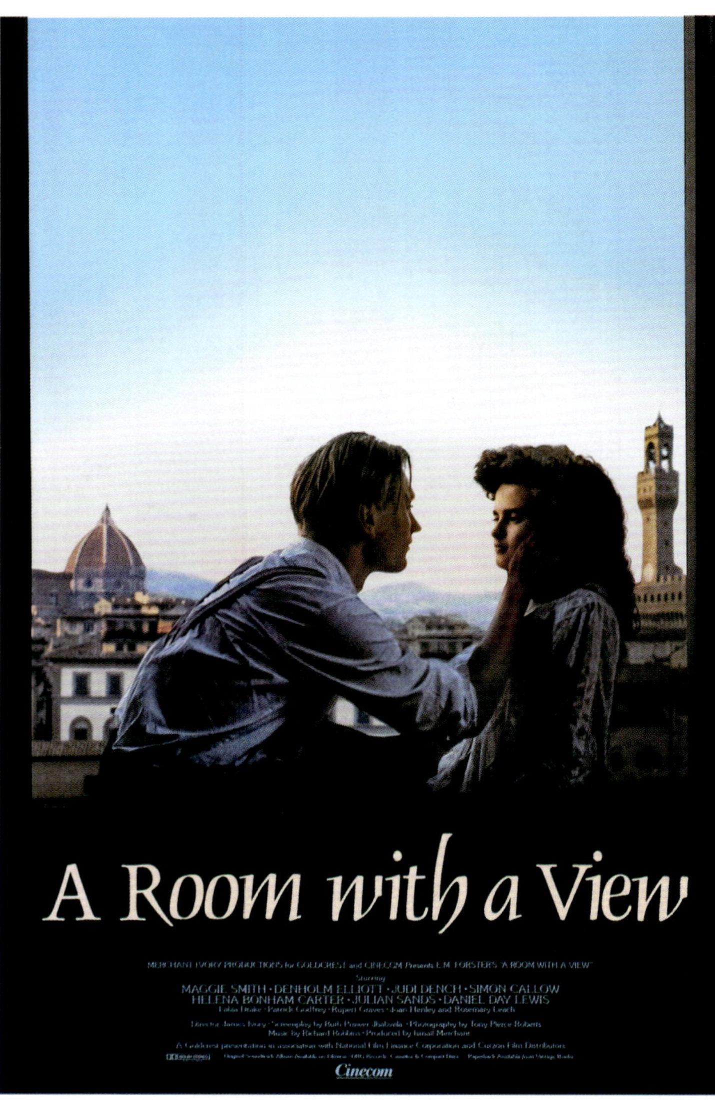

Research of pre-war Italy cityscapes, combined with Bright's expert knowledge of the period, and the rich stock of Edwardian costume at Cosprop, was the foundation in creating each character. This is especially important as the first scenes take place in Pensione Bertolini in Florence, when Lucy and Charlotte have supper and meet the other key players. The adaptation established each person in a structured manner, which helped Bright conceive each character, 'I couldn't quite get the hang of the book, as you were introduced to all these characters very quickly and I couldn't understand who any of them were. Ruth['s script] introduced them all in a much better way, and then you were able to follow the two protagonists, who had come to Florence for a holiday, and you met the other characters after that.'[14]

A Room with a View is punctuated with chapter headings separating the Florentine and English sections, with colour playing an important role in the separation of the two different environments.

There was very little influence from Jim [James] or Ismail on how we should do the clothes. Jim gave me some black and white Alinari photographs for reference. Ismail gave me some travel brochures of Florence for the locations, so we knew what the colours were going to be in the various squares. The Alinari photos gave the lead with the Italians, who were strong and forceful in the black and white spectrum, the English were a bit washed out. When the elderly ladies went to visit Lucy and Mrs Honeychurch, these people lived in a world of brown Windsor soup, I must have heard that expression in a [Terence] Rattigan play or something, it stayed with me.[15] – **John Bright**

As the costume design developed at Cosprop, the building and development of each character was an organic process. For the actors, wearing original Edwardian clothing enhanced their characterisation. Bright would put a rack of clothes together for each actor to have a 'dress-up session'.[16] Beavan called this 'a notebook of clothes',[17] explaining it was an inspirational moment when an actor would turn to the mirror and say they now knew who the character was.

Judi Dench was very clear on her character from the moment she came into the fitting room and took an active part in her wardrobe choices. For Maggie's suit for the picnic, Jenny found an extraordinary fabric, a fine herringbone linen. It's such a perfect fabric, because it holds a shape once it's created and it's there forever. Even if someone sits down, it might crease but the shape is still so strong, it holds its own **(see p.6).**[18] – **John Bright**

Christopher Prins fitted the men into their clothes and aided the younger actors, who were new to the filmmaking process. It was a period of transformation as Julian Sands recalled, 'The clothes helped me understand the people who wore them, everything we were wearing felt so comfortable and it was easy to wear, it felt so natural, and that contributes to the performance enormously (fig.53).'[19]

Beavan said, 'It was done on a minute budget so it was pretty much all done from stock, a lot of real genuine vintage clothes. We were re-stretching and re-dyeing it – as John owned it, he could do what was needed, altering it, re-accessorising it. We made very little stuff; it was all about using existing clothing.'[20] This meant that some outfits had been used, adding a lived-in quality and which costume designers strive for, as clothes must look like they have a history before they are worn. Maggie Smith's coat had been worn by Sian Phillips in the BBC suffragette drama *Shoulder to Shoulder* (1974). It was slightly aged, which Bright felt was perfect for Maggie's character: for Lucy's engagement outfit, 'It's good if a garment has a back story. Lucy's clothes were made up of a skirt and belt from stock, which we finished with purple-flowered embroidery. I found the remnants of a bodice to match, I imagined it could have been part of Lucy's grandmother's wedding dress fashioned into a blouse by her mother'.[21]

Bright attests, 'We didn't have the money to make new clothes so we used stock and adapted. If we had to strengthen something which is quite fine, we often use bra-net, a very fine net made of nylon and therefore very tough, it gets layered underneath the fragile part.'[22] For their part, the costumiers at Cosprop were expert at ensuring the period clothing could survive the rigours of filmmaking as Wardrobe Supervisor Sally Turner recalls: 'John would usually strengthen the clothes to make sure they could withstand filming and he is brilliant at finding the right item.'[23]

For the designers and the actors, creating the correct structure for the figure was an essential part of the process. Daniel Day-Lewis's snobbish Cecil Vyse was the perfect foil

53. (opposite) Publicity poster for *A Room with a View* (1985)

54. (below) Mr Emerson (Denholm Elliott), Reverend Beebe (Simon Callow) and Reverend Eager (Patrick Godfrey) in *A Room with a View* (1985)

Catherine Macteigue.
Own diamond studs. Amber collar necklace with filagree bits inbetween. + diamante.
Ochre. Silk satin original. with Black net + sequins over one Bosom. BLACK BOWS on SHOULDERS. DARKER ~~OCHRE~~ TAFF MOIRE SKIRT.

MAIDS. BROWN DRILL SKIRTS + TOPS. BLACK VELVET BOWS CF NECK. COVERING COLLAR STUDS. WHITE APRONS EMB. ANGLAIS FRILLED X Straps CB AT WAIST. BLACK BOOTS. WHITE HATS. BOW at CB + frills on Front.

PEARL STUD EARRINGS
Cream + lace Blouse
Brooch at C.F. Neck. Same Skirt
SILVER OWN RINGS.
CHAP →
pince nez w/. Black Ribbon pinned into. R. inner PKT. of JKT.
Black suit
Tex Black wkcoat
Black/white spot Bow Tie.
CHAIN. 3RD BUTTON DOWN LEFT. PKT.

BROOCH BLACK WITH SILVER PATTERN ROUND.
SILVER Rimmed specs.
Lace scarf tied Twice with Brooch
Black Blouse
grey print skirt.
BLACK VELVET BELT.

for the free-living George Emerson and is described as 'a fastidious stick insect, with his pince-nez always in need of adjustment',[24] so clothing played an important role for Day-Lewis. The formal suits and pristine jackets suited his tall and rigid frame. Likewise, Edwardian women didn't slouch or sit cross-legged, and the layering of clothes created this formality. For Turner, Cosprop provided every element required for an actor to be transformed into an Edwardian person.

For period films, you have to start from the inside and work out, corsets and underpinnings create the correct silhouette. A current reaction to anti-corsetry only confirms that an uncomfortable corset is not properly made or badly fitted. The corset should be comfortable and flexible and move with the body so that Lucy can play tennis with ease and wearing a corset should not cause her any impingement, after all women in that period played tennis in corsets.[25] – **Sally Turner**

The Italian scenes were filmed first. On location Bright and Beavan were assisted by Sally Turner and William Pierce. Italian Costume Assistant Elena Puliti provided crucial local knowledge of costume houses and resources for the English crew. On location, some members of the cast and crew stayed in the Fiesole villa Fattoria di Maiano, which was transformed into the fictional Pensione Bertolini. The experience of making and working on a Merchant Ivory was often a family affair production, as Turner discovered and as wardrobe supervisor, there were lots of practical issues that she would have to solve day by day:

You did a bit of everything, you fitted the crowd, you were on the set, there was a very small crew, you broke down the costumes, you made lots of bits. Everyone was hands on, it was teamwork. William Pierce and I helped each other, you have to be much more self-sufficient nowadays. Some of us stayed at the villa which was also the filming location. Ismail would make lunch, we would all have lunch together then go back to work ... We used some of the Italian costume houses for extra costumes that were needed and being Italy, there were a lot of black costumes, which were ideal **(fig.56)*****. There was a truck that delivered the costumes, but dressing, hair and makeup were done in the rooms that had been cleared for filming.***[26] – **Sally Turner**

One memorable scene from the film came with an unexpected twist, when George, Freddy and Reverend Beebe disrobe for a swim in a lake, with much of the action improvised by the actors (fig.54). A scene not requiring clothes might sound easier to manage but the opposite is more exact.

People always ask me about that scene and it must have been easy as they have no clothes on but absolutely not. On the day of filming we were standing with every dressing gown and every towel we could muster. Even though it looks sunny, it was freezing the day we did it. They dug the pond marginally too shallow so the bits that shouldn't show did! Even at that shooting stage they thought

55. (opposite) Costume continuity photographs for *A Room with a View* (1985). Courtesy of the Sally Turner Archive

56. (right) A scene from *A Room with a View* (1985)

Bright and Beavan's research process was inspired by the photographs of Fratelli Alinari, three brothers who created one of the world's first photographic collections in Italy in 1852 and today holds over 5 million photographs. Their images of turn-of-the-century Italy captured people at all levels of Florentine society, essential for the team to build their characters using Forster's text and Ruth Prawer Jhabvala's screenplay

'*A Room with a View* is in part a comedy of manners and the established actors added their own layer of comic timing to their roles. The actors used their clothes in their performances … I always remember Judi [Dench] flinging that cape around herself and marching through Florence. They knew instinctively how to use their clothes as part of their characters.'[27]
– John Bright

the Queen Mother would come to see the film so there was some consternation about what she might and might not see![28] – **Jenny Beavan**

During the merriment, Lucy, Cecil and Mrs Honeychurch arrive in the woodland glade and Bright conceived the scene of the arrival of the three characters in the following way, 'When the family discovered the nude bathing, they were at the top of a hill walking down. I thought of them as the avenging angels, so they all had to be dressed in their pristine white linens.'[29]

Helena Bonham Carter was thrust into the public eye with the image of Lucy Honeychurch standing in the poppy field overlooking Florence, making an indelible impression on British cinema. She became the epitome of the Merchant Ivory heroine and their screen projects became entwined, and she acknowledges that Bright had been central to her transformation, 'I'm indebted to John, my Edwardian English-rose image was entirely created by him (fig.60).'[30]

The work of Bright and Beavan on *A Room with a View* drew high praise from their peers. The film built on the turning point of historically accurate clothing being reimagined and research being the foundation to recreate a period setting, which did not go unrecognised. Triple-Oscar Best Costume Design winner and frequent Cosprop collaborator Anthony Powell remarked, '*A Room with a View* is in the same league as *Death in Venice*, it is like watching a beautiful vintage photograph of that period brought vividly to life. It lives and breathes with the wonderful performances and the eloquent script, the clothes are so true to the period that it will never date.'[31]

Seeing it again, there weren't many things I would change. I might have made one of Helena's hats not so white, the white straw ... What it brought together was an operatic strength, the clothes, although they were real, they had more than a strength because we took each one to the limit ... For a certain age group, they tell me it's still their favourite film.[32] – **John Bright**

When the film was released, it was met with glowing reviews and an unprecedented box-office result for a Merchant Ivory film, it was their most successful film to date. Made for $3 million dollars, the film grossed over $60 million dollars worldwide, an incredible feat for what was considered an art-house film. At the 1987 BAFTA awards, the film won five awards out of 12 nominations including Best Film and Best Costume Design. At the Oscars, held on 30 March 1987, Hollywood-legend Lauren Bacall announced *A Room with a View* had won Best Costume Design.

'John and I are both really good at having an instinct about character, we are so much in tune. Our goal was to transform the actors into Edwardian people.'[33] – Jenny Beavan

57. (opposite) Lucy Honeychurch (Helena Bonham Carter) and Charlotte Bartlett (Maggie Smith) in *A Room with a View* (1985)

58. (right) Jenny Beavan, Lauren Bacall and John Bright at the Oscar Ceremony in 1987, where *A Room with a View* won three awards, including Best Costume Design

Costumes for *A Room with a View* (1985)

59. (left) Charlotte Bartlett (Maggie Smith)

60. (opposite) Lucy Honeychurch (Helena Bonham Carter)

'For films such as *A Room with a View*, you can't tell what is from stock, what has been made and what is original, it's a jigsaw puzzle which John and Jenny brilliantly bring together.'[34] – Susan Hardy, Costume Maker

Maurice (1987)

Director James Ivory | Costume Designers Jenny Beavan, John Bright
Starring James Wilby, Hugh Grant, Rupert Graves, Billie Whitelaw, Helena Michell

The Merchant Ivory team were keen to follow on from the success of *A Room with a View* and turned their attention to E.M. Forster's *Maurice*, which had been published posthumously in 1971. Forster's Literary Estate were initially reluctant to give permission. Ivory said that 'the success of *A Room with a View* enabled the making of *Maurice*. The estate was shocked that we wanted to do it, they had misgivings. The estate was very protective of his legacy and they thought if the film didn't turn out well it would reflect badly on Forster's reputation. *Maurice* is the other side of the coin of *A Room with a View*, living a lie, or living the truth, both films have that.'[35]

Merchant Ivory assembled a familiar design and acting team. The design approach for *Maurice* was to research, source and collate a wardrobe of clothes for the actors to try on and explore their characterisation,

Often what we do, when someone is cast in a role, [is to] dress them up in clothes approximate to the period. If we have things we think are perfect, you get it by talking to actors, their ideas on what they think about colour and what suits them. Since you are standing looking into a mirror and they are looking at themselves, they can tell you very clearly what they like and don't like; there aren't any new designs as such, they are built up on the person, so you are designing with these specifics in mind. You work with the actor and understand what they need and try and fulfil that in terms of their characters.[36] – **John Bright**

Beavan describes the contribution of Christopher Prins, who was responsible for the sourcing and fitting a range of different suits for the film's predominantly male cast to create a textured clothing palette: 'Chris was wonderful at fitting the actors and they all adored working with him. We did it from Cosprop stock, old suits hold up incredibly well, some will be real, the cloth lasts for a hundred years (fig.61).'[37]

61. (below) Clive Durham (Hugh Grant) and Maurice Hall (James Wilby) in *Maurice* (1987)

62. (opposite) Publicity brochure for *Maurice* (1987)

AR7389

The contrasting Edwardian environments of Cambridge University, the financial heart of London and the country estate were all depicted, creating different visual signifiers and colour tones for each location (fig.62). James Ivory engaged French cinematographer Pierre Lhomme, chosen for a non-English view of traditional colleges, grand houses and cricket matches. Ivory 'wanted a cooler palette than *A Room with a View*, I wanted *Maurice* to feel more oppressive to reflect the subject matter and the English weather. I think we only had one sunny day on *Maurice* and that was the day of the cricket match.'[38]

All these visual elements, with scenes shot at dusk and at night, give the film a twilight quality, which reflects the subject matter of Edwardian Maurice Hall discovering his sexuality in a period when being gay was considered not only a mental illness but was punishable by prison and ostracisation from society.

Whilst the film did exceptionally well in territories such as the US and France (the film played for more than a year), it received a number of negative reviews in the UK, primarily from the right-wing press. Maurice and Alec's happy ending is perhaps overshadowed by the prospect of the First World War, but as the film ends, the two lovers are together; this depiction was in stark contrast to other films of the period that depicted a gay male love affair. For their design work, Bright and Beavan were nominated for an Oscar.

63. (above, left) Publicity poster for *Maurice* (1987)

64. (above, right) Alec Scudder (Rupert Graves) in *Maurice* (1987)

Howards End (1992)

Director James Ivory | Costume Designers Jenny Beavan, John Bright
Starring Anthony Hopkins, Vanessa Redgrave, Helena Bonham Carter, Emma Thompson, James Wilby, Jemma Redgrave, Joseph Bennett, Samuel West

Howards End is the last in the trilogy of E.M. Forster films by Merchant Ivory and it is perhaps regarded as their most significant film. Based on the 1910 novel, the narrative is a tour-de-force of a society in transition. The free-spirited, modern-thinking Schlegel sisters, Margaret (Emma Thompson) and Helen (Helena Bonham Carter) are swept into a relationship with the Wilcoxes, a wealthy conservative English trading family, and the Basts, a couple on a lower tier of the Edwardian class system. Ruth Prawer Jhabvala's screenplay weaves all these characters and themes into one and addresses issues of personal and societal responsibility, property and inheritance.

The film reunited a familiar and trusted design team: joining Bright and Beavan were Luciana Arrighi as Production Designer, and Merchant Ivory-regular Tony Pierce-Roberts as Cinematographer. The triple-layered social structure of the three families had to become intertwined in the narrative:

My challenge was to visually describe the different ways of life of the characters in Ruth's wonderful script, i.e. the sets and locations for the three families from the comfortable and beautiful house of the Wilcoxes, to the cultural background of the Schlegels, and then the sad poverty of Leonard Bast, to which I added references of Samuel Palmer's visionary art.[39] – **Luciana Arrighi**

Clothing creates an evocative atmosphere from the very beginning. The film opens with Ruth Wilcox walking around the grounds of her beloved home at twilight. In a luminous, Oscar-nominated performance, Vanessa Redgrave plays Ruth, a product of the Victorian age, holding fast to the vanishing England of her childhood at her country house, Howards End. Her husband, Henry Wilcox (Anthony Hopkins), is an unyielding traditionalist who must face his own past and the changing world around him.

Ruth Wilcox is the spirit of Howards End, so that first dress has to have an elemental quality to it, the green for those opening moments as Vanessa [Redgrave] moves around the garden. It was an original piece, acquired from my teacher, as part of a small collection.[40] – **John Bright**

One of the challenges for designers working in the 1970s and 1980s was the lack of availability of period fabrics. It was the work of Alan and Vanessa Hopkins (supplier of textiles and accessories to the costume design industry) that transformed the possibilities of using fabric that was as near to the original

65. Publicity poster for *Howards End* (1992)

as possible. Their pioneering work was a revolution to the costume design industry. Many of the mills that had produced fabrics from the Victorian era were dormant. The Hopkinses worked with the mill owners to persuade them to restart their work and they became a vital repository of fabric, trimmings and costume accessories, all stored in their suburban house in South London.

For Ruth and Margaret's Christmas shopping trip to London's oldest department store Fortnum & Mason, Trafalgar Square in central London was closed for filming. Beavan recalls the sounds of the horse and carriages hired to recreate the Edwardian streets, 'the noise of all the carriage wheels and horses was amazing. You didn't expect that sound in London, but that's what it must have sounded like in the early 1900s, it's something I'll never forget.'[41]

For this scene, Bright recalls, 'Vanessa told us what she wanted to wear, and she was right, she wears a light outfit, it must be light, that was very helpful, she was like a ghost, she was dying (fig.67). The blouse was real, something I had at Cosprop from the very beginnings of the company, the collar and waistcoat were from The Hopkins Collection, the skirt was made to match. We had just enough material for the lining, which I was determined to use. This mid-tone fabric, which is etched out in acid so I am told, this grey-green velvet, we used it for lining.[42]

The Shropshire wedding scene brings all the families together to create a moment of crisis. The actors were so in tune with their clothes that they used them effectively. When Helen sweeps amongst the landed gentry in a fury, her Bohemian clothes fuel her rage against the entitlement and the 'vulgar show'.

The chiffon scarf that Helena wears around her neck caused some consternation. John decided to give her a beautiful original scarf and said to her, 'Please don't handle it too much it won't last', then we watched, and 'Action!', and saw it being mangled. So it was back to Liberty to find another! [43]– **Jenny Beavan**

Margaret's outfit was a jigsaw puzzle of vintage and newly made elements formed into a new outfit. Bright recalls, 'I modelled that skirt, then added the top, whilst Emma [Thompson] was being fitted as she was discussing the role of Margaret with Jim [Ivory] and the character was forming in front of us (fig.69).'[44] Jill Harbutt, Costume Maker at Cosprop

described the bodice and sleeves were a mixture of antique lace, silk and black velvet with a corsage of original silk flowers, plus antique sleeves.[45]

Samuel West brings an assured sensitivity to Leonard Bast, whose aspirations above his class are ultimately rebuffed. His sun-drenched fantasies at his insurance clerk's desk created one of the film's most striking images. Bright said that 'for Leonard's final scene, we put Sam into a larger suit, so that he looked shrunken through poverty.'[46] *Howards End* is one of the Merchant Ivory team's most moving and perfectly realised films.

Shot on location in England from the Hertfordshire countryside to the tenements of London's East End, the film won an Art Direction Oscar for Luciana Arrighi. Ruth Prawer Jhabvala received her second Oscar for her screenplay adaptation and Bright and Beaven were nominated for a BAFTA and an Oscar for their work. The film launched Emma Thompson's international film career. She received several awards including the golden triple – an Oscar, BAFTA and Golden Globe – for Best Actress. The film was named Best Picture of 1992 by the National Board of Review, and the *New York Times* declared, 'Merchant Ivory has made a quantum leap: *Howards End* is the crowning achievement of their careers, the movie that seems to incorporate all they learnt about filmmaking and life and raised it to a new plateau. A film of dazzling splendour, powered by a dream cast, it is Ivory's masterpiece.'[47]

66. (opposite) Design moodboard for the friends of the Schlegels for *Howards End* (1992)

67. (above) Charles Wilcox (James Wilby), Evie Wilcox (Jemma Redgrave), Ruth Wilcox (Vanessa Redgrave) and Paul Wilcox (Joseph Bennett) in *Howards End* (1992)

Costumes for *Howards End* (1992)

68. (opposite) Ruth Wilcox (Vanessa Redgrave)

69. (right) Margaret Schlegel (Emma Thompson)

The Remains of the Day (1993)

Director James Ivory | Costume Designers Jenny Beavan, John Bright
Starring Anthony Hopkins, Emma Thompson, James Fox, Christopher Reeve, Hugh Grant

After the triumph of *Howards End*, Emma Thompson and Anthony Hopkins were reunited for the adaptation of Kazuo Ishiguro's Booker Prize-winning 1989 novel, *The Remains of the Day*. The novel examines the aristocracy of the 1930s, but unusually from the perspective of the staff who served them unquestioningly. Told in flashback from the 1950s, the film also details the unrequited love of the butler, Mr Stevens (Anthony Hopkins) for Emma Thompson's housekeeper, Miss Kenton, heartbreakingly depicting the cost of their loyalty.

For the production team, the research phase included Cyril Dickman, former butler to Queen Elizabeth II, who was hired as an adviser on protocol, including dress. He was an expert on the formalities of 1930s' aristocracy and provided an understanding of what was worn at particular times of the day. The film's narrative moves between the 1930s and 1950s and Beavan brought her own family history into the costume design.

***We used to go to Paignton in Devon for our summer holidays and my grandmother wore quite specific old-fashioned clothes and there was something about her headscarf. Emma at the end, in the 1950s, is dressed how my grandmother would have dressed, she was very precise, white sandals and a headscarf* (fig.70). *My father is the publican that Anthony Hopkins meets in the 1950s section, a little homage, very personal but appropriate.*[48] – Jenny Beavan**

Emma Thompson, cast as the housekeeper, also delved into her own family history for the role of Miss Kenton. Her grandmother had worked in domestic service and was able to elaborate on the many customs and duties performed by a housekeeper in the period between the two world wars. For John Bright, Jenny Beavan and Christopher Prins, the Cosprop collection provided inspiration, alongside photographs of the period of the great English houses, all of which had been well documented. Bright says, 'You just know when someone looks completely natural in a suit, what is the suit being worn for? The higher up they are in a profession, the better the suit is cut, some actors need a well-cut suit. With Anthony, we tried six different jackets and it wasn't the smartest one that won.'[49]

***For* The Remains of the Day *we had lots of tailcoats in stock, black waistcoats, striped trousers so we put a number of those on Anthony Hopkins to see how and what they did to him. I don't think anything was made for him for that film, they were all stock items. His butler's dress is his suit of armour, which he hides behind, he is completely held in, so when we see him in something entirely different, a pullover, he is very, very vulnerable. I can almost not look at that scene because I feel embarrassed for him, he wants to hide but he's not got his uniform to hide behind and this piece of storytelling is achieved through costume. For Emma's Miss Kenton, it's not a uniform but it has to be dark, unobtrusive and the shoes created the all-important walk she adopts.*[50] – John Bright**

The fictional Darlington Hall is a composite of several English stately homes including Dyrham Park, Badminton House and Powderham Castle. *The Remains of the Day* contains several scenes with large groups of actors in conferences or parties so the challenge for the designers was how to differentiate between actors wearing dark suits photographed in heavily panelled stately homes, surrounded by dark furnishings (fig.71). Also returning to the Merchant Ivory troupe was Christopher Reeve – portraying an American journalist in the 1930s section and later on as the new owner of Darlington Hall in the 1950s – was once again costumed by Christopher Prins. Beavan said, 'Chris sourced clothes from stock and fitted all the actors. We made Chris Reeve's suits because he is so tall and period clothes didn't fit him.'[51]

One of the most memorable moments in the film is when Miss Kenton discovers Mr Stevens quietly reading a book in his butler's pantry. Intrigued to know what he is reading, and to understand him a little more, she backs him into a corner and forcibly removes the book from his hand only to be disappointed at the 'silly romance' he is reading. The tension throughout the scene is palpable:

***It was filmed in the butler's pantry, which is a minute space, there was only room for the actors, the director and cinematographer, so the tension those two produced, the chemistry between them is phenomenal as the camera must have been next to them.*[52] – Jenny Beavan**

The film struck a chord with audiences and critics and it was nominated for eight Oscars including Best Costume Design for Bright and Beavan, and Anthony Hopkins won a BAFTA for his emotionally starved Mr Stevens.

70. (opposite, above) James Stevens (Anthony Hopkins) and Sarah Kenton (Emma Thompson) in *The Remains of the Day* (1993)

71. (opposite, below) Dining scene in *The Remains of the Day* (1993)

'Anthony Hopkins is ... such a natural actor and in a fitting he will put on the clothes, a straightforward suit of the period and he can hunch his shoulders and almost fall into the character, his whole body language will adopt the character he is playing.'[53] – Jenny Beavan

Jefferson in Paris (1995)

Director James Ivory | Costume Designers Jenny Beavan, John Bright
Starring Nick Nolte, Greta Scacchi, Thandiwe Newton, Simon Callow, Seth Gilliam, Michael Lonsdale, Daniel Mesguich

Set in France between 1784 and 1789, when Thomas Jefferson (Nick Nolte) was the American ambassador to France, the screenplay explores his relationship with a beautiful Anglo-Italian painter and musician, Maria Cosway (Greta Scacchi; figs 73, 74). While he was still exchanging letters and romantic sentiments with Cosway, he was forming another attachment with his daughter's enslaved maid, Sally Hemings (Thandiwe Newton).

The screenplay depicts France on the verge of revolution at all levels of French society, from the royal court of Louis XVI and Marie Antoinette to the servants' quarters. The film was made in France and with a large international cast to clothe and accessorise, this was one of Cosprop's largest productions.

The stories are real, the whole history surrounding it was fascinating. On location, we used a school, on the edge of Paris, it was an old primary school. It has all these rooms around a central courtyard, so we had different rooms for uniforms, the lower classes, etc.[54]– **Jenny Beavan**

Once more, the collection at Cosprop provided inspiration. Bright recalls 'I had bought quite a few coats from that period which proved useful and I modelled one of Michael Lonsdale's jackets on something I had seen at the MET in New York, it was encrusted with real diamonds.'[55] For pre-production, Bright was based in India making jackets and base garments, which were then sent to Beavan and her team in Paris to decorate. Due to the enormous cast, the clothes were sent 'by the bale load', with French and Italian costume houses providing further costumes for the lavish production. The Parisian costume houses supplied costumes for the extras and the Italian costume house Peruzzi provided the military uniforms.

When they were making clothes in the eighteenth century, if they were embroidering an outfit, it would have been done before the garment's material was cut, so people sat and embroidered. There might be eight women doing this level of work and we wanted to replicate this craftwork on the film.[56] – **John Bright**

Merchant Ivory collaborator Carol Hemming designed the hair for the film and created an approach which was accurate for the period but did not overwhelm the image.

Through the 1980s and 90s, the design partnership of Bright, Beavan and the support of Cosprop, particularly Christopher Prins, gave British cinema some of its most memorable images. Their work created characters and stories that set the template in the presentation of period costume on the screen and transformed the visual identity of the films of Merchant Ivory. Throughout the 1990s, the Merchant Ivory 'effect' was felt across cinema. Charles Sturridge's *Where Angels Fear to Tread* (1991) reunited Helena Bonham Carter and Rupert Graves. Martin Scorsese lavishly filmed Edith Wharton's *The Age of Innocence* (1993) and *The New York Times* commented, 'we live in the age of Merchant Ivory'.[57]

72. (left) John Bright fitting Seth Gilliam for *Jefferson in Paris* (1995)

73. (opposite) Thomas Jefferson (Nick Nolte) and Maria Cosway (Greta Scacchi) in *Jefferson in Paris* (1995)

'Carol Hemming researched the paintings of the period, which are an interpretation of that time. She realised that this era could be hideous, with all that artificial hair piled up and then a hat placed on top. She was able to create something that presented a character in a much more nuanced way.'[58] – Greta Scacchi

Costumes for *Jefferson in Paris* (1995)

74. (opposite) Maria Cosway (Greta Scacchi)

75. (right) Franz Mesmer (Daniel Mesguich)

CHAPTER THREE

THE WORLD OF JANE AUSTEN

Designing for the Regency Era

'In the 1950s, when period films were made, they were an adaptation of what people wore in the 1950s. In the 1960s costume designers thought we need to go to another way of thinking about period.'[1] – John Bright

Attention to period authenticity or 'the truth of the period' as John Bright describes it, has been a challenge to designers whenever a precise timeframe is recreated. Since its inception, the work of Cosprop has adopted this ethos rather than being influenced by the prevailing trends of the era. Period timeframes present opportunities and challenges for designers: the balance between the script, the director's vision of the story and input of actors, and the creation of characters is combined with the designer's creativity to bring the people in the story to life.

Works by Jane Austen and other Regency-set stories have been adapted for theatre, film and television for every generation. These historic settings offer writers the chance to explore timeless themes through a modern lens. For actors it is an opportunity to portray some of the most famous figures in literature, and for filmmakers and costume designers, it is an opportunity to put their own creative stamp on a familiar period. With every new adaptation, costume designers are presented with a story that is indelibly etched onto the public's imagination and puts their work under microscopic scrutiny, as Michele Clapton, Costume Designer for the 2008 BBC adaptation of *Sense and Sensibility* reflects:

Any Austen adaptation will open you up for criticism, people are so passionate about her work. I worked with John on the costume design, and I tried not to be too restricted by the period. I looked at other Austen adaptations, I think if you are doing an Austen, you almost have to.[2]

The Regency period (1795–1837) has been interpreted in a variety of ways across film and television. The MGM film of *Pride and Prejudice* (1940; Costume Designer Adrian) is one of the few early Hollywood adaptations of a Jane Austen novel. Although set in 1813, the design referenced the fashions of the late 1930s. Fashion historian and former Director of the Fashion Museum in Bath, Rosemary Harden said, 'it's very tempting to be pompous about the MGM film, but I'm sure the same thing will happen when you look at newer versions of Jane Austen adaptations in the future.'[3]

Early television productions of Austen adaptations were often studio-bound and had a tendency to resemble filmed plays with pristine sets and costumes. In the 1990s designers were embracing exterior filming and had the opportunity to depict the period as it might have been experienced. Alexandra Byrne designed *Persuasion* (1995) for the BBC and the approach was liberating from the earlier stage-bound productions. Byrne said, 'Period pieces tend to be over-costumed; they can't have too many clothes, they had no washing machines. Which is why we did the scene [in *Persuasion*] with the characters walking through the mud, this was the reality of their lives.'[4]

Throughout Cosprop's history, they have had to recreate Regency clothing. For the Cosprop making team, it was a similar making experience to other periods, except that in the early days of the company, there were few original clothes to copy. Most BBC designers had used the collection in some form, as the BBC wardrobe department did not contain good stock for this era.

Bright's approach to period has always been to begin with the construction of the correct silhouette. Once the silhouette is in place, the outer layers are built up. Underpinnings and corsetry are essential for period clothing. For the 1983 BBC production of Jane Austen's *Mansfield Park* (Costume Designer Ian Adley) Cosprop provided the clothes for Anna Massey and Sylvestra Le Touzel. Actor Anna Massey recalled working on *Mansfield Park* and how the wearing of a corset dictated everything.

I invented a walk for Mrs Norris, she was what I call somebody who wants to come into a room earlier than they're there, leaning forward, listening at keyholes, etc. Ian and John at Cosprop helped me create all that. I am so thin I don't really need to wear a corset, but John made me wear one and he was right, because if you don't, you will make a move that you couldn't make if you had a corset.[5] – **Anna Massey**

Researching this period of history can be challenging for designers; artistic impressions mostly present depictions of high fashion and are not always accurate. It is only by looking at real clothes (where they exist) that designers can create a nuanced vision for their design work, as Alexandra Byrne does when designing.

Today we can use the fashion engravings as a primary source. These engravings are very detailed but can lead towards overbuilt costumes. By looking at the actual garments I learnt how individual they were, depending on the maker's skill, style, taste and budget. The clothes are not machined, bound and overlocked; they are hand-sewn interpretations of fashion plates or copies of clothes seen on other people, and sometimes clothes adapted to reflect the latest fashion.[6] – **Alexandra Byrne**

76. (opposite) Marianne Dashwood (Kate Winslet) and John Willoughby (Greg Wise) in *Sense and Sensibility* (1995)

Sense and Sensibility (1995)

Director Ang Lee | Costume Designers Jenny Beavan, John Bright
Starring Emma Thompson, Kate Winslet, James Fleet, Alan Rickman, Hugh Grant, Greg Wise

According to Producer Lindsay Doran, *Sense and Sensibility* had been planned for around 15 years before it came to fruition. Emma Thompson was approached to write the screenplay whilst she was preparing for the role of Margaret in *Howards End*.

The script directed that Bright and Beavan design for the 1790s rather than the 1810s, when most Austen adaptations are set, and this gave the film a distinct contrast to the contemporaneous television productions. Creating contrasting features between the two lead female roles, Elinor (Emma Thompson) and Marianne Dashwood (Kate Winslet), was the initial design brief for Bright and Beavan.

You look at one of the sisters and you think, 'that one is more practical than the other one', that comes out in the characters and that was always at the back of my mind when we were looking at them, the separation between the two sisters. With Kate, there was a more romantic image; with Emma, there was a more direct, grounded image.[7] – **John Bright**

Bright and Beavan avoid sketching, the characters are created through trying period clothes on the actors to see what suits them, and what will work for their character's journey through the narrative. Bright's view is, 'if you do a drawing, you've already committed to an image. If you try clothes on somebody at the beginning, they're already in the right frame of mind to think of them as their clothes'.[8] Actors working at Cosprop engage with their clothes as if they belong to them and not as garments imposed on them as Bright attests, 'at the beginning of the process, you try clothes on a person to see how they relate to them'.[9]

For the Cosprop making process, fabrics are the building blocks to recreate the period:

For a Jane Austen, the fabrics were mostly very fine, and often the specialised fabric suppliers Hopkins were used. They stocked beautiful fabrics of natural cottons and silks and often they had printed in beautiful authentic designs that were specially woven.[10] – **Jill Harbutt**

The changes in men's fashions were also integral to the costume design process, Greg Wise believing the point of his character [Willoughby] is that 'he's the breeze of modernity coming in',[11] especially in relation to Alan Rickman's character, Colonel Brandon, who is still dressed 'in the old world'.[12] For his entrance into the narrative, Wise's John Willoughby wore a dark green greatcoat (fig.78). The scene dictated that he arrives on horseback in the rain and discovers Marianne, who has fallen and strained her ankle. Greg Wise remembered, 'I suggested to Ang Lee that at this stage, we have to meet a superhero, we have to meet the 1800s equivalent of Batman, so can I have a cape or something? It's also about Marianne's head and in a way, Willoughby is a manifestation of her dreams'.[13] The fitting and wearing of period clothes informs everything for a character intellectuality and physicality.

The period is very much about constraint, which is very important – you are constrained emotionally, you are constrained with what you are wearing. You have a waistcoat which is tight, a topcoat which is always buttoned up, you do feel that you are being held, and therefore you have to hold yourself in a certain way as a result of that, the clothing informs everything you do.[14] – **Greg Wise**

Colonel Brandon's military uniform symbolises a transformation in Marianne's perception of 'an old man' into a dashing husband.[15] Throughout her books, Austen's female characters are often impressed by men in uniform who were a common feature moving around the countryside during the Napoleonic Wars (1803–15).

Marianne and Colonel Brandon's wedding completes the narrative (fig.79). Bright drew inspiration for the dress from a straw-trimmed dress from the Hermitage in St Petersburg, the exquisite embroidery was hand crafted by Katharine Swailes (fig.80).

The film was a commercial and critical success, Bright and Beavan were nominated for their sixth Oscar for Best Costume Design and a BAFTA for their work. Thompson and Winslet both won BAFTAs for their performances and Thompson made history by becoming the first person to win Oscars for acting [*Howards End*] and screenwriting.

The wave of Austen-mania continued with one of the most celebrated productions in the history of the BBC, *Pride and Prejudice* (1995).

77. (opposite, above) The Dashwood family in *Sense and Sensibility* (1995)

78. (opposite, below) John Willoughby (Greg Wise) in *Sense and Sensibility* (1995)

'Marianne's wedding dress was a rare opportunity to work with a completely new material: straw. It appeared on my worktable in a carrier bag, as an unfathomable knot of delicate, beautifully crafted straw pieces. It took time to assemble the pieces to work out how this could be used. The main focus of the dress was the neckline.
A combination of netting and wire was used to create a shape to place the straw on. As the straw work moved down the front into the skirt, the embellishment became more open and allowed the silk supporting fabric to billow and move freely.

The silk dress fabric had an interesting weave, that created a slight firmness, this allowed the fabric to fill with air so the train of the dress lifted and floated, the straw acted as weight on the edge, grounding the outside edge of the longest part of the train.'[16] – Katharine Swailes, Costume Maker

79. (above) Marianne Dashwood (Kate Winslet) and Colonel Brandon (Alan Rickman) in *Sense and Sensibility* (1995)

80. (opposite) Costume for Marianne Dashwood (Kate Winslet) in *Sense and Sensibility* (1995)

Pride and Prejudice (1995)

Director Simon Langton | Costume Designer Dinah Collin
Starring Jennifer Ehle, Colin Firth, Alison Steadman, Benjamin Whitrow, Julia Sawalha, Polly Maberly, Susannah Harker

Everything we are doing is an interpretation in the end, we are not making a documentary, the clothes have to look attractive to a modern audience. I like to find that step between them and us, translating between the two flavours, it has to appeal to people in the modern day.[17] – **Dinah Collin**

Pride and Prejudice occupies a unique place in British literary and cultural life. BBC adaptations of the novel had been staged since 1938, when it was filmed and broadcast live at Alexandra Palace in North London. The BBC has subsequently filmed *Pride and Prejudice* in 1952, 1958, 1967 and in 1980 (Costume Designer Joan Ellacott).

After a 15-year absence from BBC programming, *Pride and Prejudice* was commissioned as a six-part Sunday night serial adapted by Andrew Davies, who had become synonymous with 'classic' adaptations. His distinctly personal approach often involved highlighting sexual tensions and he would reshape and create scenes where he felt the original novelist was restricted.

None of the previous adaptations had taken Jane Austen seriously, they were presented as light social comedies, when they are about love, sex and money and how to survive in a cruel world. Previous BBC versions looked artificial and studio-bound and they hadn't presented the characters as fully rounded people – rather like us.[18] – **Andrew Davies**

Director Simon Langton had a strong vision for how fabric, clothes and character could tell the story of the *Pride and Prejudice* characters:

What struck me most of all was the obvious sense of freedom afforded by the light, soft materials. I wanted pale colour or creamy whites for the girls to reflect both their zest and their innocence* (fig.84)*. This meant we could keep the darker, richer colours and exotic fabrics for the Bingley sisters or Lady Catherine de Bourgh.[19] – **Simon Langton**

When writing the screenplay Andrew Davies wanted to draw out several elements not present in previous productions, 'Mr Darcy is a misunderstood character. I wanted to emphasise the men in the story. We began with Darcy and Bingley on horseback, that set the tone, I wanted to remind the audience of the physicality of these people, so they weren't standing stiffly in ballrooms all the time. I pushed the boundaries of so-called "costume dramas" at the BBC.'[20]

For Davies, it was important for contemporary audiences to connect with a period setting:

One of the things I've always thought is a drag in so many period adaptations is that they are always buttoned up to the neck ... I'm always looking for excuses to get them out of their clothes. I wanted to see Elizabeth running, like she does in the book, I wanted to show her energy, I showed Mr Darcy in his bath.[21] – **Andrew Davies**

BBC Costume Designer Dinah Collin was commissioned to design the adaptation and the challenge for Collin, Bright and his team at Cosprop was a lack of stock for this period, even in their reference museum, in 1995.

I didn't know the novel and I hadn't worked in that time period before, so it was a challenge. I explored the world of museum collections and I collected lots of reference material and images for the different families depicted in the story. I wanted something fresh for the Bennet sisters, to show their youth and energy and I wanted to create something that also felt contemporary. For Colin Firth's Mr Darcy, I wanted clothes that didn't overwhelm him. The rails of clothes at Cosprop from the 1850s and 1860s went on forever, but the early 1800s, the rails were empty. This meant that I was going to have to make most of the costumes, so most things had to be created from the ground up.[22] – **Dinah Collin**

Collin's research process took her to the Fashion Museum in Bath and textile collections in Winchester and at Manchester's Platt Hall, which contained examples of Lancashire printed cottons 'which were hugely valuable to the fabric research.'[23] Curators at the Victoria and Albert Museum in London also provided examples of period clothing.

At the V&A, curator Avril Hart told me they had just been given a coat made out of a fabric they had never seen before. It's called partridge, a sort of fleck with a stiff cotton weave. When I went to Cosprop, I found they had been making a 1780s' coat out of a fabric

82. (opposite) Moodboard (above) for Elizabeth Bennet (Jennifer Ehle and (below) for Fitzwilliam Darcy (Colin Firth)

'I've never drawn. I like to see things develop. I create moodboards ... My boards tend to be a collection ... of images from various points in time, as long as they have a way into what you want to talk about.'[24] – Dinah Collin

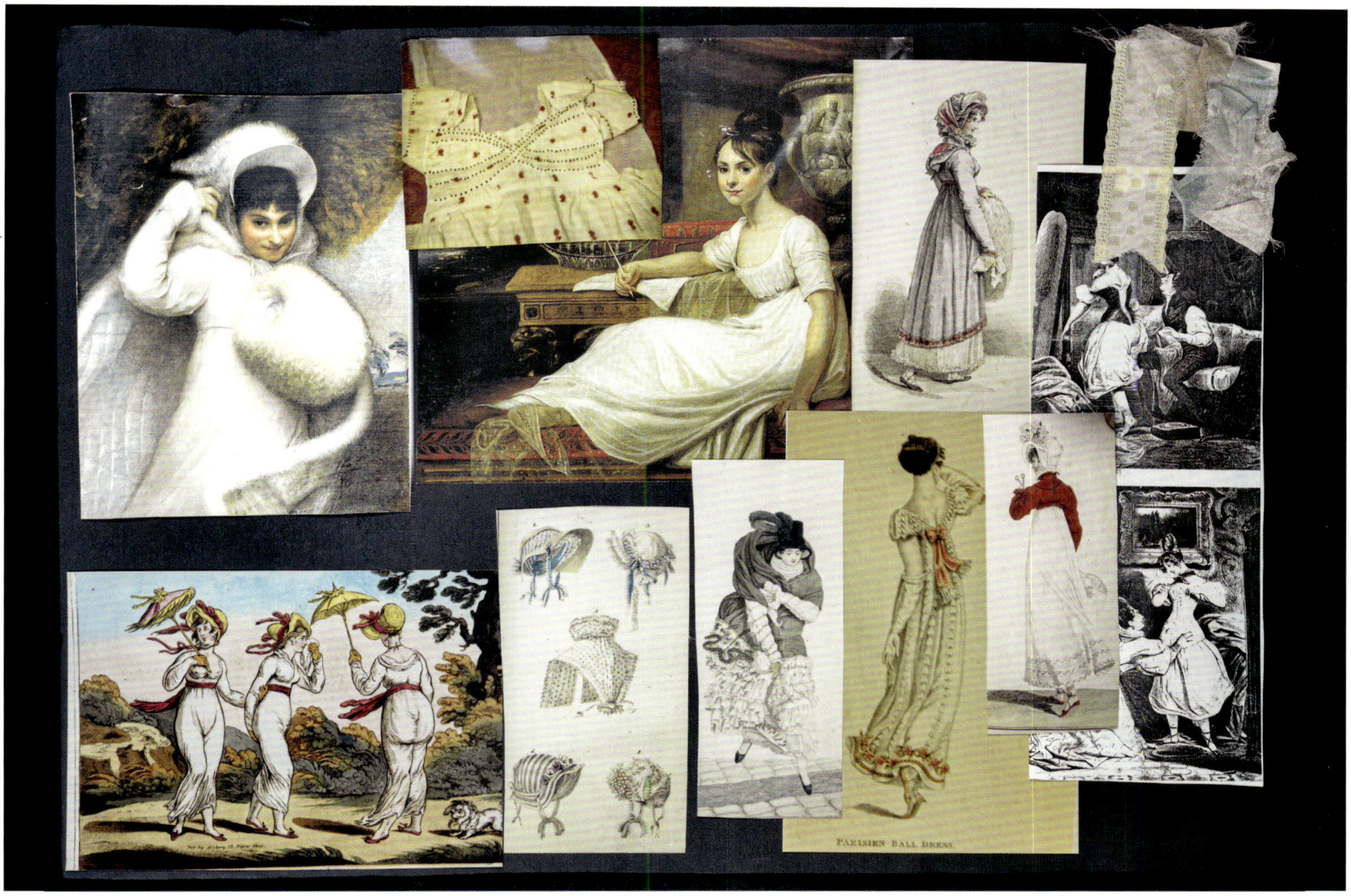

PARISIEN BALL DRESS.

Afternoon Dress for March

called India, which was very similar. We made one of Mr Bennet's long coats along those lines because it had exactly the right look.[25] – **Dinah Collin**

Dinah is one of the few designers who will commission fabric to be printed to make sure it's right for the period. Sometimes when you buy a print, and it's on heavy cotton, perhaps it's been sold as furnishing fabric, this is just too heavy for someone's clothes. But Dinah chooses her fabric and her print and makes the two work together.[26] – **John Bright**

Collin contacted Amy Caswell, who had just completed a textile and print course at the School of Art, Design and Textiles in Bradford. The principal of the college, a Jane Austen fan, suggested they could use the college's printing facilities. Collin found cotton saris in Bradford, working closely with Caswell, to have them then dyed to achieve the correct effect. The design concept for *Pride and Prejudice* explored an authentic narrative of hand-made patterns being passed between families (fig.86).

The muslin dress was a very important part of a woman's wardrobe during this period. While women would often wear the printed 'washing-frocks' as they were called, these were not considered appropriate for the evenings or for visiting. The muslin dress was worn with a petticoat of a different colour underneath.[27] – **Dinah Collin**

Collin created moodboards for each character and drew from the resources and the skill of the Cosprop Workroom staff. The designer enjoyed the collaboration and being able to drop in and consult them on any of the processes.

Authenticity was at the heart of the production, the key being to make the clothes look like real clothes from a wardrobe, rather than a set of costumes worn by actors.

Collin worked out a costume plot for each character and then discussed with the actors how they'd like to wear the clothes.

For Elizabeth Bennet (Jennifer Ehle; fig.83, above), Collin created 'the direct and practical aspects of her character' with lots of browns and a curry-coloured coat she wears on her visit to Pemberley.[28] Collin was inspired by a hat she had seen on display in Jane Austen's house in Chawton, Hampshire: 'I wanted a straightforward look that was very pretty and not fussy, Elizabeth was very active, and it was important that her clothes allowed her to move easily and naturally.'

There was one dress that I used to wear a lot – just as today you would pull on a favourite pair of Levi's or a well-worn T-shirt – you don't often get the chance to have a choice like that, and I was very grateful, my daily mix-and-match became part of the pleasure of making the series.[29] – **Jennifer Ehle**

The collection at Jane Austen's house provided inspiration for the smallest of details. Collin said, 'I saw two crosses on display at Chawton, and I commissioned jewellery-maker Dinny Hall to copy them, they were worn by Elizabeth and Jane.'[30]

The contrast between the Bennets and Bingleys was paramount in establishing their class differences. Collin dressed the Bingley sisters wearing 'the equivalent of Gucci' to stand out against the simplicity of the Bennet sisters.[31] Evening head-dresses were more elaborate and reflected their elevated status. To establish Mr Bingley as an instantly likeable character, Collin dressed him in warm colours and soft textures such as tweed. The Italian costume house Peruzzi provided the military costumes.

Equally important as the Bennet sisters was dressing the hero of the story. The fitting process with Colin Firth allowed Collin to explore several options to create Mr Fitzwilliam Darcy. 'Colin Firth is very strong and has a virile quality, and I wanted to make sure he wasn't diminished by the clothes. We looked at various colours on him, we decided to keep the warmest tones for Mr Bingley. Colin wanted to be saturnine but not wear black.'[32]

There was also the challenge of making Darcy, who begins the story aloof and unapproachable, into an object of desire both for Elizabeth Bennet and for the viewer. Costume was integral in making him more relatable, Collin describing his wardrobe as having to feel like jeans and a T-shirt when it's actually breeches and boots.

Collin designed clothes in dark greens and greys, but half-way through filming schedule, Firth said that he'd now like a black coat. For Collin, one of the advantages of filming over a long period is that it allowed the actors to adapt their wardrobes as they become more comfortable in their roles. Head of Men's Wardrobe at Cosprop, Christopher Prins, worked with Collin to source costumes, fit and dress Firth, 'I said to him, 'Let's get you dressed. It was the second fitting. We got him into his classic look, trousers and boots and olive-green coat and he turned towards the mirror and Mr Darcy was born, it was a thrilling moment.'[33]

83. (opposite) Jennifer Ehle being fitted into her hat for her role as Elizabeth Bennet in *Pride and Prejudice* (1995)

84. (right) The Bennet family in *Pride and Prejudice* (1995)

85. (below) Fitzwilliam Darcy (Colin Firth) in *Pride and Prejudice* (1995)

One of the most celebrated moments in BBC's television history came about through collaboration as the original script called for Darcy to dive into the lake naked (fig.85).

Mr Darcy's 'wet shirt moment' was never scripted. It came about in discussions between myself and Christopher Prins. In the scene Mr Darcy is spied emerging from a lake having taken a cooling swim on a hot summer's day. Because on-screen male nudity was not permitted (taking into account the BBC watershed and US broadcasts) – the idea of the 'wet shirt' was born. Our way round this was for Colin Firth to be filmed three-quarter length, wearing just the Irish linen shirt, copied from an antique original, which clung to the body ... The scene transformed Colin Firth from a respected classical actor to something of a sex symbol overnight![34] – **Dinah Collin**

It was such a sexy moment because suddenly Elizabeth is aware of his physicality. Whereas, if it had happened as scripted, he would then have been dressed again and you would not have had their meeting and that's the moment when they really fancy each other.[35] – **Christopher Prins**

Firth felt it would be unrealistic to strip to a pair of drawers and was correct in his research; men rarely wore underwear in this period. They wore a long shirt, which was tucked under the legs, 'like a nappy' as actor Greg Wise recalled when he was being costumed in *Sense and Sensibility*.[36] This clothing element was revealed further when in the 2020 film adaptation of *Emma*, Mr Knightley (Johnny Flynn) is shown being dressed by his manservant and shows this undergarment being tucked between his legs.

Collin ensured that Firth's coats were fitted closely to his body, revealing his athletic physique, as projection of his marriageability.

The women were bejewelled, silked and coiffed and the men can see exactly what they are getting in terms of looks and wealth. The men, with their fine tailoring, the women will know what they are getting in terms of wealth and status.[37] – **Christopher Prins**

Period footwear is essential for actors to carry their performance but can be challenging to recreate as Jenny Ireland, Cosprop's former Company Manager recalled,

I was responsible for the ordering and making of shoes, in conjunction with the designer. At Cosprop there was a list of the usual shoemakers that we used. We tended to go to different makers for different periods. Whether it was Duke of Wellington boots with one company or 1920s' shoes with another. The boots for **Pride and Prejudice** ***and*** **Sense and Sensibility** ***were a challenge because nothing existed outside of a museum. Eventually we found someone who worked on his own in Northampton, the UK home of shoe and boot making.***[38]

Textile expert Ruth Caswell, who had also been a costume maker for theatre, found a tiny, single shoe in a repertory theatre. Julia Sawalha, who played Lydia Bennet, tried it on and it fitted, so a pair was made and is now in the John Bright Collection.

Screened on the Sunday night autumn slot, the series was watched by an audience of 11 million people. At the peak of home entertainment, 200,000 VHS boxsets of the series were sold after the broadcast, making it one of the most successful programmes in British television history. Dinah Collin won an EMMY Award for her work.

For many audiences and commentors, the 1995 version of *Pride and Prejudice* remains the definitive adaptation of the novel. Its costumes would ultimately go into Cosprop's stock on a 'new to hire' basis or into exhibitions. The popularity of the programme resulted in many of the costumes touring around the country and being exhibited in a range of venues, such as the *Jane Austen: Film and Fashion* exhibition staged at the Fashion Museum in Bath (2004).

In 2022 the BBC marked its centenary with 100 objects that had come to shape and define the organisation and its place in British culture. Collin's shirt for Mr Darcy was one of the costumes that was chosen to represent the BBC's worldwide celebration of classic adaptations. The scene was referenced in the Regency fantasy *Bridgerton* (2020–), which depicts Anthony Bridgerton (Jonathan Bailey) emerging from a lake in a soaking wet shirt.

The impact of *Pride and Prejudice* was global, and it changed the life of one future Cosprop maker.

Part of my Cosprop journey was watching **Pride and Prejudice** ***in Australia as a teenager and being captivated by the costumes. I watched it with my mum who loved costume dramas. She was very proud when I moved to the UK and started working at Cosprop, which was a dream come true.***[39] – **Emma Burke, Costume Maker**

Ten years after its impact, director Joe Wright embarked on a feature film adaptation – the first since the 1940 MGM version.

86. (opposite) Costumes for Elizabeth Bennet (Jennifer Ehle) and Catherine Bennet (Polly Maberly) in *Pride and Prejudice* (1995)

Pride & Prejudice (2005)

Director Joe Wright | Costume Designer Jacqueline Durran
Starring Keira Knightley, Matthew Macfadyen, Brenda Blethyn, Rosamund Pike, Kelly Reilly, Donald Sutherland

Things go in cycles; audiences want new writing but those classic books are so brilliant, what's the point of reinventing the wheel? A different set of actors want to try those roles and there's always a different interpretation. With the Jane Austens, the Dinah Collin 1995 version is so different to Jacqueline Durran's 2005 version, a different director such as Joe Wright will bring something new to it, even if it's the same story.[40] – **Ross Braganza, Senior Men's Costumier**

Directors and writers can reimagine a period, and pinpoint accuracy is not always important to directors. Joe Wright wanted to release the narrative from a formal Regency setting and explore the ebullience of the Bennet sisters, describing his vision as a 'teen movie.'

Although the novel was published in 1813, Jane Austen wrote her first draft, then called 'First Impressions', around 1797. So, we used the fashions of the earlier period, where the waist on dresses was lower and more flattering. When Caroline Bingley appears, she would obviously be wearing the latest creation. But Mrs Bennet's dresses are earlier than 1797 and Lady Catherine's are even earlier, because those two would have the best clothes from previous years in their wardrobes. Jacqueline, working with Mike Leigh, comes from a very character-oriented British realist style of filmmaking.[41] – **Joe Wright**

Wright and screenwriter Deborah Moggach also opted for a 'muddy hem version' of the Bennet's family home Longbourn,[42] presenting it in a more rural setting than in previous adaptations out of a desire to depict the Bennets in 'very close proximity to their rural life and to emphasise their relative poverty'.[43] This would contrast to the opulence of the Bingley's bringing their London life to the country (fig.87).

Jacqueline Durran's approach to the costume design was to bring 'variation into the world, between the different families, because the world has variation',[44] so the two family strands in the *Pride & Prejudice* world would be served by having different costume sources. She made the decision to have Mr Darcy's and the Bingleys' costumes made at Cosprop and those of the Bennets at a different costume house, explaining that styles of costume houses differ and that can inform the look of the characters. Durran also brought a layer of authenticity to the clothes in the form of handmade skills. 'I thought about how a local dressmaker would've made something, the fabric choices she would have had, what a provincial family would do with their clothes'.[45]

The long opening panning shot of Elizabeth Bennet (Keira Knightley) returning to Longbourn in a brown dress established the idea of a close family and clothes that would have been handed down (and repurposed) from sister to sister. This would then contrast with the wealthier characters. At the Meryton Ball, Wright wanted Caroline Bingley (Kelly Reilly) to wear the height of London fashion so when she enters, the crowd stops as she deliberately stands out against the rural – behind the times – fashions.

Durran developed Mr Darcy's clothes for Matthew Macfadyen, working closely with Christopher Prins.

Christopher had a knack of finding the correct costume, exactly what you needed, he knew the period so well and he knew the stock so well, so he could find the right thing you needed. A fitting with him was always a pleasure, something surprising would always happen, he was great with actors, explaining the form that something should take in that period. It's a very subtle thing, it's not only finding the right garment but it was also what was right for the character.[46] – **Jacqueline Durran**

Mr Darcy's narrative arc was as crucial as Elizabeth Bennet's, with Durran complementing his change in attitude through clothing.

***Darcy's costume has a series of stages. The first time we see him, he's at Meryton, where he has a very stiffly tailored jacket on, and he's quite contained and rigid* (fig.87)*. By the time we get to the proposal that goes wrong in the rain, we move to a similar cut, but a much softer fabric. The nth degree is him walking through the mist in the morning, completely undressed by eighteenth-century standards* (fig.88).**[47] – **Jacqueline Durran**

This image of Mr Darcy appeared on all the marketing material associated with the film, capturing a contemporary vision of a classic novel. Durran was nominated for an Oscar and BAFTA for her work.

87. (opposite, above) Caroline Bingley (Kelly Reilly) and Fitzwilliam Darcy (Matthew Macfadyen) in *Pride & Prejudice* (2005)

88. (opposite, below) Fitzwilliam Darcy (Matthew Macfadyen) in *Pride & Prejudice* (2005)

Sense and Sensibility (2008)

Director John Alexander | Costume Designer Michele Clapton
Starring Hattie Morahan, Charity Wakefield, Dan Stevens, Janet McTeer, Dominic Cooper, David Morrissey

Austen's popularity showed no sign of abating, and in 2008 the BBC commissioned a new adaptation of *Sense and Sensibility*. Building on the legacy of *Pride and Prejudice*, Andrew Davies once again adapted the novel and added several scenes, which had been only suggested in the original text. Beginning the research process, Michele Clapton decided to make the clothes from the ground up, working with Bright to create a lot of the costumes together. The stock and the Museum Collection offered sources of inspiration for the design palette.

***My initial research into the period clothes for* Sense and Sensibility *included visits to Cosprop, not only to look at their original pieces and stock of the period, which by that time was quite extensive but to also speak with John, whose knowledge of the period and support for designers is unrivalled ... I adore looking at the cut of original garments they have there. I can look at the construction, the original colour still present in the areas hidden from sunlight, also the nature of decoration, be it embroidery, beading or pleating. These conversations with John are wonderful and informative and later, as we create costumes, they are key to the understanding of fit and movement.*[48] – Michele Clapton**

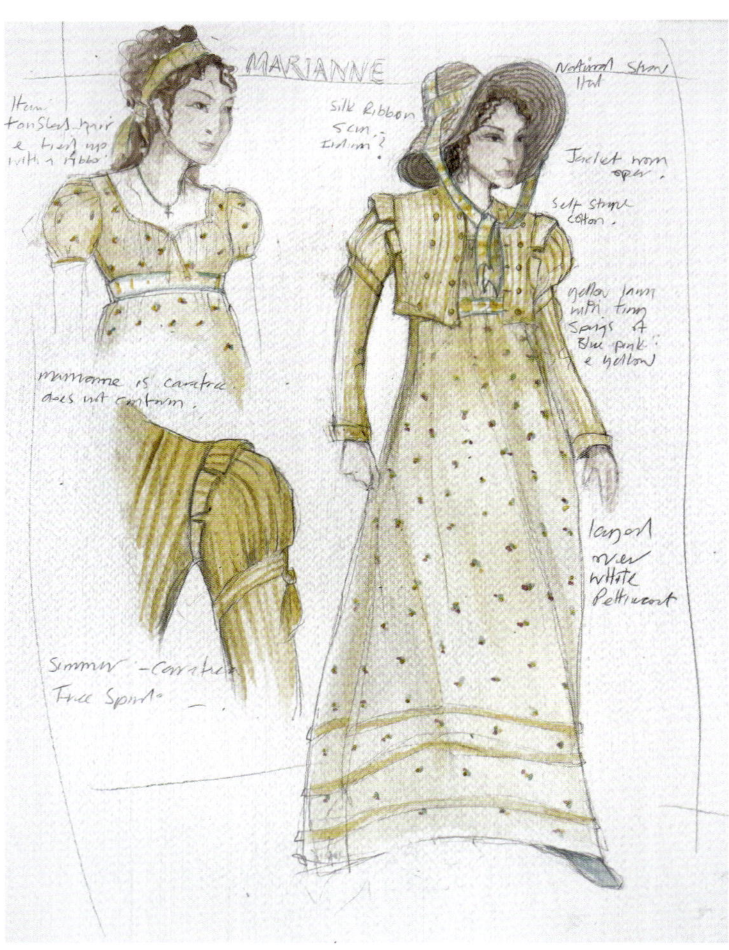

Clapton decided to give the Dashwood sisters contrasting wardrobes. The artistic, romantic Marianne wears strong colours compared to Elinor, who has a different personality and expectation. Assistant Costume Designer Alex Fordham revealed that with Marianne being younger and a 'wild child', her wardrobe contains a lot of buttercup yellows, which suited Charity Wakefield's complexion and her character's freshness.

***On any project I love to create a palette of dyed cloth samples in particular shades. I find it to be a 'way in'. Colours to me are like the underpinnings of a costume ... they provide the structure on which everything else sits, it's a shared language for the creative team. It helps me build a particular visual sense of the story, I can then share these with the director and production designer to see if our ideas align. Once this is established, I can then use them in the preliminary principal fittings as part of the conversation with the actor and John around character.*[49] – Michele Clapton**

For the making team at Cosprop, the starting point for the costumes is the selection and use of fabrics. The balance between how costumes strive for authenticity but need to be relatable to a modern audience is also reflected in hair and make-up.

***Female characters in nineteenth-century dramas would all have their hair done in very precise ringlets, all neat and perfect just like in the portraits. Now we're trying to achieve a more believable, natural look, especially when the Dashwoods are at home.*[50] – Michele Clapton**

For the men's wardrobes, the need to distinguish between suitors was similar to the approach to defining the different sisters. Clapton explained that Willoughby's (Dominic Cooper) wardrobe was designed to reflect his 'poetic and fashionable' nature, while Edward (Dan Stevens) was more suited to eighteenth-century rural colours. Colonel Brandon (David Morrissey) being a stronger character, had costumes that were halfway between the two, his clothes were designed to be out of date.

During the Cosprop fitting process with Bright and Clapton, Morrissey commented that the period costumes were uncomfortable for modern life, but as soon as the cast were riding horses or walking across fields, he realised why they were made that way. 'When you're dancing, they're quite restrictive, but that's quite good for posture – posture was

89. (left) Costume design for Marianne (Charity Wakefield) in *Sense and Sensibility* (2008)

90. (opposite) Mrs Dashwood (Janet McTeer), Elinor (Hattie Morahan) and Marianne (Charity Wakefield) in *Sense and Sensibility* (2008)

'One of the things you do at a fitting, as soon as somebody's got a corset on, is to ask them to sit down in the underwear before you put the dress on, so that you know if the corset is going to dig in or if it lifts at all on the body. You make sure that the base is right before you move on to the next stage.'[51] – John Bright

different then, and that's important. But they give you a feel for the character which is really an advantage to you as an actor'.[52]

In fittings at Cosprop once we establish the underpinnings we can start to explore character in shapes and cuts from existing stock to get an idea of direction. This time is of paramount importance for all involved. For the actor to meet and develop with us their character. To get a sense of the feel and restriction of a costume, this informs the posture and gait of the time. I continued to explore the period and its levels of society, and in particular our character's place within it. How they might move, their individual style. For me, it's also about the modern audience relating to these characters, it is not a documentary, it is a drama, it is story-telling. But there is always a certain expectation from purists around the interpretation of a Jane Austen story![53] – **Michele Clapton**

Michele Clapton was nominated for Best Costume Design at the Costume Design Guild Awards.

Emma (2020)

Director Autumn de Wilde | Costume Designer Alexandra Byrne
Starring Anya Taylor-Joy, Johnny Flynn, Mia Goth, Bill Nighy, Miranda Hart

Emma has been filmed regularly since *Pride and Prejudice* (1995) ignited a wave of adaptations of Austen's work. In 1996 a feature film starred Gwyneth Paltrow (Costume Designer Ruth Myers) and following the success of *Sense and Sensibility* (2008), the BBC revisited *Emma* with Romola Garai (Costume Designer Rosalind Ebbutt) in 2009.

For the 2020 version, Alexandra Byrne examined clothing at the Fashion Museum in Bath, an important repository of Regency fashion and explored other museum collections to inform her design process. Byrne had designed the BBC 1995 production of *Persuasion* and used the original novel as a source of inspiration.

I always read the novel, a lot of the audience will have also read the novel, if you can add to anything, another layer, that's important ... When you investigate the clothes closely, when you go into the seam allowance where it hasn't seen daylight, you see the real colours, there's a tendency to go very sepia and faded with period films, their colour combinations were vibrant so I tried to respect that.[54] – **Alexandra Byrne**

The museum at Cosprop also informed research and inspiration for the design concept. Piecing together a visual picture from this range of sources, Byrne created a world for each character that reflects the eclectic wardrobe of the modern viewer. She also appreciated the talents of the Cosprop makers, who bring their own interpretation when making costume, acknowledging that, 'you can give them the same character and they can make a difference.'[55] For *Emma*, Byrne developed the visual design concept of using the seasons to inform the structure of the narrative.

This story takes place in a calendar year, and I used Emma's extensive wardrobe to define the colours of the season. She is wealthy and entitled; she has a dressmaker rather than sewing and embroidering her own clothes. She has access to fashion magazines and is a big fish in a small pond.[56] – **Alexandra Byrne**

One of the fashionable garments of the 1790s was the spencer, a short jacket worn over a gown to provide warmth. Cut like the bodice of the gown, usually with long sleeves and a high neck, spencers could be made of silk as well as woollen cloth and were often worn with a beautiful shawl.

Costume Maker Jill Harbutt was one of the makers responsible for recreating a spencer for Anya Taylor-Joy.

The Jane Austen period is not a difficult period to make for in general. Quite often the dresses have the petticoat incorporated in the dress, so the bodice was made as one (two layers) then the skirt's two layers are free flowing. Alex [Byrne] wanted the two layers separate so it was a petticoat and a dress. They had to sit well together so as to look good. Piping was used a lot during this period, often as a drawstring channel under the neckline to control the gathering when on the body, and then tied to correct the shape. They were quite a delight to make as they are small and precise, with piping and the period seam lines and a little collar.[57] – **Jill Harbutt**

A mustard-coloured coat worn by Anya Taylor-Joy became the lead image for the film's global marketing campaign (fig.92). Julia Buckmiller, created the costume working from Byrne's costume design and research (fig.91).

Alex gave me two fashion plates of the period, one of them was* Costume Parisien, *1809, No. 1025, that shows a similar back with radiating pleats and has a similar colour. I developed the pattern myself and the fabric was dyed to Alex's specification, it was one of my favourite costumes that I made at Cosprop and I'm always delighted that people like it so much as well.[58] – **Julia Buckmiller, Costume Maker**

Most designers only come to a particular period once or twice in their whole career, so we should be able to offer some sort of support system, in that way the museum has developed over the years and we now have a large collection to draw from. We are better covered for periods such as Regency than we were when Dinah [Collin] was doing* Pride and Prejudice *in 1995. For* Emma *(2020) there was a lot more for Alex to look at, little jackets and things.[59] – **John Bright**

The reconstruction of the period was celebrated by the media when the film was released in 2020. Byrne received an Oscar nomination for Best Costume Design.

'About two weeks into filming, I started relying on my corset to help me get the work done. The second my corset was put on, I was like, "I know what I'm doing. I've got this. It's all going to be fine." I just had to be laced in first.'[60] – Anya Taylor-Joy

91. (above) Fashion plate, 1800s, similar to the coat worn in *Emma* (2020)

92. (right) Emma (Anya Taylor-Joy) in *Emma* (2020)

CHAPTER FOUR

INSIDE THE COSTUME HOUSE

The Workrooms

THE STOCK

'Clothing you have selected from stock forms the foundation for costume design then you adjust and build up layers. You might be the first person the actor has met on the film and you may never have worked with them before. It's important to win their confidence and to look at them in different clothes.' – John Bright

The stock at Cosprop provides costume designers with everything they need to bring their characters to life. Designers strive for their characters to have a lived history, a life prior to the beginning of the narrative. Like the clothing we wear on a daily basis, costume design has to be infused with the same lived-in history. Cosprop provides this service, which is part of its success and why it is beloved by the costume design community and by actors.

Cosprop's stock of clothing and accessories are the beating heart of the organisation and business. What began as a rail of clothes in John Bright's parents' dining room, Cosprop now holds more than one million items of clothing, hats, shoes, handbags and other accessories and has been built up over decades to create a unique museum-worthy collection.

In the early 1960s, you could pick up fabrics, handbags, parasols and scarves at markets for virtually next to nothing. The Cosprop stock has always consisted of genuine period clothes, or what Maggie Smith liked to call 'clothes off dead people!' **– John Bright**

Company Manager Chris Garlick explains the importance of the stock: 'Cosprop has always used original pieces to guide how they create newly designed outfits, where possible using the same period techniques and materials ... The stock at Cosprop is very, very good quality and this often gives us the edge over the competition.'

The stores at Cosprop are a living history of dress, unseen outside of a major museum such as the Victoria and Albert Museum in London or the Metropolitan Museum of Art in New York. For costume designers, there are thousands of costumes to hire. Cosprop Costume Maker Thaïs Demontrond believes that 'costume designers love Cosprop because each garment has history, a story. It's in every fibre, that's why they keep returning to Cosprop over and over again because they know they will find the ideal garment for their project.'

Early in my career, I was on a film set dressing a crowd scene and, on the rail, was a group of beautifully finished, clean, organised costumes and I knew they were all from Cosprop, they just stood out from the rest, you know you have quality from Cosprop because the standard is the best in the industry.
– **Michael O'Connor, Costume Designer**

Keeping track of what stock has been selected by what design team, whether an item of clothing needs to be fitted or altered, when they need to be checked and booked out to go to set is part of the day-to-day work. When an actor is in front of the camera or goes on stage, their clothes must be correct. With actors often not cast until the last minute to save the cost of paying them before they need to start work, there is often a dash to the finishing line. Cosprop costumiers and the design teams work closely together to ensure nothing is overlooked.

The costumiers are the bridge between the Cosprop stock and the designer, their assistant and the supervisor. Chris Garlick explains that once a production's look has been established, 'the wardrobe supervisor will pull costumes from stock with the support of one of the costumiers, assigned to the project. There's an art to the pulling of stock, a costume palette begins to form itself on a rail.'

Costume designers will show us their moodboards and designs and we will discuss the time period of the piece, the character and the plot. Depending on what is needed, I can also advise on the correct historical costume and we will have an initial look in the stock. We tend to look at the principals first and the crowd later. If the costumes are being made in our workroom, we look for shapes to try on the actor as a starting point, and if they are just using stock, we can pull together rails. – **Hannah Monkley, Senior Costumier, Womenswear**

The quality of the garments, original or made in-house with utmost care and attention from quality fabrics, has meant that they continue to provide great service even after several decades. For designers, faced with less time and smaller budgets, they can combine to create an outfit. With the help of the costumiers, all of whom have an expert knowledge of historical dress, shows can sometimes be pulled together almost entirely from stock.

Because we know the stock so well, some designers trust us to find something for them. If they've got something in their mind, we can help find a particular look for them. With other designers, they might have a feel for the character and it's useful for them to go and look themselves for inspiration.

Sometimes there is an actual design or sketch for a character, or reference material mood boards, though this happens less and less. Some designers are really hands on and want to go and look for items in the stock. Things are not in cases like a museum, at Cosprop they can look closely, handle clothing, turn it inside out if needed to see how it's constructed and put together.

If they are looking for something really specific, John will show them the way, he knows everything in the building, he is a walking encyclopaedia! – **Ross Braganza, Senior Costumier, Menswear**

When we fit costumes that need repairing or do not fit and are in between an alteration and a remake, we make a decision on that along with the Workroom. The Alterations team are magicians in the way they can turn a costume around. Their knowledge of sewing construction is extraordinary and they continually surprise me with their skill and ingenuity. – **Hannah Monkley**

The art of the costumiers is to understand what the designer may like and build it up over a period of time through knowledge of their work and the designer's aesthetic.

I was working on a rail of costumes for a production, my assistant had pulled some clothes but it wasn't quite working. I changed a couple of items. John notices everything that is going on at Cosprop and said to me 'the rail is looking better than it did last week.' – **Michael O'Connor**

Sourcing the correct fabrics is also an essential part of creating the authenticity of a character. Fabrics from the early part of the twentieth century tended to be heavier than they are today. For designers, fabric is key.

Monkley elaborates on the pre-production process: 'We will be pulling clothes and putting them onto rails, along with the designer and their team. We book everything out by hand, we photograph everything and maintain a meticulous

record. We are currently coding the stock, which is a mammoth task, but we are chipping away at it. In the future, there will be a database and it will be a brilliant resource'.

As an organisation, Cosprop evolves with changes and new demands of the film, television and theatre industries. ***We are also thinking about size-inclusive stock, many of our clothes are for a particular body shape. Casting has become more inclusive and diverse over the past few years so our stock has to reflect those changes and offer options to designers. –*** **Hannah Monkley**

A production with a large cast will also require all the accessories to complete the wardrobe: underpinnings, corsets, shoes, trousers, coats, belts, waistcoats, collars, bags, ties, gloves and hats. This can comprise around 15 separate pieces for each ensemble which all need to be booked out.

The staff at Cosprop play an important role in textile conservation. The maintenance, care and attention of a collection this size is a momentous task and requires specialist skills. With a large collection of clothing to maintain and to ensure their future survival, the issue of pest control (moths) is an everyday concern for the staff at Cosprop. Fogging is a practice that aims to ensure the stock is protected. The stock at Cosprop must be constantly replenished to ensure it remains current and resourceful for future designers and productions. Monkley, for example, manages the women's returns and works closely with stock management to know exactly what is coming back in the building, and to then organise any necessary repair or cleaning. New costumes that are created in the Workroom must be future-proofed, so they join the stock and be reused for a new production. Cosprop is the ultimate example of textile recycling, adaptation and sustainability, an important concern in the disposable world of filmmaking. Clothing and all essential accessories to complete a character – hats, belts, shoes – are all recycled and reinvented for future productions.

Bright says 'If a costume is a particularly good shape or representative of a specific period, it will often go from show to show.' Costumes worn in *Brideshead Revisited* (1981) were later worn by Greta Scacchi in *Heat and Dust* (1983), and then later the costumes reappeared in the television series *The Orchid House* (1991). Costumes from *Dangerous Liaisons* (1988) were repurposed and worn by Saskia Wickham in the BBC production of *Clarissa* (1991). The costume for Daniela Denby-Ashe for the BBC's *North and South* (2004) was also worn by Gillian Anderson in the BBC's *Bleak House* (2005) and then by Michelle Dockery in *Return to Cranford* (2009).

THE MUSEUM AND THE LIBRARY

'John will often show an original piece to a designer, and it will fire their imagination. A designer can see inside a historical garment to see the construction, which is hugely important to understand fabric and cut.' – Chris Garlick

Traditionally called 'The Museum' by the staff, Cosprop's reference collection is an archive of surviving antique garments and is used as a 'library of dress'. Its most precious items are kept separate from the stock in two dedicated rooms – but its continued growth has populated other parts of the building with archive-quality boxes holding seemingly endless sources of inspiration. It is a testimony to John Bright's passion for collecting, preserving and curating. It also illustrates the origins of his 'period-accurate' designs and some of his – and Cosprop's – working methods. Today it is known as the John Bright Collection and more than 400 key items are available on the Heritage Lottery-funded John Bright Collection website.

Bright has always had a fascination with the past. Like many costume designers who were emerging in the 1960s, such as Shirley Russell and Anthony Powell, Bright would explore antique markets in and around London. He would visit Bell Street, Alfie's Antique market and the famous Portobello Road which, in the 1960s, was a treasure trove of clothing from a bygone age. Building up this collection has been a life's work and pieces have come from a variety of places and collaborations. In the early days of Cosprop, some of the original garments in the collection were hired out for productions, a practice that strengthened Bright's and Cosprop's reputation for authenticity. However, it also showed that these pieces could not withstand the demands of a production, so it was decided that the originals should become a reference collection and a template for the Cosprop stock.

In 1985 Cosprop appointed Elizabeth Owen as the first curator to organise the Museum Collection, which she oversaw until 2023. Over the decades of her curatorship, it was extensively developed and underrepresented areas, such as the post-Second World War period, were added to and strengthened. The collection's profile was raised as external dress and textile historians were made aware of its quality and importance. Research undertaken during this time became the basis for the John Bright Collection website, established to bring highlights of the collection to a wider audience.

On occasion, garments of historical significance have been found amongst the stock and have been transferred into the Museum Collection with the permission and blessing of the members of the Men's and Women's Departments. This was the case, for example, with a number of block-printed garments by the firms Cryséde and Footprints, as important examples of the revival of interest in traditional craft techniques in the fashion world after the First World War. – Elizabeth Owen, Historic Collection Curator

It remains a constant challenge to determine which 'vintage' items can still be safely used in stock and it is a team effort to ensure that fragile originals make their way into the collection. It is thanks to the attention and expertise of the costumiers, Returns Department and stock maintenance staff that important pieces are spotted in stock and suggested as additions to the collection. Thus, the costume stock itself 'feeds' the archive, making it an ever-growing resource and a safe haven for fragile garments that often have gained additional historic value through their use on well-known productions.

Today, original dresses from the 1920s are still used as hire stock, but they are a hundred years old and need to be monitored. The same was the case for Victorian dresses in the early days of Cosprop. When John used an original late 1870s dress on Vanessa Redgrave in the 1984 adaptation of The Bostonians, *it was roughly of the same age as 1920s' dresses are now in the 2020s. –* Barbara Kloos, Historic Collection Curator

The appreciation of verisimilitude taught Bright that the costumes we see on the screen should be clothes for real people, and by developing a truthful style, started a trend in the 1980s that has been considered by many a new and unique national genre: British Heritage Cinema. The museum now holds around 8,000 historical pieces and is a valuable and highly regarded asset. Several generations of designers have used the collection for research, inspiration and recreation of a particular item of clothing.

It is not only garments that can inform design direction, often accessories and even patterns might ignite a designer's imagination. When researching the film *The Duchess* (2008), Michael O'Connor was shown a late eighteenth-century printed dress sash, known as a Versailles Sash. The film's classical scenes inspired his design for a gown worn by Keira Knightley in the title role. Costume designers Jacqueline Durran and Susannah Buxton also often start with the museum. Buxton states, 'Looking at originals is the most important part of the preparation, the more research you are able to do, the more the production value of the drama benefits.'

When I show items to designers and makers, what strikes me most is the impact of the realisation that someone really wore it in the past. It opens a door to the physical world the characters lived in – and it shows that people were not unlike us. We see their sweat, evidence of their changing bodies in alterations, and also of their vanities and beauty standards in body-enhancing paddings, etc. Some pieces in the Museum Collection are very influential, like a wonderful 1830s' man's coat that also features on the website. It has been used as inspiration by the tailors many times, for example for Ralph Fiennes' costumes in Onegin *and for Suranne Jones in* Gentleman Jack *(p.170). Although these coats differ in design, the original coat has clearly been very helpful to achieve the striking silhouette of the period. –* Barbara Kloos

Since Cosprop's creation, costume designers have also offered clothing to Cosprop as former Company Manager Jenny Ireland recalls, 'Clothing was often donated from costume designers and dealers such as Judy Moorcroft, Frances Steidelman, Margaret Wicks and Joanna Marsh. They all had a discerning and knowledgeable eye, and each one knowing that their things would be going to a grateful home.' Similar to a museum collection such as the Victoria and Albert Museum in London, Cosprop has built its collection from a range of sources.

A neighbour clearing a relative's house found a dustbin bag, containing an 1830s' dress and petticoat that she donated to the collection. The petticoat was later copied to be worn by the young Queen Victoria in a scene from the series Victoria (2016–19) – Elizabeth Owen

Over Cosprop's 60-year history, numerous items have been given by illustrious donors, such as the actors Helena Bonham Carter, Joanna David, and the Cadbury Family.

Whilst working on a new digital in-house catalogue, a 'new' oldest piece of the archive was recently identified by the collection team: Assistant Collection Curator Sage Foley spotted the 1620s–30s' men's leather doublet in a box labelled as 'historic fancy dress'. The team invited an expert on the period, Jenny Tiramani, who founded the School of Historical Dress in London, to view it and she confirmed their suspicion, 'much to the joy of the entire staff who immediately set off on a pilgrimage to see this survivor'.

The museum collection also holds clothing worn by members of the British Royal Family, including dresses originally belonging to Queen Mary. The royal garments were acquired in 1981 from the Theatrical Ladies' Guild (now the Theatrical Guild). Apart from being important collector's

93. (opposite) Jacket, early 1890s; altered 1940s. Given by Doris Langley Moore to Dame Margot Fonteyn

items, these royal dresses are of surprisingly frequent practical use. As period dramas often feature royal characters, they have been used as reference for their technical intricacies and materials. One example is the film version of *Downton Abbey* (2019) when Queen Mary (Geraldine James) visits the Crawley family. Access to these garments is not only crucial to recreating an item of clothing but a revelatory experience for a designer.

Aside from clothing, Bright has been a life-long collector and has also amassed children's toys, porcelain, paintings, costumes designs, books, furniture and other ephemera. These influences all inform the design process at Cosprop.

We have a display of porcelain at Cosprop, which shows researchers how the various aspects of a period can come together. I have a piece of 1800s' fabric, and it is similar to the porcelain of the period, so the shape of a teapot sometimes echoes the shape of a sleeve. – **John Bright**

In 2022 Bright's collection of children's toys, dolls' houses, train sets, puppets and games formed part of the Bright Foundation Museum and Barn Theatre in Hastings, Sussex. These displays are part of the creative offer to children and young people and offer inspiration and creativity as part of workshops and performance-making.

The Cosprop library is also a vital resource for designers and dress historians to research and recreate a moment in time through dress. Cosprop staff also use the library to inform their thinking and to research period dress.

When I started at Cosprop, John really encouraged me to do my own research, so I spent time in the library and researched period clothing. I photocopied images I liked the look of and generally read about costume. I would get a stand and dress it to see what the clothes looked like and this was so helpful when it came to fitting an actor seeing how clothes looked on a body. – **Ross Braganza, Senior Costumier, Menswear**

Research is the foundation of every costume designer's process. The library at Cosprop is more than a collection of reference books, it is also a history of the organisation. Bright says that he has collected books like he has collected clothes and accessories. Reference material includes vintage photographs, costume designs, fashion plates, periodicals, period newspapers, archives of costume designers, such as Shirley Russell, and copies of the *Radio Times* where the cover photograph is a Cosprop production. Its wide range of books covers film, fashion, television, theatre and many historical periods.

MUSEUM COLLECTION FOCUS: **THE BALLET RUSSES**

The Ballet Russes company has long held a fascination for John Bright. Sergei Diaghilev founded the Ballet Russes in 1909 and over the next 20 years developed one of the most influential dance companies of the twentieth century, and its work still resonates in dance, choreography and design. In the 1920s, the company's design aesthetic filtered through fashion and interior design.

The first collection of Ballet Russes costumes I bought in the early 1980s was from someone who had bought them in 1967 from a sale at Sotheby's. I bought around ten. One of the dealers I knew from the Portobello Road said she might have something in her attic. Searching through the material, I found a yellow felt-like jacket with a Russian name label in it and further investigation showed that all the clothes were labelled in French and Russian and were from the ballets **Le Pavillon d'Armide** ***and*** **Giselle.** ***They are extraordinary documents of an extraordinary period.*** – **John Bright**

The two principal stage designers for the Ballet Russes were Léon Bakst, whose bejewelled colours, swirling Art Nouveau elements and sense of the erotic envisioned dance productions as total works of art and Alexandre Benois, who was equally seminal in exerting an enormous influence on popular taste.

When you look at early stage costumes they are often restrained and safe but these new ballet costumes were altogether more expressive, using seemingly never before explored techniques with paint and texturing. Fashion designers such as Paul Poirot picked up on these new designs immediately and by the early 1920s, the Ballet Russes had influenced fashion, film and interior design. Other artists become involved with the Ballet Russes including Pablo Picasso, Natalia Goncharova, Giorgio de Chirico, Coco Chanel and Jean Cocteau. – **John Bright**

94. (opposite) Costume for *Schéhérazade* (1910; Costume Designer Léon Bakst)

THE DYE ROOM

'Colour is something that you arrive at by looking at people in certain clothes and seeing what it does to them. Some people can wear red, some can't. Yellow does terrible things to some people's skin. Some actors don't like green – there's a superstition, especially in the theatre. I rely on the reaction from the dressing up session and how actors respond to colour.' – John Bright

The colour palette of a production – in film, television or theatre – creates its mood, atmosphere and overall visual language. Colour is crucial in communicating character to an audience. The Dye Room at Cosprop is central to the transformation of clothing and production of the correct interpretation of the characters' clothes. A broad range of skills and techniques are used in the Dye Room. The technicians dye and breakdown fabrics, complete jewellery and accessories repair and revamp costume stock.

For this job you need to understand colour theory in order to correctly mix colour together to create other shades. When dyeing fabric you also need to understand the dyeing process, preparing the fabric for the pot, timings, dye quantities and water temperature need to be monitored and adjusted throughout. The time it takes to dye something can vary, from as little as ten minutes to seven hours or occasionally more depending on fabric type and colour depth etc. – **Stacey Liddall, Dyer and Breakdown Artist**

We don't write colour recipes, so we do all the colour matching by eye. It takes experience and knowledge of the individual dyes and how they combine to work with each other as well as creating opposite tones. We also rely on our confidence in colour mixing and memory to previous times when we might have tried to achieve similar colours. – Nicolina Griffiths, Dyer and Breakdown Artist

In the Cosprop costume workflow, the Dye Room is usually one of the first points of contact for designers. Fabric needs to be the correct colour before it can be cut by the workroom staff; costumes from stock may need to be colour-matched to new elements added by the alterations team and costume pieces might need to be dyed after work by the makers. The process is a visual jigsaw puzzle and all Cosprop staff work closely together to achieve the designer's vision. The costume designer will occasionally provide a costume bible with swatches, sketches and images for their design concept.

A dye job may come about by consultation with John, a designer or a member of staff. This usually involves colour swatches to match to. Occasionally we get asked to dye samples in various fabrics and tones around a chosen colour idea then the designer or John would pick their favourite. Sometimes it's a verbal description where we translate what we feel a designer is communicating, it really varies. – Nicolina Griffiths

Before dyeing material, a small area of fabric is rinsed, spun and pressed numerous times to make sure the desired colour is achieved.

The dyes we use at Cosprop and the many types of materials we dye have their own personality with unique characteristics. Each responds differently when in the dye vat. This is due to the individual dye pigments and chemical profiles, fibre types, fabric weight, the weave and processing finishes play a part too. Each type of fabric needs its own treatment, there are a few things to consider depending on what fabric you are dyeing. For example, delicate silks that may damage easily will be handled more gently than a calico cotton, which is more robust. Rinsing wool should be treated carefully to avoid felting. This can be achieved by air cooling the fabric a little first before transferring the fabric from hot water into colder temperatures. – Stacey Liddall

After the fabrics have been dyed in the Dye Room and cut and made into costumes in the Workroom they may come back to us to be broken down. Breaking down costume is a technique used in film and TV to manipulate costume to look worn, damaged or emphasise the profession, internal state, surroundings or experience of the character. – Nicolina Griffiths

The process of breaking down clothes, making them appear lived in and to have had a life before the narrative began is driven by the script, the character and the designer's concept. The Dye Room staff will ask questions about aspects of the character's narrative journey and in particular the scenes where the item of clothing is worn to work out how heavy the breaking down should be. Breaking down theatre costumes can be heavier; for film and television, the practice must be more subtle. It also can help to make the character become more believable to the audience.

We did a project which involved a young girl living on the streets during the Second World War, her jacket had to show the effects of what that would look like. We would sand down certain parts of the costume; after the sanding, we would paint in highlights and shadows, spray into the garment and apply wax or greasing or other breakdown details if needed. We take it to a point and on purpose don't go too far, as that can be done on set when they are in the moment and they can see what is needed with the scenery and lighting for that specific scene. – Nicolina Griffiths

Sustaining and maintaining the stock is an important part of the daily workflow. Over time, items can show signs of wear and tear, with visible marks to be removed or concealed. This may involve spraying or painting techniques or a whole re-dye.

We also dye and spray items of clothing to refresh and renew. A designer might want a costume to be a different colour entirely. Perhaps a piece is too bright and the colour would need to be knocked back slightly. If the item is white, say a shirt for example, then we would dye that too, often to a cream if it wants to read as white on screen. – Stacey Liddall

The effect of dyeing clothing has to be carefully considered depending on the medium, and crucially the effect of lighting which differs between television, film and theatre. In theatre, lighting can change the colour of some fabrics, especially when gels or colour-changing fixtures are used.

The staff also mend all clothing and accessories, including belts, handbags, canes, spectacles, parasols and jewellery. The work is often exacting. New buttons on a jacket are individually painted to soften their shine or to distress, or to create a tarnished effect, to bring out a particular colour in the costume. Beaded embellishments on costumes are often painted individually if a particular colour is required. Each project presents new challenges and learning experiences, and in the era of high-definition cameras and televisions, costume elements should not distract the audience.

THE FITTING ROOM

'There is a marvellous moment in fittings when you can see the character, when the scales fall from the eyes of the actor and they know who they are. It's terribly exciting. You know when that moment arrives. When I see that, I just pat the actor on the back and say, "that's it, that's you".' – John Bright

The most transformative and intimate of spaces at Cosprop is the Fitting Room, where an actor becomes the person they will be portraying. Depending upon the schedule and at what stage the casting happens – which can be late in the process – there may be several fittings with an actor. A fitting room is the most private of spaces inside the costume house, where the fusion of actor, design and clothing all comes together to create a magical whole.

A fitting room must be practical as well as comfortable, so the size of the space is important for designers, makers and costumiers.

The Fitting Room is not a tiny cubicle like in a shop, you want as big a room as you can get, with a large mirror so you can see the actor full length. You stand behind the actor, out of their view in the mirror. If you're doing something of a particular period you concentrate on the shape of it before anything else. Some actors naturally have a certain posture that's useful for some period but not for others. You try to use what you're given and accentuate it where you can; bustles, corsets, whatever it takes. This is where a knowledge of the different periods is essential, homework as far as the shape goes is the starting point. – John Bright

The space you first notice when you first come into Cosprop is

the mirrors and the skylight. It's not there by chance, it's because John is so brilliant. It's the perfect place for photographing actors in their costumes during the fitting process. It's perfect because John knows what would work best, John knows what we need as designers. – Jacqueline Durran, Costume Designer

In the Fitting Room, actor, designer, maker and costume are all brought together under the supervision of Bright's expert eye. For the costume makers, the fitting process can be a nerve-wracking and exciting moment seeing a garment brought to life and created in cloth.

I enjoy fittings, you have had the actor's measurements but until you have the living, breathing, moving body, you never know until the fitting happens. It's always interesting to see how an actor responds to the costume, the dynamic changes when they put something on. – Emma Burke, Costume Maker

The first fitting can be a little rough as it is the first time you see your garment on the real body. After the fitting you might have to take the costume apart to readjust something fundamental that hasn't worked and correct it according to what you learnt from the actress. The second fitting is crucial and that's when you know if your approach is correct or not. – Thaïs Demontrond, Costume Maker

Cosprop costumiers play a central role in the fitting process and their understanding of the extensive stock is essential as new characters are created and refined through cloth throughout the fitting period.

During fittings, if an actor has a lot of clothes to wear, you might build a whole wardrobe, the designer will think it through for each scene. Sometimes an actor will have one key look because they don't have lots of scenes, for the actor, they have to feel right and the actor has to look at the character and not themselves. Fitting actors in an artform which John has perfected, I've learnt so much from him. – Ross Braganza, Senior Men's Costumier

There comes a moment when you put on something, whatever it is, it doesn't matter if it physically fits or not, it doesn't matter if it's the wrong colour, what matters is that it immediately helps the actor become this other person. Often it can be a hat or even the angle at which a hat fits or doesn't necessarily have to be the whole thing. And at that moment something magical happens, and I describe it as another person, the character steps through the mirror into the room. It's like opening a box and out steps this character. – Tom Rand, Costume Designer

The fitting room can often become quite crowded with myself, an assistant designer, John and his team of cutters and makers bustling in and out, but throughout this John maintains an air of reassurance that the actors adore, they feel in safe hands, many of them have worked with him before so there is this rapport. With his support here it also allowed me the space to experiment that I might not have had elsewhere. – Michele Clapton, Costume Designer

The number of fittings required for an actor can vary from the scale of the production to how many changes they have in the production's narrative. A photographic record of the fitting process is captured by designers and their assistants so they can reflect on what might be required and what changes need to happen to compete an outfit. Over the past sixty years, the move from analogue to digital photography has enabled a quicker recording of the session and these photographs are archived in the costume bible. For Bright, they are an essential reference folder in the costume design process: 'The photographs from a fitting remind one of certain aspects of the garment on the person. You may not be thinking of everything at once – a photograph shows you the thing you might have forgotten.'

Actors are dressing and undressing, so they have to feel relaxed and comfortable. You might have a lot of people in the fitting room, it's not what we do, we don't normally undress in front of other people but at a costume house you do. John has created a unique space for this. Each fitting room has its own feeling. It's not just a room with a mirror and a rail, each space has its own relaxing atmosphere ... John is so natural at fittings, he brings something else to the fitting ... He might change one small detail and everything comes together and everyone is thrilled – the actor, the designer, everyone – I don't know anyone else in the world who can do that like him. – Ross Braganza

You're having to look at your own image because you're standing in front of a mirror. Then they put something on you and we have got a long way to go, and then John comes in and he just does a few adjustments. He's staring at me and staring at the reflection of me. And then he'll just do one or two things, and then after a bit it's okay. It's perfect, and that's the magic. – Helena Bonham Carter

Cosprop has a calmness, a space to be creative, that has always been important to John. He created this space away from the hustle and bustle of the Holloway Road. Actors adore John, there's a trust between them and Cosprop. John has the ability to combine the needs of the actor, the designer and the character, which is key, and that combined with his knowledge and skill creates something really special. It's a pleasure to witness. – Hannah Monkley, Senior Costumier, Womenswear

THE WORKROOM

'Work that is started from the truth in some form is much more interesting than superficial, decorative work.' – John Bright

Before the costume making process begins at Cosprop, a conversation takes place between the designer, John Bright, Company Manager Chris Garlick, and Head of the Workroom Nancy Knapp. The scope and scale of the project is assessed, costed and factored into the Cosprop costume workflow. There are two making teams at Cosprop: one for womenswear and one for menswear.

At Cosprop, each maker creates a new piece of clothing from start to finish, from the delivery of the fabric to the moment it leaves the building. This approach has created the 'Cosprop look', and Garlick confirms that 'Many actors request that Cosprop make their clothes; they know they will get the best possible quality of making and fitting.'

The work at Cosprop is unique in that each costume is created by one person. This differs from other costume houses or organisations which have making departments, where a costume would pass from department to department for each stage of its process. Some makers are trained in flat pattern cutting, then seamstresses take over, that's not the Cosprop way. – **Nancy Knapp, Head of the Workroom**

The Workroom at Cosprop is a place of methodical creative calm and quiet transformation. Under natural skylights, the room is made up of several workspaces, each with a mannequin at the end. It is on these mannequins that new characters are formed and created through cloth.

John's ethos is that they are clothes to be worn, they are not

STOCKMAN

costumes to be paraded around in. Everything is draped on a stand as it would be moulded to the actor's body, and we work from that to create a piece of clothing. – **Nancy Knapp**

John Bright oversees every costume project that passes through the Workroom. Nancy Knapp supervises the work and the makers and liaises with designers and manages the fitting process. The work is allocated to a member of staff whose skillset is best suited to the demands of the project. Part of the Cosprop ethos is to train and develop a person's skill, these are then passed onto the next generation. Costume Maker Thaïs Demontrond says 'We came to Cosprop with our skills but we learnt so much from each other and that's how it works here.'

I was taught the Cosprop way when I began. I sat next to Jill Harbutt and Jill taught me. I was surrounded by these incredible makers. When you come to Cosprop, you learn in a very concise way. The Cosprop way is passed on through each generation. You are also allowed at Cosprop to find your way and make mistakes. – **Nancy Knapp**

Cosprop has an egalitarian feel and the notion of hierarchy is absent, particularly in the workroom – starting with the way work is distributed, with each person responsible for seeing their costume through from beginning to end. – **Pippa Cleator, Costume Maker**

Once the work is allocated, costume designers discuss the demands of the script, character and director. Costume Maker Heather Woad says that the Workroom staff are rarely given a script, as sometimes it is not finished when work has to begin. All these factors have an impact on the work, and casting is also an endless topic of discussion as the Workroom staff are often forced to work 'in the dark', without an actor in mind, so the costume has to be imagined onto the uncast role. In previous years, costume designers were mostly given 12 weeks to prepare, but today casting is getting later and designers often only have five weeks or less.

The costume designer will provide a costume bible with duplicate sketches, photographs, diagrams and research material for each costume being made. The designer will explain the concept and the character and what is required, bibles are allocated to the person working on the project so they can understand the designer's thought process and decision making.

The pattern and fabric are then crucial to the next stage of production. Designers often supply fabric, sometimes Bright provides what is required. For designers and makers, his fabric archive offers a unique resource of material, some of which is no longer made or produced. They also use special suppliers such as the Hopkins Collection (Alan and Vanessa Hopkins, suppliers of textiles and other accessories to the costume design industry).

One of the wonderful things about making at Cosprop are the fabrics. John has collected fabric for over 60 years, it's a fabric archive but he allows it to be used, and also braid, trimmings and everything else you might need to make an item of clothing ... John is not precious about his collection; he allows you to inspect and explore a garment, you can see the mechanics of it, that's so important when you are a maker and recreating something for a project. – **Dan Ashworth, Tailor**

Costume makers are adept at understanding fabric and the way it can be cut, draped and used to create costume. Over time, different makers became experts at cutting certain fabrics and would be allocated the necessary materials. As elements of a costume are cut, they are then draped onto the stand, sewn into place, then resewn because something doesn't quite work.

Jill [Harbutt] was brilliant with chiffon, which has a life of its own; if I went near it with scissors, it just moved! We all developed our own special skills and John encouraged that. – **Diana Thomas, Costume Maker**

Some designers come with their fabric already sourced. The quality of the fabric we work with is crucial because each fabric is different and has its own challenges. Often costumes are dyed. The dyers are magicians, they transform pieces and sometimes garments are broken down so they do that work as well. We all collaborate closely together. – **Thaïs Demontrond**

With the measurements, the stand is padded to the actor's size. Then we drape it with a toile fabric to make the pattern before we cut the real fabric. I rarely do flat-pattern cutting – **Emma Burke, Costume Maker**

The Workroom staff are resourceful and have endless patience with the twists and turns in the creation of each new production. They work tirelessly to ensure the workshop delivers what is required and is created to the best possible

'Cosprop' standard. The era of streaming has brought opportunities and new demands on costume houses like Cosprop and a shift in the design process.

The designers used to have the final word on design. Designers now have to do 'show and tell' to the producers but producers don't understand the process, what is involved, the director might be more involved now. The making process is very personal, you become very attached to the person you are creating, we think of them as people, like members of your own family. That personal touch is embedded into every costume that is created at Cosprop, which sets it apart. – Nancy Knapp

Similar to an atelier, Cosprop has to work through the fitting process, allowing for the actor to become the character. The costume needs to serve the purpose of the script, what kind of movement is required, does the character have action sequences, is there any major physical kind of activity, will there be stress points on armholes? All these considerations must be factored into the making process.

Nancy Knapp manages the fitting system, liaising with designers and their assistants, and ensuring that costumes are ready for a first, second or third fitting. Each fitting can generate further work to ensure the costume can move, suits the character and actor and each alteration can require multiple staff to complete each stage of the process. Makers keep a record of their projects, from swatches to photos, notes and diagrams. These are not only a record of each production that passes through the Cosprop Workroom but they also detail the design decisions behind every costume that has been created.

When makers are working on the same production, creating womens- and menswear, the making team compare and exchange thoughts and ideas. The progress, challenges and solutions to a particular garment are discussed.

I was making a frock coat for the film Emma *designed by Alex Byrne, and Emma [Burke] was making a dress and we realised that they were in the same scene so we could see what they would look like next to each other as we were making them.* – Dan Ashworth

It's hard to let go of costumes sometimes, you have been involved in its creation, sometimes from scratch, but it has to go at some point and the next time we see it is on the screen or on the stage. Which is always a thrill when you see it in action and you think, I did that. – Thaïs Demontrond

When I've had costumes made at Cosprop, I know that the techniques and materials used will be completely correct – I have learnt over the years that no matter how good a design is, if it isn't made in the right fabric and in the right way, it will never come across in a way that is altogether natural. Costumes made in Cosprop have an inarguable humanity to them – made by humans for humans. – Michael Wilkinson, Costume Designer

THE ALTERATIONS ROOMS AND THE RETURNS DEPARTMENT

Every film, television and theatre production that Cosprop works on will pass through the Alterations Rooms and there are separate departments for womenswear and menswear. There is virtually no item of clothing that leaves the premises that has not been worked on and condition-checked for quality control by the staff.

Alterations are an essential department in the costume house; as no two actors are the same, it is rare for an item of clothing not to be modified in some form for a production. The department is primarily divided into three main focuses: alterations, maintenance and organising.

Both costume designers and actors have varying requirements and preferences, all of which are dependable on the nature of the production, body type, turnaround time and aesthetic tastes. These factors will be advised on and discussed during bespoke fittings, with any compromises agreed on before changes take place. A theatre actor who uses wide arm gestures on stage may need extra fabric in the sleeve for ease, or a designer may favour a lace trim over fringing. It is the role of the Alterations team to meet the needs of all parties involved whilst upholding the Cosprop ethos – to maintain the longevity and structural integrity of the costume so it may be used for future productions. David Lothian in Alterations confirms that even when a dress is beyond saving, any salvageable trimmings or fabrics will be kept for future use.

Options for alterations are endless and can be hugely variable day to day. Monday could involve a simple hem turn up, whereas Tuesday may call for a dress to be let out a few inches, be retrimmed and restyled from a soft late 1860s' silhouette to a sharper, mid-1880s' bustle look. However, to increase the longevity of the piece, no fabric from the original garment can be cut away, leading to the team coming up with imaginative solutions and methods to disguise this limitation. To further achieve this practice, fabric offcuts from the Workroom are saved for modifying and mending.

Cosprop's stock includes a selection of original garments dating back to the Victorian era, older costumes made by the company's very first team of makers and newer items that are repeatedly favoured and hired by incoming productions. Due to time and use, pieces will inevitably succumb to deterioration and damage. Alterations staff will check every item that leaves the building, mending as they go, to ensure hems are not ripped, fastenings are secure and trimmings remain attached. Repairs are a crucial part of the overall lifecycle of a costume and can sometimes take weeks to complete to a standard that captures the original essence of each piece.

When a costume needs a makeover, John frequently lends our department his expertise, finding the perfect lace to redecorate a bodice for example. With his keen eye for detail, he never fails to give tired garments a breath of fresh air. – **Hannah Curtis, Women's Alterations**

For the costume house to run smoothly, fabrics and haberdashery must be easily accessible to designers and workers. In quieter periods, the department will meticulously sort and clearly categorise Cosprop's vast stock of treasures. This varies from original eighteenth-century lace to Edwardian mother-of-pearl buttons or endearing mid-century Mickey Mouse ribbons. The similarly abundant stock of fabric ranges from supple silk taffetas to charming, printed cottons, all of which have been contained into orderly boxes. The collection is catalogued into folders, with samples and quantities for designers and staff to explore and refer to.

Working through rails of costumes chosen by productions makes no two days the same. You can go from a selection of Regency corsets to quaint 1930s' woollen swimsuits, straight onto an 1890s' velvet beaded cape. It's exciting being part of the journey of bringing a character to life. – **Annalise Clark, Women's Alterations**

Once our job is complete, garments are passed on to the costumiers who prepare and package all items leaving the building. These can be sent across the world to the outback of Australia or closer to home to a theatre in London. Cosprop's outfits are well travelled. – **Julia Fallon, Head of Women's Alterations**

With a continuous cycle of clothing and accessories moving in and out of the building, the system of exit and re-entry is an essential part of the day-to-day job of the costume house staff. The costumiers at Cosprop are responsible for any costumes that leave the premises to go to the set or the stage. When the costume is finished with, the Returns Department is the point for entry back into the building.

I manage anything that comes back after it has been worn in a film, in a television programme or on stage. We ensure that once it is back in the building, there is a system for the costume to be processed and returned to stock or wherever it needs to go. – **Peter Costen, Returns Manager**

Diligent paperwork underscores the returns process, and a paper trail is essential to recording all parts of the costume – from top to toe – and ensuring every element is accounted for. Therefore, for Costen, 'labelling is an important part of our work, in returns, we check all labels, we sometimes receive costumes from other costume houses, we make them aware and return them in the process.'

Each costume that is returned has to be deconstructed by the returns staff and every part is checked for cleanliness and damage before it can return to stock for future use. Any damage is assessed, and items may have to go to the Alterations Room or the Workroom for repair, with associated costs for damage passed onto the production company.

An important aspect of the Cosprop workflow is the embargo of costumes, held until a film or television programme is released. Some costumes will be acquired by the Exhibitions Department for future display options. Once a costume has been assessed and all necessary work has been done to ensure its future, it can be returned to the stock and reused for a future production and its journey can begin again for a brand new character.

THE MILLINERY ROOM

The art of millinery and headwear has been central to the costume house since its creation in 1965. For the period projects worked on at Cosprop, most costumes have to be completed with headwear. Hats and headwear are fitted during the costume fitting process, unless there is a special make required and the milliner would be present for the fitting.

Period dress doesn't look finished without a hat, most people of all classes wore hats up until the 1960s, people even went to bed in a hat – a night-cap. However, hats can interfere with their close-up shots and hide the face so brims, especially with bonnets, end up getting shorter and shorter, changing the shape of the hat, and the way the period is being interpreted. In certain periods, an outfit is not complete or finished without a hat, it unifies the costume. Some modern productions prefer very few or no hats, choosing elaborate hair or small hair pieces instead.
– **Kat Goodall, Milliner**

The Milliner at Cosprop works closely with the costume designer, who may have reference images or a mood board, and will also conduct their own research to ensure the shape and material is correct for the period and for the actor. Goodall explains that 'there are many different processes, and materials to create a hat. You can create some in one piece, two or many pieces. Using wool, fur-felt, hoods, straw, wire, fabric, buckram just to mention a few.'

The fitting of hats is an exacting art form, as actors need to feel comfortable and to be able to move their heads with freedom and not feel constrained or self-conscious with headwear.

Trying to get head measurements is often difficult, it seems to be the one thing that gets forgotten. Head sizes can be tricky to cut out. A large person can sometimes have a small head and vice-versa. We are not used to wearing hats today so, for some actors, it can take time to get used to wearing something on their head, and it affects the body's movements. – **Kat Goodall**

Goodall discussed her work for the television series *Poldark* starring Aidan Turner as Ross Poldark (2015–19; see right and p.166). 'I created most of the Tricorn hats for his character across the entire series. The designer found something from stock and it was copied to fit Aidan's head. The hat forms part of the visual image of his character.' The process of creating a Tricorn hat involves a complex series of steps.

For Aidan's Tricorn, I blocked a peach bloom fur-felt in two pieces, a crown and a brim. It was then stiffened with felt stiffener. Once dried, the crown and brim are cut down to the desired size and the brim edge wired. Then I attached the crown to the brim and trim to the edge and around the base of the crown with Petersham ribbon and turn up the brim to create the three corners, hence the name Tricorn. Lastly, I put in a Petersham head band and lining. – **Kat Goodall**

For a television series such as *Downton Abbey* (2010–15), many characters were required to wear several hats throughout the narrative, depending on script and character.

We made all the hats for* Downton Abbey *at the beginning. For actors such as Maggie Smith, because John knew Maggie so well, he knew what would suit her for the role. There were other hats we used from stock and it would be a conversation between myself and the designers on what would work for each character. – **Kat Goodall**

Costume designers often research the Cosprop Library and Museum, the Exhibition section or the stock to explore what might be available and what can be adapted and reinterpreted. The stock is another invaluable resource for Goodall as 'the designer can see what it looks like, rather than looking at images, hats need to be seen in 3D and from different angles.'

The Oscar- and BAFTA-winning film *The Duchess* (2008; p.206) starred Keira Knightley and was designed by Michael O'Connor, and required several late eighteenth-century hats. 'We took the idea of Knightley's hat from a painting – it was a portrait, not of Georgiana, but for one of her friends, but it was ideal for Keira.'

Some characters' personas are intrinsically linked to wearing hats. The headwear for Penelope Wilton when she was playing The Queen Mother in the play* Backstairs Billy *(2023) was central to her costume design. Two period hats were designed by Tom Rand for the play. 'The hat is a classic Queen Mother straw hat in vivid green, with a turned back brim. We don't usually do 1979 at Cosprop, it's a bit late for us. The other hat was a 1950s' hat in a black fur-felt. – **Kat Goodall**

As with other departments, recycling materials in millinery is part of the Cosprop ethos.

Everything gets reused in this department, every part of a hat can be repurposed, I rarely throw anything away. We can always do something with all the materials I have, even if the hat has had a battering on the set, I can repair and preserve and reuse for a future production. – **Kat Goodall**

Film and television favour the closeup, where actor's faces and their hats become part of the marketing campaign. For a series such as *Peaky Blinders* (2013–22), the headwear can have an immediate effect on popular culture. The flat caps and bakerboy (or newsboy) caps worn by the fictional gangster family contributed to a resurgence in the popularity of these styles some 100 years after the series was set. Costumes from popular and award-winning projects will be stored in the Exhibitions section, hats included, for future display.

THE ACCESSORIES ROOM

'When I showed people around Cosprop, I used to leave the jewellery room to last. Whatever building we were in, it was always painted black, without windows, with a dark-red carpet and twinkling lights. You would put on the light and there was this gleaming treasure house!' – Jenny Ireland, former Company Manager

The Accessories Room is a testament to a life of collecting by John Bright, and an extraordinary resource for designers to draw from, providing the flourish to the 'top to toe' outfits for each character that are created.

We have everything a designer might need to complete a character's look: hatpins, handbags, cigarettes cases, pipes, lighters, smoking compacts, glasses, sunglasses, medals, crucifixes, cufflinks, rings, opera glasses, necklaces, earrings, canes, parasols, tiaras and crowns. – **Kate Anderson, Costumier**

All these separate items have to be sourced, signed out and added to the booking system, which accompanies each costume before it leaves the Cosprop premises. The return process is equally as challenging as all items need to be checked for damage with certain objects vulnerable to loss. Anderson says, 'Pocket watches and watchchains are the most vulnerable, as they can get put into a pocket of a costume after filming is completed and not seen again.'

The creation of the Accessories Room was carefully designed by John Bright and Jenny Ireland and has been recreated in the various premises that Cosprop has occupied

COSPROP

over its decades-long history.

For costume designers, details are essential to piecing together the whole character.

***When Anthony Powell designed* Indiana Jones and the Temple of Doom *(1984), for the little Maharaja character, we made the whole costume and we got the jewellery from a wonderful Indian shop in Southhall in London, and they had lots of authentically shaped and styled jewellery, but it did fall apart as they were only stuck on! Anthony preferred the faceted stones, because they twinkled better. For a Spielberg film, you have to have the right twinkle!* – John Bright**

The correct accessory can often be used to serve a film's narrative and play an important role to underscore a dramatic scene. Janet Patterson used a striking parasol for Nicole Kidman's Isabel Archer in *The Portrait of a Lady* (1996) where John Malkovich's character uses the parasol to hypnotise Isabel into marriage.

***With the parasols, almost all of them were genuine, the earliest ones were from around 1840, so that's something that has existed for all that time, still being used.* – Jenny Ireland**

Like the Cosprop Museum Collection, John Bright's knowledge of dealers and antique markets and his discerning eye has led to the creation of an extraordinary treasure trove used by designers. 'If you've got something authentic, within the whole look of someone, it always gives it a stamp of reality, it is an enormous help to designers. You couldn't make some of the handbags we have in the collection, they would be too expensive, but you could find them in antique markets.'

EXHIBITIONS

Costume exhibitions are an opportunity for audiences to see costumes worn by their favourite characters and actors. Exhibitions are also a chance to appreciate the quality of outfits often only seen fleetingly on the screen. Exhibitions are managed by a team of staff at Cosprop who facilitate the curator's expectations, mount the costumes onto mannequins and send objects out on tour. Cosprop has been loaning costumes to international exhibitions since the 1980s and has been creating its own touring exhibitions since the 1990s.

It was an exhibition in 1956 that inspired a young John Bright when *The Observer Film Exhibition: Sixty Years of Cinema* was staged in central London. 'The exhibition was organised by Richard Buckle, it displayed all manner of things including costumes, props and backdrops. It was marvellous. It also set me off on my obsession with the Russian Ballet.'

In 1985 British Film Year was created under the Presidency of Sir Richard Attenborough and it marked the first time that the entire British film industry united to highlight the international impact British film had on culture, with a touring exhibition, *The British Film Year Roadshow*. A series of stamps were issued to celebrate important figures in British film history including Charlie Chaplin, Alfred Hitchcock and Vivien Leigh.

The celebrations were also an attempt to highlight the range of skill and production facilities that the UK offered to international filmmakers. Cosprop was integral to the promotion of the work of the costume house and the art of costume design. Costumes from *Tess* (1979), *The French Lieutenant's Woman* (1981), *The Bostonians* (1984), *A Passage to India* (1984), *A Company of Wolves* (1984) and *The Shooting Party* (1985) were displayed.

Cosprop's first General Manager Christine Hill organised the costume displays and toured the UK with Costume Designers Tom Rand and Judy Moorcroft, who were part of a series of talks to promote the understanding of their design process to audiences. The roadshow visited Brighton, Liverpool, Edinburgh, Swansea, Norwich and Aberdeen.

I toured in a mobile lorry with the costumes along with a make-up artist, a stuntman and visiting film directors, the tour was to spread the message that cinema was the best place to see a film. – **Christine Hill**

When the British Film Institute opened the Museum of the Moving Image in London in 1988, John Bright and Christine Hill worked on the installation and display of the costume design section of the museum, lending costumes and objects from Cosprop for the display. Since then, Cosprop has loaned costumes to many exhibitions as well as curating its own displays celebrating and exploring the costume design process.

In the United Kingdom, Cosprop has loaned costumes to a range of exhibitions including *Starstruck in the Cathedral* (2009) staged in Worcester Cathedral. Farther afield, *Fashion in Film: Period Costumes for the Screen* (2004–7) toured the United States and featured costumes from *Dangerous Liaisons* (1988), *Elizabeth* (1998), *The Portrait of a Lady* (1995) and *Onegin* (1999).

In the twenty-first century, costume exhibitions have grown in popularity as audiences become more aware of the contribution costume designers make to the filmmaking process. In 2012 the major exhibition at London's Victoria and Albert Museum, *Hollywood Costume*, borrowed several important costumes including *The French Lieutenant's Woman* (1981), *Out of Africa* (1985) and *A Room with a View* (1985). The exhibition then toured to Australia and the United States, including Los Angeles in 2013–15.

High-profile television productions such as *Poldark*, *Downton Abbey* and *Peaky Blinders* have also generated their own costume exhibitions, which have toured internationally.

EXHIBITION CASE STUDY: **RECONSTRUCTING CORNELIA VANDERBILT'S WEDDING DRESS**

The Biltmore Estate in the United States is owned by the Vanderbilt family and was one of the largest private estates in America, and today the estate is a visitor attraction. In 1924 Cornelia Vanderbilt married John Francis Amherst Cecil, it was the social event of the year. To celebrate the 90th anniversary of the wedding, in 2014, The Biltmore Museum commissioned Cosprop to reconstruct Cornelia Vanderbilt's wedding dress.

The commission took Bright and his team 12 months of work before they were able to begin the making process. The research images from the era and newspaper accounts were sourced to achieve an authentic reconstruction (see opposite). The fabrics used for the original dress did not exist so Bright and his team had to experiment to match the original. The museum collection offered inspiration for fabrics until the right piece was found, dyed and used. Ultimately, a satin foundation was chosen, combined with antique lace, which provided an outer layer.

The wedding veil was also reconstructed, the attention to detail was extended to orange blossoms being sewn onto the headdress. Bright added a layer of nylon tulle underneath the silk veil as silk tulle is prone to wilt in humid conditions. This ensured the veil remained as airy and voluminous as worn in 1924. The gown was featured in Biltmore's *Fashionable Romance: Wedding Gowns in Film* exhibition in 2014 and now forms part of their permanent collection.

CHAPTER FIVE

MAKING A GOLDEN AGE

Television Costume Drama

'There were so many serials made from classic novels, people may not have read the book, but they saw the television adaptation and that's what often remains in the public's imagination.'[1] – Elizabeth Waller, Costume Designer

As Cosprop was building its collection and reputation in the late 1960s and early 1970s, television programming in the United Kingdom was also expanding. This era is now considered a 'Golden Age of Television'. One of the most popular formats was the 'costume drama': this template combined British literary tradition, acting prowess and excellence in costume design. These programmes were sold internationally as the 'British heritage export'.

In the twenty-first century era of global streaming and home entertainment, it is hard to underestimate the impact that BBC programming had on the cultural life of the UK in the 1960s through to the 1980s, in particular the adaptations of classic and popular novels into television series. Cosprop's early creative input in television began with the creation of Miss Havisham's wedding dress for the 1967 adaptation of *Great Expectations* (p.13; fig.4), followed by a long-running television series that created the hugely popular episodic template: *The Forsyte Saga* (1967).

BBC2 had launched in 1964 but had failed to establish itself; in order to receive BBC2, viewers needed to have their TV sets adjusted to access the ultra-high frequency 625 channel, which was not immediately available in all parts of the country. BBC2 programmers needed to create something to attract viewers and 'event television' changed its profile. *The Forstye Saga* (1967) established the Sunday night costume drama format which continues to the modern day.

As television producers begin to experiment and transition from black and white into colour in the late 1960s, John Bright was approached by ABC Television to collaborate on tests for colour television. This opportunity enabled Bright to develop expertise about the challenges of working in this new medium that he could pass on to costume designers. The experience gave Cosprop the edge by catering for colour cameras at such an early stage.

For black-and-white costume design, designers had to think in terms of tonal qualities. All the great Hollywood designers like Adrian, Travis Banton and Edith Head were able to contrast characters by using a range of colours and tones of fabric like grey, green and black.[2] – **John Bright**

95. (opposite) Violet Crawley, Dowager Countess of Grantham (Maggie Smith) in *Downton Abbey* (2010–15)

Buxton sourced the fabric, which was a silk brocade with a self-pattern that was dyed at Cosprop to a deep purple colour. 'It was the second colour worn by women after black, in the stages of mourning for a relative. Widows often stayed in mourning much longer than young people, if not indefinitely, but Maggie wasn't keen on staying in black.'[3] – Susannah Buxton

It was important for costumiers, designers and their assistants working in colour to share their experiences of what would work in this new emerging area of transmission.

We discovered that no two cameras recognised colour in the same way. There's a shade of blue that's a very mechanical colour and it really 'zings' out. What you found with some early BBC productions is that it looked fine in the studio but when they filmed outside, it was on the older OB video and it didn't match at all. Even with colour film, sometimes it is filmed in one colour, like Eastman colour or Agfa colour and then because it is cheaper to then print it on Fuji colour, all the colours go kaput. Because when you look at the fact of Fuji film, it is slightly pink. So it will make any blues and reds much stronger than they were.[4] – **John Bright**

In its aim to deliver ambitious programming, John Bloomfield recalls that the BBC drama department recruited more than 50 full time costume designers to cope with this new workload, and 'we were all learning on the job how to cope with the challenges presented'. In the late 1960s, BBC dramas were filmed live, so costume designers were not only present for the recording, they had to manage the cast's costume changes. Bloomfield remembers this challenge: 'It was being broadcast live, so it was terrifying, you had to make sure you weren't caught on camera if you were doing a costume change for an actor.'[5]

'The BBC were hiring young designers and I was part of a group that included Dinah Collin, Charles Knode, John and Ann Bloomfield, James Acheson, Raymond Hughes and Robin Fraser-Paye. We were all from theatre backgrounds and many of us had trained at Wimbledon School of Art. At the same time, the BBC was providing creative challenges that might not have existed in film or theatre' as Elizabeth Waller reflected. 'We were all young designers, I was designing shows such as *Elizabeth R* when I was 25. In film, designers would have been in their fifties doing that scale of show, so you were given opportunities, in a different landscape that would not have been possible.'[6]

The regime change at the corporation reflected a change in the times as Vanessa Hopkins, former BBC Costume Supervisor, and co-founder of The Hopkins Collection, recalled,

The old guard of costume designers at the BBC were attached to the established style of theatrical glamour; they wanted gilt chairs and velvet curtains for grand actresses at fittings, and they went to the long-established costume houses such Nathan's or Bermans. Then this new place called Cosprop appeared on the scene, quickly gaining attention among the younger designers, and it was a new approach to costuming.[7]

War and Peace (1972)

Director John Davies | Costume Designer Charles Knode
Starring Anthony Hopkins, Joanna David, David Swift, Alan Dobie, Angela Down, Basil Henson, Rupert Davies

The BBC landmark production of *War and Peace* took two years to make and was broadcast in 20 parts, creating a milestone in British television history. Set from 1805 to 1812 (with a later epilogue), costumes ranged from French and Russian military uniforms to the Russian aristocracy, and from Tsar Alexander I to Napoleon.

Projects such as *War and Peace* allowed emerging costume designers to flex their creativity. BBC Costume Designer Charles Knode, then only in his twenties, designed thousands of costumes for the production (fig.96).

Charles had an interest in European royalty, he knew so much about the period, he immersed himself in research for the project. My responsibility was costume supervision, I also did research, I chose fabrics and organised the costuming of the military scenes, it was an epic production and great experience.[8] – **Christine Rawlins, Costume Supervisor**

Costume designers from this period – Anthony Powell, David Walker, Charles Knode – had been trained by the best teachers including stage designer Doris Zinkeisen, they were taught painting, technique, historical references and this comes through in their costume design drawings.[9] – **John Bright**

Epic in scale, it was filmed in Yugoslavia (in areas now in Serbia) for battle scenes, both in summer and again in winter, with a thousand extras from the Yugoslav Territorials playing the soldiers. Cosprop created all the civilian menswear clothes for the series.

Organising a thousand men into their costumes when you don't speak their language is no joke ... we had to create an assembly line and then a passing out parade.[10] – **Charles Knode**

Interiors including a recreation of the Kremlin, and many stately homes, were filmed back in England, with Knode costuming 160 principals. Ballroom scenes also had dancers and an orchestra and were filmed on location in Kedleston Hall, Derbyshire, and Ragley Hall, Stratford-upon-Avon.

At almost 15 hours long, *War and Peace* remains the most ambitious large-scale drama ever made by the BBC. It thrust its young lead Anthony Hopkins into stardom and he won the BAFTA for best actor in 1974. After *The Forsyte Saga* (1967), *War and Peace* cemented the BBC's reputation for literary, opulent drama which continued through the 1970s.

96. (opposite, left and right) Costume designs and fabric swatch by Charles Knode for *War and Peace* (1972)

97. (right) Costume for Prince Vasili Kuragin (Basil Henson) in *War and Peace* (1972)

Television 1970s–1980s

Television in the early 1970s provided Cosprop with a range of projects that added to their growing collection and making prowess, including *Bel Ami* (1971), *The Pallisers* (1974) and *Shoulder to Shoulder* (1974).

For Costume Designer John Bloomfield, *Bel Ami* was an opportunity to work with John Bright.

I was working for Century Theatre in 1967 and our stage manager told me about his neighbour John Bright, who had opened a costume hire business. So I went to Cosprop and stood outside and thought to myself this is not a costume house, but then I went inside, and it was like a Tardis, as he had collected so much stuff, it was an absolute treasure trove of original things.[11] – **John Bloomfield**

Bel Ami was serialised in six episodes, set in Paris at the end of nineteenth century, 'although all filmed at the BBC, there was very little location filming then, you filmed an hour-long episode in one day'.[12] John Bloomfield commissioned Cosprop to make costumes for Elvi Hale, Peter Sallis and Margaret Courtenay.

The BBC was wonderful for light entertainment but for the period shows, we had to go to Nathan's or Bermans and eventually many of the BBC costume designers got to know John and Cosprop and began going there, because they were making clothes and not 'costumes' as people might think of them.[13] – **Elizabeth Waller, Costume Designer**

Witnessing the immense popularity of costume dramas, BBC rival ITV commissioned *Upstairs, Downstairs* (1971–75; Costume Designer Sheila Jackson), an original work not based on historic fiction. This Sunday night drama set in the Edwardian period offered interweaving narratives of upper- and working-class characters. The above-stairs-below-stairs series was hugely popular and became the genesis for ITV's *Downton Abbey* (2010–15).

The BBC continued its ambitious programming with a major series to begin the new decade. *The Onedin Line* (1971–80; Costume Designers June Hudson, Dorothea Wallace, John Bloomfield) ran for the duration of the 1970s, keeping Cosprop busy with regular commissions.

The 1970s also experienced economic instability, industrial strikes, and a three-day week when the UK's electricity was rationed due to fuel shortages. The social unrest of the era impacted on series such as *The Pallisers* (1974; fig.98) starring Susan Hampshire, Philip Latham and Anna Massey. Designed by Raymond Hughes and broadcast over 26 episodes, the series offered an antidote to the turbulent period and became a casualty of the political unrest of the era. Strikes at the BBC meant the last two episodes were not finished in time and not shown until five months after the original broadcast, diminishing its impact. Costumes from the series returned to stock and found their way into new productions. A costume worn by Susan Hampshire in the series was eventually reworked and adapted by Penny Rose in the 1990s for *Evita* (1996), worn by Madonna.

In 1974 the BBC commissioned Winston Graham's eighteenth-century Cornwall-set *Poldark* (1975–77; Costume Designers John Bloomfield, Penny Lowe). The epic romantic series captured audiences' imagination and with its use of location filming, freed the visual impact from the stage-bound quality of other BBC productions.

My approach to* Poldark *started with reading the books and not just the scripts, and going to look at tin mines and images in the Royal Cornwall Museum. I talked with Janet Arnold, whose book series* The Patterns of Fashion *are so useful to understand the cut and shape of period clothes. She said I should go and look at Snowshill Manor in Warwickshire, which has a really interesting collection of late eighteenth-century clothing. Then I got down to doing the drawings of costumes made for Robin Ellis as Ross.[14] – **John Bloomfield**

98. (opposite) Costume design by Raymond Hughes for *The Pallisers* (1974)

'In the BBC Allocations Office, there was a huge chart on the wall and you were commissioned projects according to your abilities, so they played to your strengths. The fashion designers tended to design light entertainment. I was given classic serials and *Play for Today*.'[15] – Elizabeth Waller

Sc. 11 & 12 EP 21.
c 1884/5
black velvet
black satin

The 1970s' range of productions and periods allowed Cosprop to expand their collecting remit. This expansion would necessitate the company moving from their first premises on Gloucester Avenue in 1975 to a former Victorian Boys Home on Regent's Park Road where it was based for five years.

Whilst period costume dramas were associated with the BBC, the different franchises of ITV also commissioned adaptations. ATV produced the 13-part *Edward the Seventh* (1975) featuring Timothy West as Edward and a BAFTA-winning Annette Crosbie as Queen Victoria. With a huge cast of British acting talent playing royalty, politicians and the military, and covering Edward's birth in 1841 to his death in 1910, Cosprop's expertise in formal Victorian and Edwardian clothing was essential.

Francesca Annis played Lillie Langtry, the actress who was Edward's mistress, in two episodes and was dressed by Cosprop. She made such a success of the role that LWT (London Weekend Television) commissioned a separate series *Lillie* (1978) using many of the same writers and directors. Alongside her royal connections, this also covered her theatrical life with characters including Oscar Wilde, Sarah Bernhardt and James Whistler portrayed. For this 13-part series, Cosprop made all of Annis's costumes, who won a BAFTA for Best Actress for the role.

Cosprop's range of productions moved beyond the Sunday night 'classic' slot to some of television's cult programmes.

***When I was designing the* Doctor Who *episodes, 'The Talons of Weng-Chiang' (1977), John made some costumes for Louise Jameson* [*as Leela*]. *It was set in mid-nineteenth-century London, so it was ideal for a Cosprop project.*[16] – John Bloomfield**

Vanessa Hopkins was one of several new costume assistants taken on by the BBC Costume Department in 1970.

***The Cosprop approach was so good, it was so different to what had gone before, and it was in tune with a new design generation, who wanted something different from the theatricality of costume design.*[17] – Vanessa Hopkins, former BBC Costume Supervisor**

Hopkins would eventually leave the BBC at the end of the 1970s and, with her husband, Alan, founded The Hopkins Collection, a supplier of fabric and accessories to the costume design industry. A 'cottage industry' in the design chain, the business was run from their South London home and, over time, every costume designer would visit their vast resource for advice and to source material for their projects.

Beginning at a time when fabric production was disappearing in the UK, they realised that what costume designers needed were fabrics appropriate for period costume, and they sought out textile manufacturers who could reproduce period fabrics and trimmings. In time, The Hopkins Collection became an essential part of the design process and John Bright was a regular customer.

This shift in costuming was beginning to take place on the small screen, although the impact would eventually find its way into feature films. Many of the costume designers who developed their design skills with the BBC would go on to have careers in the film industry – among them James Acheson, John Bloomfield, Dinah Collin and Elizabeth Waller.

John Bright, Christopher Prins and their teams were nurturing the next generation of costume designers:

***I went to Cosprop with my sketches, John was so encouraging and interested, he looked at my sketches carefully. I was based at the BBC for a few years. You were put onto different projects so it was a good training ground, it was very valuable but it was like working for the civil service, the BBC calendar was different to other calendars. You were assigned constant design projects to work on so you were always busy.*[18] – Phoebe de Gaye, Costume Designer**

By the end of the 1970s, the Regency and Victorian set dramas were about to give way to a new era of costuming. The new decade would bring further opportunities for not only the organisation but also for John Bright, as he began to establish himself as a costume designer for stage and screen whilst still overseeing the organisation, collecting and being a costumier for every project that passed through the Cosprop premises.

99. (opposite) Costume design for Ross Poldark (Robin Ellis) in *Poldark* (1975–77; Costume Designer John Bloomfield)

'I used Cosprop for *Poldark*, I had a couple of costumes made for Robin Ellis as Poldark and Ralph Bates as George Warleggan. Also one-off costumes for Mary Wimbush and Paul Curran as the Poldark household servants, I also hired quite a few costumes from Cosprop.'[19] – John Bloomfield

'POLDARK'
ROSS
Robin Ellis
BBC TV
John Bloomfield

Brideshead Revisited (1981)

Directors Charles Sturridge, Michael Lindsay-Hogg | Costume Designer Jane Robinson
Starring Jeremy Irons, Anthony Andrews, Diana Quick, Laurence Olivier, Claire Bloom, John Gielgud

Brideshead Revisited (1981) had the cultural impact of a major feature film when it was serialised. Broadcast over eleven weeks during the autumn of 1981, after a summer of civil unrest in many UK cities and towns, the series offered a nostalgic narrative of upper-class privilege. Its romantic themes of a world that was disappearing appealed to audiences; it remains one of the most watched series in British television history.

Jeremy Irons, Anthony Andrews and Diana Quick were all newcomers to television audiences and were supported by a roster of British stage and screen household names including Laurence Olivier, John Gielgud and Claire Bloom. Whilst ITV franchises had made *Upstairs, Downstairs*, this lavish production and stellar cast propelled them into a different league.

***I worked with many designers. I worked on* Brideshead Revisited *with Jane Robinson, she was a delight to work with. I created a couple of Diana Quick's 1920s' evening gowns. Cosprop was all about using different skills and applying this to different time periods.*[20] – Jill Harbutt, Costume Maker**

The production values and budget of *Brideshead Revisited* were of film quality, and was the most expensive television production ever created on British television. This was immediately evident in the critical and cultural acclaim of the series. At a preview for the industry's leading figures, film director John Schlesinger was heard to say 'this is where the British film industry is'.[21]

The costume design of *Brideshead Revisited* benefited from a long shooting period, which had been disrupted by a strike by staff at ITV. It also afforded the designers and makers at Cosprop a period of time to develop a character's wardrobe and provide continuity to the visual identity of a character.

Because it was shot over such a long period of time, the clothes really became the actors' wardrobe, they belonged to them

and became moulded to their bodies.[22] – **Jane Robinson, Costume Designer**

The impact of the weekly broadcast of *Brideshead Revisited* was similar to that of *The Forstye Saga* 14 years earlier. London restaurateurs reported low bookings on Monday nights when the series was screened and 'looked forward to its conclusion by Christmas 1981'.[23] The impact of the series' costume design was immediate on fashion. Throughout autumn 1981, fashion magazine *Harpers & Queen* was 'adopting the Brideshead look.'[24] Menswear magazines also promoted 'wider ties, cravats, bow ties, Panama hats, braces and polka dots as a homage to Brideshead.' Visits to Castle Howard in Yorkshire, where the series was filmed, trebled, and cricket sweaters and Oxford brogues also enjoyed a revival.

John Mortimer, who adapted the novel to the screen reflected on its success, 'we struck a chord with *Brideshead*, the end of the 1970s were bleak, anarchy in the UK and all of that, but the locations, the beautiful costumes and acting talent elevated audiences.'[25]

100. (opposite) Costume designs by Jane Robinson for Julia (left) and Sebastian (right) in *Brideshead Revisited* (1981)

101. (above) Sebastian Flyte (Anthony Andrews), Julia Flyte (Diana Quick), Charles Ryder (Jeremy Irons) in *Brideshead Revisited* (1981)

50 Dr. Jaeger's Sanitary Woolen System Co.
Men's Dressing-Gowns
AND
SMOKING (OR LIBRARY) JACKETS
Men's Smoking (or Library) Jacket.
Men's Dressing-Gown.
MEN'S DRESSIN
MEN'S SMOKING (or LI
Sole Importers and Exc
PURE CAMELHAIR SLEEPING-BAG.
The "JAEGER" Sleeping-Bag was used by Field-Marshal Lord Roberts, General Lord Kitchener, thousands of Officers, the late Sir W. MacCormac, Bart., and others during the South African War.
Sleeping-Bag.
KAISER
MUSTACHE TRAINER.
BEFORE.
If You Want a
IN USE.
AFTER.
Nice Well-Trained Mustache
Use this wonderful trainer. Worn five minutes in the morning trains any mustache for all day to the shape desired, and permanently after using a few times, assuring comfort and improved appearance.
It will be found that nearly all gentlemen with nice and well-trained mustaches use one of these Kaiser Trainers.
It overcomes every objectionable feature of a mustache.
Sent to any address on receipt of 50 c
Bartitsu is an eclectic martial art and self-defence method originally developed in England during the years 1898–1902. In 1901 it was immortalised (as "baritsu") by Sir Arthur Conan Doyle, author of the Sherlock Holmes mystery stories.[1]
Poirot—3.

Agatha Christie's Poirot (1989–2013)

Original Costume Designers Series 1: Linda Mattock, Sue (Susi) Thomson | Subsequent Costume Designers Sheena Napier, Barbara Kronig, Robin Fraser-Paye, Elizabeth Waller, Andrea Galer, Charlotte Holdich, Sharon Lewis
Starring David Suchet, Hugh Fraser, Philip Jackson, Pauline Moran, Zoë Wanamaker

Hercule Poirot has appeared on stage and screen since his creation in 1920, and has been portrayed in all-star Hollywood films by Albert Finney in *Murder on the Orient Express* (1974) and Peter Ustinov six times starting with *Death on the Nile* (1978). When David Suchet took the part in 1989, the lesser-known short stories were filmed first, and he researched all the books as he 'wanted to be the character that Agatha Christie wrote'.[25]

Although written from 1920 to 1975, the decision was made to set the stories in the mid-1930s, often considered a golden age of detective fiction, and allowing an Art Deco sensibility to influence set and costume design.

From his bowler hat to his patent leather shoes, the costumes created by Cosprop were incredibly detailed. For this 'small, dandified man',[27] Suchet's own shape had to be modified and he wore complex padding of foam rubber including separate breast plates and belly, which folded when the character sat down. A small hump was added to the back to push Suchet's head forward; Suchet had to wear all the padding for all fittings at Cosprop.

Christie describes Poirot's silhouette as 'an inverted pear' so, alongside the padded torso, the trousers were cut wide so that there was no visible gap in between the legs.[28] Supplemented with his swan-topped cane – Poirot's 'prized possession' according to Suchet – the actor was able to create Poirot's distinctive gait.[29] On set for later series, the weight and warmth of wearing the padding and bespoke suits meant that Suchet had to use a leaning board to avoid sitting down and creasing the costumes, remarking, 'my suit gets special treatment, not me.'[30]

Suchet's encyclopaedic knowledge of Poirot afforded him 'a huge input into costume design – and moustache design'.[31] He would never appear outdoors in 24 years of filming without a hat. The look was completed by a small flower vase brooch, worn throughout the series with miniature flowers. In the only flashback episode to Poirot's previous life as a Belgian policeman, 'The Chocolate Box', we see him being given this by the woman he secretly loved.

With their rich stock of 1930s' clothing, Cosprop supplied many other costumes. The brocade dressing gown worn by Poirot from 2003 had previously been worn by Hugh Laurie in *Jeeves and Wooster* (1990; Costume Designer Dany Everett). Cosprop also dressed one of Agatha Christie's favourite characters, the flamboyant novelist Ariadne Oliver played by Zoë Wanamaker in *Cards on the Table* (2006; Costume Designer Sheena Napier).

In filming all 70 Poirot stories over 24 years, *Agatha Christie's Poirot* was a landmark of British television. Both Series 1 Costume Designers, Linda Mattock and Sue Thomson, were nominated for a Best Costume Design BAFTA (with Mattock winning). The series was shown in more than 100 countries to an estimated 700 million viewers, in no small part thanks to Suchet's incredible performance and attention to detail, matched by the exquisite costumes.

102. (opposite) Moodboard of 1930s' men's fashions and facial hair

103. (right) Hercule Poirot (David Suchet) in *Agatha Christie's Poirot* (1989–2013)

'Classic books and period adaptations have been our bread and butter over the years, but it's important to get the right look and the right feeling of the book.'[32] – John Bright

Tipping the Velvet (2002)

Director Geoffrey Sax | Costume Designer Susannah Buxton
Starring Rachael Stirling, Keeley Hawes, Jodhi May, Anna Chancellor

The 2000s experienced global instability with the war on terror and the financial crash of 2008 affecting the film and television industries. The rise of international satellite channels – Sky, Home Box Office (HBO) – also began to impact the central place that organisations such as BBC had played in television hierarchy. As a response to these creative challenges, the BBC began to diversify its programming.

The BBC adaptation by Andrew Davies of the popular Sarah Waters novel featured a female-led story set in Victorian England, with female-to-male impersonation and the strata of high and low society. Susannah Buxton's research process began with the resources at Cosprop.

***The idea of looking at originals in John's Museum Collection is not to copy them, the intention is to create a character. For that actor in that drama, things will be different. You're taking the inspiration and understanding – but it would not necessarily work to recreate a costume. The characters have a life of their own and are taking part in a story.*[33] – Susannah Buxton**

104. Kitty Butler (Keeley Hawes) and Nan Astley (Rachael Stirling) in *Tipping the Velvet* (2002)

The costumes for lead Nan Astley (Rachael Stirling) needed to chronicle her journey from provincial oyster-girl to London society via cross-dressing on the music hall stage. From full-length dresses to male dinner suits, seen both dressing and undressing, getting the complete Victorian look from the underwear up was key to creating each silhouette.

When I was doing my research for* Tipping the Velvet *I looked at the history of the music halls and particularly at the cross-dressing performers like Vesta Tilley. The world the series wanted to create was very much a theatrical world so I was keen to see many photographs of the time. John Bright has also collected some original costumes from different theatre productions to give me ideas of colour, shapes and texture.

All the uniforms and suits for Rachael and Keeley were made in the workrooms at Cosprop with huge help from Christopher Prins and the tailor there. We took really good patterns from original 1890s' suits and had to scale them down in size to fit the actors, added padding to change their shapes, and bust flatteners as Vesta Tilley would have done at the time.

***The art of making a historical costume is one of collaboration with all the different skills involved. There can be as many as five or six technicians brought into one fitting at Cosprop, and that's not including the dyers and breaking-down artists who work behind the scenes. The main people in a fitting will be the designer, the assistant and the costumier, but coming in can be the corset maker, the seamstress, the tailor and the milliner. All are invaluable to the designer and are rarely given the accolade they deserve.*[34] – Susannah Buxton**

Lead press images from the series included Rachael Stirling and Keeley Hawes in the underwear they wore beneath their masculine suits. The show was a ratings triumph, and was particularly well-received by the LGBTQ+ community. Buxton's skilful designs led her to work on the next BBC Waters' adaptation of *Fingersmith* in 2005.

The Forsyte Saga (2002–3)

Directors Christopher Menaul, David Moore, Andy Wilson | Costume Designer Phoebe de Gaye
Starring Damian Lewis, Gina McKee, Rupert Graves, Corin Redgrave, Ben Miles, Amanda Root

A landmark BBC production in 1967 and one of the first large-scale costume dramas, *The Forsyte Saga* fused together the essential ingredients for the BBC costume drama: it was based on a series of well-known novels by John Galsworthy, staged in period settings (1870s–1920s), and featured costumes designed by Joan Ellacott. Six months after it first aired, the series was repeated on a Sunday evening on BBC1, with an increased viewing figure of 18 million, a third of the UK population at the time. Some churches altered their evening services so that parishioners could get home in time to watch it.

John Bright became involved with the series when the narrative moved into the 1920s. Some of the clothes that were being used had been given to him by fashion historian Doris Langley Moore (p.12). It was an early learning experience of using original clothes, as one of the beaded dresses began to disintegrate because of the heat of the lighting on the fragile decoration.

With such a legacy of success, in 2002 ITV revisited John Galsworthy's trilogy to engage a new generation of viewers. Cosprop, in its infancy, had been involved in the original and were the obvious choice for the remake.

I had seen the original, filmed in black and white, at the time when it was made. In 2001 the hairstyles seemed very 1960s, but perhaps the version I worked on would now seem very 2001! Joan Ellacott, who was the Costume Designer, had borrowed some items from John. The BBC period stock tended to be heavy and theatrical, built to last by a workroom that operated 24 hours a day in two shifts, catering for a huge number of programmes. At Cosprop I could find lighter, more detailed costumes, which felt more authentic.[35] – **Phoebe de Gaye**

The Forsyte Saga is the story of three generations and covers five decades. Costume played a significant role establishing the timeframe of the story. The large cast and the actors' appearance changed greatly with the passing of time and fashions.

An advantage of Cosprop's large stock is that outfits can be retrimmed and repurposed with great sensitivity and skill. For instance a decorative blue and gold waistcoat worn by Corin Redgrave in 2002 was later modified with different buttons and an altered fit for Adam James in* Belgravia *in 2023. Sometimes these costumes can seem like old friends![36] – **Phoebe de Gaye**

An elegantly embroidered coat and matching scarf was created at Cosprop from an antique tablecloth and was worn by the actor Beatriz Batarda in *The Forsyte Saga*. This had been seen previously in *The House of Eliott* (1991–4), *Mrs Dalloway* (1997), *The Grand* (1997–8) and by Elizabeth McGovern in *Downton Abbey* (Season 3, 2012).

105. Montague Dartie (Ben Miles) and Irene Forstye (Gina McKee) in *The Forstye Saga* (2002–3)

'I have learnt so much from seeing John at work. He is always so focussed. Particularly about proportion and the importance of keeping your lines clean – some period outfits can become very complicated. Gina McKee, whose many costumes were overseen by John when they were created, would refer to him as a kind of doctor! This was because of his forensic analysis of problems, and his unswerving ability to solve them.'[37]
– Phoebe de Gaye

Downton Abbey (2010–15)

Directors Brian Percival, Andy Goddard, Brian Kelly, Ben Bolt, James Strong (Series 1, 2)
Costume Designers Susannah Buxton, Rosalind Ebbutt, Caroline McCall, Anna Mary Scott Robbins
Starring Hugh Bonneville, Elizabeth McGovern, Maggie Smith, Penelope Wilton, Lesley Nicol, Jim Carter, Phyllis Logan, Michelle Dockery, Dan Stevens, Jessica Brown Findlay, Laura Carmichael

Downton Abbey heralded the return to a narrative of the English country house, its aristocrats and the staff who serve them. Using a format devised by *Upstairs, Downstairs* in the 1970s, and building on the acclaimed *Gosford Park* (2001), writer Julian Fellowes created the series that would become not only a phenomenon in the UK but its high-quality production standards, acting and script were globally successful.

Maggie Smith and Hugh Bonneville led the ensemble cast, which included Elizabeth McGovern, an important casting decision for the export possibilities for American audiences.

When I began my research for the first series, I looked at contemporary design elements to incorporate to make it accessible to modern audiences. The wardrobe of Heather Firbank held at the Victoria and Albert Museum in London was also a huge source of inspiration. The show was set in an interesting period, the end of the Edwardian era before the outbreak of the First World War, which would change everything; this time has been called The Golden Summer.[38] – **Susannah Buxton**

For Buxton, designing a major period production was not about creating eye-catching costumes:

The clothes are a complete part of that character, so you're accepting what they're wearing without thinking. I don't want everyone looking at the frock. That's the hardest thing. Some of the costumes I'm most proud of are the ones you wouldn't necessarily think about because the clothes naturally belong to the character. They don't look like actors in costumes, they look like real people.[39] – **Susannah Buxton**

Fellowes based Violet Crawley, The Dowager Countess of Grantham (Maggie Smith) on 'his own Great Aunt Isie'.[40] Buxton recalls the process of bringing her to life.

Queen Mary came to mind for Maggie Smith's character Violet Crawley, I was inspired by her shape. Queen Mary always had a certain look and it was right because we wanted a really strong, positive look for Maggie Smith. She's the dominant character in the series. You want a costume to help emphasise the character, to be part of who that person is. It's almost totally different from fashion, which is all about the clothes but not about the person. It's about making them look thin and beautiful, whereas a costume is about helping that character develop.[41] – **Susannah Buxton**

Cosprop's input into the design of* Downton Abbey *was led from the very beginning of the series. For Maggie's outfit (fig.95), the blouse was from John's special stock for principals; we re-lined the neck to keep it as soft as possible, and the jewellery was from Cosprop Accessories Room. The workroom at Cosprop made the outfit based loosely on a jacket shape we had tried on Maggie at the first fitting. I am not sure if the workroom made a toile* [a version of a costume made in cheaper material] *initially to save cutting the fabric until we were sure of the shape, if it's an expensive fabric this is often the best practice. The jacket has fine lace inner sleeves to cover her wrists. The hat base was entirely retrimmed with dyed silk tulle but John came in with the strange cotton-filled bobbles which he had taken off a damaged original hat years before, and which I thought were genius.[42] – **Susannah Buxton**

For Maggie's clothes, I found the black coat she wears in Episode 1 at Camden Market, it was an extraordinary Parisian coat. At the end of the first series, she is in an Alpaca cream coat, with a beautiful hat. I had to wash it and do things to it but to get something of that quality for a series like that is rare.[43] – **John Bright**

Buxton had a strong female cast to design a narrative and character arc for; designing the three Crawley daughters – Mary, Edith and Sybil – exemplifies the jigsaw puzzle nature of costume design for *Downton Abbey* as Buxton reflects,

These three dresses demonstrated well the different ways in which we brought the costumes together for the show* (fig.106)*: Mary's dress was made for her; Edith's was hired – it was previously used in* A Room with a View (p.64) *and Sybil's is an original Edwardian dress.

106. (opposite) The Crawley sisters: Edith (Laura Carmichael), Mary (Michelle Dockery) and Sybil (Jessica Brown Findlay) in *Downton Abbey* (Season 1)

107. (overleaf) Mrs Patmore (Lesley Nicol) in *Downton Abbey*

SALT

I really tried to get the difference between the three girls. For Lady Sybil I tried to show she is more of a free spirit – slightly bohemian for her time, and not so interested in high-end fashion. Her style is slightly more individualist. Lady Mary is very much high-end fashion. The Crawley family have got money, so they go to London, which already has big department stores. And since her mother, the Countess of Grantham, is American, I tried to show both of them as very keen on the latest fashions.

As for Lady Edith, she tends to not get it quite right because she's the more awkward girl. I didn't want to make her frumpy because that would be predicting her character. She wasn't supposed to be frumpy, just the less beautiful girl. I tried to avoid cliché. Sometimes she looks stunning, but sometimes odd, so that Mary can make scathing remarks.[44] – **Susannah Buxton**

As the series was being filmed, it emerged that a major television event was taking shape.

The end of Season 1 was the declaration of the First World War, the news is announced during a garden party, it marks the end of 'The Golden Summer' era as the Edwardian period ended. I dressed the characters in creams, blacks and whites. The day we filmed the scene, we had the perfect natural light, everyone stood still and the cast and the crew had goosebumps (fig.109).[45] – **Susannah Buxton**

Downton Abbey chronicled the interplay between the ruling

'Most of Mary's clothes were made, a few were originals; Susannah keeps it simple and never likes to overload us with too much jewellery, the dress is the thing.'[46] – Michelle Dockery

aristocracy and their household staff, cutting between above-stairs and below-stairs life, and their narratives were interwoven throughout the series. The impact of the show was immediate and the clothing had an influence on contemporary fashion.

***There's a tweed suit that Lady Mary wears during a hunting party in the Christmas Special* (fig.108). *People would happily wear it now. It looks good, but it also fits comfortably in the era where it's supposed to sit.*[47] – Susannah Buxton**

Downton Abbey ran for six series and has spawned several feature films. Susannah Buxton won a BAFTA and an EMMY for her work. Costumes from the show have been on continual display since the series premiered and have toured internationally. Several publications have also been produced reflecting its ongoing status as a high point in British television history. Parallel with the success of *Downton Abbey*, was the premiere of one of the most discussed and ground-breaking series of the era, *Game of Thrones*.

108. (opposite) The hunting scene in the *Downton Abbey* Christmas special (2012, Season 2)

109. (below) The garden party scene in *Downton Abbey* (finale, Season 1)

'Over the dozens of productions I have worked on with Cosprop, John has usually been called upon at some stage of the process. As if from nowhere, he suddenly appears in the fitting room, like some twinkly, avuncular wizard. He tweaks, he adjusts, he suggests ... confirming an experienced designer's ideas, educating a newcomer with warmth and clear advice based on his decades of experience. A magician of his craft.'[48] – Hugh Bonneville

Game of Thrones (2011–19)

Director Tom McCarthy (pilot) | Costume Designer Michele Clapton
Starring Sean Bean, Mark Addy, Michelle Fairley, Nikolaj Coster-Waldau, Lena Headey, Iain Glen, Peter Dinklage, Kit Harington, Emilia Clarke, Sophie Turner

The landmark television series *Game of Thrones* was based on a series of fantasy novels by George R.R. Martin, set on the fictional continents of Westeros and Essos. The series was created by David Benioff and D. B. Weiss and featured several interlinking story arcs and a huge cast of actors.

My initial ideas grew out of those early conversations with David (Benioff) and Dan (D. B. Weiss), I also began re-reading the first two novels, the show's scripts would become the most important road map. From the books, we took the sigils and colours for each house, among other important details, but we were really setting out on our own path.[49] – **Michele Clapton**

To anchor the characters in a believable fantasy world, Clapton immersed herself in research and studied a vast range of historical, cultural and ethnological sources.

I explored the influence of religion on clothing along with ancient ideas about beauty and accessories and the uses of applique and embroidery. I looked at clothing from cultures around the world over many centuries: Japanese, Flemish, Siberian, Afghan, Persian and Native American to name a few. Nothing could look like it came from any one specific historic era.[50] – **Michele Clapton**

The different environments depicted in *Games of Thrones* were also key in the costume design process and informed the development of the different family clans.

I began studying how people lived in various climates historically, I looked at how they protected themselves from heat or cold and enemies. Which materials and trades were available to them and which colours of dye they were able to create. The other element that I really had to explore, and in a way this was probably even more daunting, was how to produce my designs.[51] – **Michele Clapton**

Michele came to see me with the script for* Game of Thrones. *Michele's ideas were very clear, I knew it was going to be a massive hit, I had a strong feeling about it. There were five factions, represented by a different actor. We made the initial costumes for the leading male characters, we made leather tunics, padded and quilted costumes.[52] – **John Bright**

Game of Thrones was a significant move away from the Cosprop timeframe and making remit which, until the series, had not included 'fantasy' costuming. Bright said that it was good to get away from what Cosprop normally does and that 'it gave us a wider understanding of what we are doing, and the experience gave me a wider knowledge'.[53]

At that time I didn't have the experience of setting up and running a large costume and armour department, and we were to work out of Belfast where I knew very few crew. It was important to me that the costumes reflected my research and that they were rooted in reality and constructed in an appropriate way with the correct materials, to be clothes. Having worked with John on period projects in the past, I felt that his support and passion for helping to create thoughtful, beautiful principal costumes would enable me to realise key pieces. These examples would then help me to set the sense of the costumes for the workroom I was creating in Belfast. I did worry that the series was not something that John would even consider.[54]– **Michele Clapton**

110. (left) Tyrion Lannister (Peter Dinklage) in *Game of Thrones* (2011–19)

111. (opposite) Eddard 'Ned' Stark (Sean Bean) in *Game of Thrones* (2011–19)

'"Fantasy" was not something that was associated with Cosprop at the time. John saw something in it, and my passion for it, and indeed he gave me a safe and supportive place amongst friends to explore and realise the essence of costuming *Game of Thrones*.'[55]
– Michele Clapton

I worked on costumes for Iain Glen, Sean Bean and Peter Dinklage. Not only were the designs unusual for us to work with, but the fabrics were also too. All period designs are based on real clothes, but Michele's designs were only limited by her imagination – which was limitless![56]**– Susan Hardy, Costume Maker**

With multiple, parallel storylines featuring a huge cast of characters, informing the audience of the hierarchies within these groups, the costume design 'communicated the history, culture and a myriad of characters and factions'.[57]

The impact of *Game of Thrones* was global, the characters and actors became household names and the storylines – though often controversial – were acclaimed. The costume design for the series elevated the artform for a television series and was lauded as one of the most important features of the series' dramatic narrative. Clapton won several awards for her work including a BAFTA, a Costume Designers Guild Award and several EMMYs.

Series such as *Games of Thrones* and *Downton Abbey* changed the landscape of costume design for television. Content for television challenged the dominance of film, and multiple streaming services were creating new opportunities for writers, actors and designers.

Poldark (2015–19)

Directors Ed Bazalgette, William McGregor (Season 1)
Costume Designers Marianne Agertoft, Susannah Buxton, Howard Burden, Ros Little
Starring Aidan Turner, Eleanor Tomlinson, Jack Farthing, Heida Reed, Luke Norris

The BBC commissioned a remake of *Poldark* as a response to the success of *Downton Abbey* on ITV in the Sunday night slot. The first adaptation of *Poldark* was one of the most successful series of all time for the corporation. Set in 1780s' rural Cornwall, Aidan Turner was cast as the eponymous hero; the original Ross Poldark (Robin Ellis) was cast as Reverend Halse.

With its painterly qualities, sweeping cinematography and a central charismatic performance from Turner, it was an immediate hit with audiences. Susannah Buxton joined for series 2, taking over the design template from Marianne Agertoft. A long running series offers designers scope as established characters are given new storylines and new characters are added. The timeframe also shifts, and this is reflected in the changes in fashion and the impact this has on a character's journey.

I did watch all of Season 1, I wanted to see how characters would evolve and how the new cast members could become part of the same visual world. I liked how the first costume designer had established the colour palette and the silhouette so I took her ideas forward, with changes and additions from my own designs.

The series had moved to the year 1790 and fashions had changed, although these are country people and would not be in high fashion. Even the local aristocracy would not be in court dress, which is so often considered to be the main fashion of the time, because these are often the only clothes that have survived and are seen in costume collections.

The question of wealth, status and age has to be taken into consideration when designing costumes. Ross Poldark's financial position was precarious and Demelza [Eleanor Tomlinson] would have had only work clothes, she needed changes once she was married but still had a basic mix and match of hard wearing bodices and blouses in a similar silhouette. I added more colour and gradually added more styles. We also altered and adapted first series' makes, particularly when she became pregnant. I designed a completely new jacket and breeches for Ross as the male silhouette was slimmer and sharper but the tricorn hat remained the same (see p.135).

Cosprop provided all of the crowd costumes from stock and continued to do so throughout the series (fig.113). *They made principal costumes for Morwenna and their workrooms made most of the costumes I designed for the second series. It was invaluable to have the original costumes from the Museum Collection there, to look at for reference. Although the designers source and buy the fabric for each individual costume, the huge range of sample books at Cosprop reduced the hours spent sampling in the fabric stores.*[58]
– **Susannah Buxton**

112. (opposite) Ross Poldark (Aidan Turner) in *Poldark* (2015–19)

113. (right) Costume for Ross Poldark (Aidan Turner) in *Poldark* (2015–19)
Courtesy of Kerry Taylor Auctions Ltd

Victoria (2016–19)

Creator Daisy Goodwin | Costume Designers James Keast, Rosalind Ebbutt
Starring Jenna Coleman, Tom Hughes, Peter Bowles, Catherine Fleming

The ITV series *Victoria* offered a different narrative to the prevailing image of Queen Victoria as an elderly figure in mourning, exemplified by Judi Dench in the film *Mrs Brown* (1997). The series began with Victoria's accession to the throne aged just 18 in 1837, covered the Great Exhibition of 1851, and ended by foreshadowing Albert's early death in 1861.

***We tried to reflect in Victoria's clothes the emergence of the young queen from an inexperienced teenager, and onward to betrothal and marriage. The changing fashion of the time also helped reflect this, as the wide puffed sleeves of the late 1830s gave way to tighter sleeves, lower waistlines, and more bell-shaped skirts.*[59] – Rosalind Ebbutt**

Cosprop's wealth of nineteenth-century material and expertise in the period made them a favourite choice for original Costume Designer James Keast, and for Rosalind Ebbutt who took over from him during the first series. Perhaps the most famous costume was the wedding dress worn by Jenna Coleman as Victoria, which took several weeks of making at Cosprop.

***Victoria wrote a lot about it in her diary, about how she wanted to dress in white and look more like a real woman and less like a queen. She wrote about the orange blossom and the fact that Prince Albert had given her a beautiful brooch. She wanted to be an English bride. Victoria was very keen that everything would be from her country.*[60] – Rosalind Ebbutt**

***The wedding dress for Victoria was exciting to make because it required making a faithful recreation of the real thing as possible and it's from a historical moment. I had reference images from when the original had been on display. I also had a couple of drawings from the time of the wedding itself. The dress was a simple design to make, created in a heavy silk satin. It was all about the lace. Victoria had Honiton lace on her dress so John and I worked with the designer to find the best possible match for the laces we were going to use. Victoria also needed a rather long train that had to be detachable for some of the following scenes.*[61] – Emma Burke, Costume Maker**

The bridesmaids' dresses were based on drawings that Victoria had sketched in her diary, and were made at Cosprop alongside the bridal train that they carried. The uniform Prince Albert (Tom Hughes) wore at his wedding to Victoria was made by Dan Ashworth, Tailor (fig.115).

***I went to Kensington Palace to conduct my own research and saw an original uniform and this made me rethink how I would approach the construction* (fig.116). *I then referred to Norah Waugh's* The Cut of Men's Clothes *for reference using the 1824–1825 section for the pattern. This uniform was a one-off for Albert as he didn't belong to a regiment.*[62] – Dan Ashworth**

Ebbutt acknowledges that whilst historical accuracy is important, the actors must feel comfortable in their clothes. Hughes had wanted his costume to be very fitted; contemporaneous paintings show Albert in what would be considered today skin-tight trousers.

***It was during the second fitting that Tom realised it was going to be too tight for him. But at the third fitting, when Tom put the uniform on it fitted perfectly ... you have a realisation that something works.*[63] – Dan Ashworth**

The wedding couple featured in the *Radio Times* (fig.114) and Cosprop's costumes including other uniforms made by Ashworth featured in *Vogue*. As he commented, 'The clothes speak for themselves, we are rarely – if ever – credited so it's very personal when your work is acknowledged.'[64]

114. (left) *Radio Times* cover featuring *Victoria*, April–May 2019

115. (opposite, above) Costume and fabric research from the workbook of Dan Ashworth, Tailor, for *Victoria* (2016–19).

116. (opposite, below) Prince Albert (Tom Hughes) and Queen Victoria (Jenna Coleman) in *Victoria* (2016–19)

'Every stage of the process is photographed and recorded in the costume bible. For a recurring television series or a film franchise, the bible is a vital record of the costume construction process. If a series designer changes, the character and costume are the bridge between the series' visual identity.'[65] – Nancy Knapp, Head of the Workroom

Gentleman Jack (2019–22)

Directors Sally Wainwright, Sarah Harding, Jennifer Perrot (Season 1) | Costume Designer Tom Pye
Starring Suranne Jones, Sophie Rundle, Gemma Whelan, Gemma Jones, Timothy West, Joe Armstrong, Amelia Bullmore

Gentleman Jack was based on the diaries of Anne Lister, written in 1830s' Yorkshire and she is described by historians as 'the first modern lesbian'. She came from a minor landowning family and the show follows Lister returning to her ancestral home in Yorkshire to find herself a wife. From its opening credits showing Anne Lister getting dressed in male attire; costume plays a key role in *Gentleman Jack*. Together with Bright and his team, Costume Designer Tom Pye dressed Suranne Jones both as a man and as a woman, and said that 'the men's clothes just worked so much better.'[66]

Lister's diaries – many of which needed to be decoded – detailed both her conquests and her clothing.

We were fascinated by the balance between male and female, the ambiguities that could be explored by going into close detail, and the interesting juxtapositions that could be created between garments, such as male drawers worn over female corsetry. So much of what Anne wore would have been dictated by the strict social conventions of the time, such as corsetry and ankle-length skirts. I found it fascinating to imagine how she may have complied with these restrictions and how, at the same time, she might have subverted them, creating what must have appeared as a very masculine silhouette to earn her the nickname 'Gentleman Jack.'[67] – **Tom Pye**

Pye went back to the diaries, which included a packing list for a trip to Denmark, to learn that Lister's male wardrobe included a spencer, a greatcoat, wool waistcoats, gaiters and stays. The greatcoat was a particularly important piece, worn for formal meetings, and was based on an original 1830s' coat from the John Bright Collection (fig.118).

Pye was able to also draw on Cosprop's expert makers and tailors to mix and match male and female details to ensure the perfect fit for both the period and the actor.

I worked closely with one of the tailors at Cosprop, Dan Ashworth, to design Anne's greatcoat to fit Suranne in very particular ways. I wanted its length and construction to give Suranne the ability to move easily, and it was also essential for me that the coat itself would move in an exciting way. This was achieved through the choice of fabrics and also through a specific construction that allowed the coat to billow behind as she strode about.[68] – **Tom Pye**

Ashworth recalls his interest in the project stemmed from the fact that Lister's real clothes would have been made by a male tailor but worn by a woman.

In the fitting room, putting the garment on Suranne Jones for the first time, she became Anne Lister, it was extraordinary. You are nervous, it's your work, you have spent time talking to the

117. (left) Ann Walker (Sophie Rundle) and Anne Lister (Suranne Jones) in *Gentleman Jack* (2019–22)

118. (opposite) Wool coat, trimmed with silk velvet (1830s), John Bright Collection

designer, you try and understand what they want. When you know the actor is happy, it's a great moment, you see your work brought to life by the actor in character **(fig.120).**[69] – **Dan Ashworth**

I worked closely with Tom from the offset. He came in and showed Gina [Women's Costumier] and me his designs and ideas ... We both then went through the stock ... pulling out interesting shapes that complemented the look he was going for ... The fittings with Suranne were really interesting with the mix of corset, skirt, shirt, cravat, waistcoat and frockcoat, top hat etc. Some items used were stock and other items were tailor-made for her in the workroom.[70] – **Ross Braganza, Senior Men's Costumier**

The gender mix was brought out in the details, whilst adhering to source material. Within the fitting room, pantaloons were tried on Suranne, but rejected as being too unlikely for Lister to have worn, and there would have been mention of it in her diaries or in contemporaneous accounts. Pye's research found that the women's garments mentioned in her diary include petticoats, skirts, corsets and at least one pelisse.

However, I believe she toyed with breeches in her youth and we reflect this occasionally in flashbacks, using them to suggest Anne was a rather precocious teenager.[71] – **Tom Pye**

When we do see Lister in conventional female attire at a ball, we are so accustomed to her androgenous look and masculine mannerisms that Pye's intention was that the costume, though beautiful, would look 'wrong'.

I wanted to deliberately exaggerate Suranne's silhouette, so that the more traditional dresses she wears emphasise the line and width of her shoulders as a way to make her appear more masculine. All the lines of Anne's white ball gown are very horizontal, with large epaulettes capping the sleeves that widen the shoulder line still further ... and the sash at her waist is a reference to a hussar uniform.

The two birds-of-paradise feathers in her hair are straight out of the diary – she wrote about one falling out in the carriage on

119. (below) Costume design sketch by Tom Pye for Anne Lister in *Gentleman Jack* (2019–22)

120. (opposite, left) Suranne Jones being fitted for the role of Anne Lister at Cosprop, 2020

121. (opposite, right) Anne Lister (Suranne Jones) in *Gentleman Jack* (2019–22)

her way there! I chose a particularly large, rather absurd pair of feathers. And Sally directed Suranne to adjust the feathers as she entered the ball, reflecting the mention in the diary. Much of the work to make Anne look 'wrong' was achieved through designing clothing for Suranne to inhabit uncomfortably.[72] – **Tom Pye**

To contrast with Lister's stylish masculine attire, Pye also considered the costumes of the actors around her (fig.119).

The challenge was that I was worried about Anne looking a bit normal to a contemporary audience. Just wearing black and sort of men's clothes isn't that surprising for us.

I came across a cartoon of 1830s' fashion, a satirical cartoon of how absurd the fashion was, and I thought 'that's what I want to do,' that's how I want to make the straight people look daft, make them look as ridiculous and extreme as possible to show what was normal then. That gives context to show how Anne, in quite simple clothes, was extraordinary. It was so daring to wear what she wore because what most women were wearing was absurd. They were dressed up like Christmas trees. It's about context really.[73] – **Tom Pye**

With six million UK viewers, *Gentleman Jack* captured the public imagination, especially in the quality and detailing of the costumes. Since the show premiered, the costumes have been exhibited at the Bankfield Museum, Halifax, and the Holy Trinity Church, Goodramgate, York, where Lister and Walker took the sacrament in 1834 before starting their life together.

'Eventually we came to this place in the fitting room where we liked this look which was top-half male and bottom-half female, so she's still wearing skirts, and then we added a top hat so she stuck out in a crowd. Then we gave her a cane which, for the day, is obviously very masculine. We didn't try to beautify me in any way.'[74] – Suranne Jones

Peaky Blinders (2013–22)

Directors Otto Bathurst, Tom Harper (Season 1)
Costume Designers Stephanie Collie, Lorna Marie Mugan, Alexandra Caulfield, Alison McCosh
Starring Cillian Murphy, Helen McCrory, Paul Anderson, Sophie Rundle, Joe Cole, Tom Hardy

For the Peaky Blinders, the clothes were about them showing their worth. They would go without to have that fantastic suit because for them it is all about status. It shows where they stand in their neighbourhood.[75] **– Stephanie Collie**

Set in Birmingham after the First World War, *Peaky Blinders* showed a different working-class side of the Roaring Twenties from the familiar aristocracy or flapper girls. Telling the story of the rise of the volatile Shelby clan, it was inspired by the real Peaky Blinders gang (1880–1910), although changed to the post-war period.

Research at Cosprop helped create the distinctive looks, and Collie was able to hire many of the suits worn by the cast. The authenticity Cosprop offered helped embed the characters in the narrative.

Cosprop adapted stock costumes for Collie by shortening trousers and tailoring them to give a narrower look. Collie was delighted by 'how much the boys loved their clothes, and I think you get a feel of that by the way they walk; they have a swagger about them.'[76] Collie was also able to make copies of clothes inspired by real stock, changing the colour to suit the set decoration or character. She would always use original designs when possible. 'The red dress that Annabelle [Grace] wears at the races was also a copy of an original dress. It was actually blue but we knew we wanted it red for that scene – she was the scarlet woman.'[77]

Just as the Shelby clan became more successful, so did the series, and it was recommissioned several times, with four costume designers covering the six seasons. Each costume designer added to the story as it progressed through the 1920s, with Alison McCosh designing the final three seasons set from 1927 to 1933.

I wanted to bring the female characters forward stylistically and really make them present and on an equal level to the men. Tommy Shelby (Cillian Murphy) was still at the forefront but I'm always interested in who's behind, and who is that in this show? It's the women.[78] **– Alison McCosh**

Central to this vision was the change in Polly Gray (Helen McCrory) making bolder choices in keeping with her strong character and an equal to the men, inspired by Marlene Dietrich (fig.122).

I really loved the idea of putting her in trousers and a suit just to make a real statement. You can really see the transition in Polly from Season 1 – each season and costume designer have added something to reflect her growing wealth. Now the whole family is at the height of money, of course, and Polly is really embedded in that wealth and power and that really projects now, with the fabrics, the colours, the intricacies of the materials. There's a portrayal of status now projected through their clothes.[79] **– Alison McCosh**

Cosprop's wide stock for the period was used for clothing many of the crowd scenes. Even stock items would have to be carefully distressed if that was necessary to reflect the character's status, such as for Alfie Solomans (Tom Hardy).

We didn't make anything for the first series, it was all stock. In later series we made most of Paul Anderson's suits and made for Adrien Brody and Daryl McCormack. I also fitted Tom Hardy, Alexander Siddig, Jordan Bolger, Finn Cole and others. Crowd stock was also taken for this show.[80] **– Ross Braganza, Senior Men's Costumier**

Because it covered 14 years, new fashions were always required: by the sixth series it was 1933 and the styles – and the wealth – of some characters had changed. But from the start it was the suits that captured the public imagination (fig.123).

What I like about this period is that really, it could almost be now. You can go out now and buy stuff like that and wear it like that. I've said this before, but fashion always repeats itself. Three-piece suits look good on everyone. With* Peaky Blinders, *we did actually want to create a look that would then translate into autumn and winter ranges this year for* [high street stores]. *They could actually translate the look from* Peaky *into the shop window.[81] **– Stephanie Collie**

Collie's prophecy came true. The show's costumes are thought to have revived the interest in 'baker boy' flat caps, increased sales of overcoats, and David Beckham created a fashion line inspired by the show.

Cosprop have seen many projects reimagined and revived for twenty-first century audiences. The show that created the template for all dramas to follow, *The Forsyte Saga* made in 1967 by the BBC, was remade in 2002 by ITV, and had a third version for PBS in production in 2024. Bright and his team have been involved in all three versions.

'These men probably only had one or two suits which is how we worked as well. The clothes are there to be part of the story, but you don't want anyone to go "oh wow!" when they see them. They can never be more important than what's going on in the scene.'[82] – Stephanie Collie

Changing modes of consumer consumption have brought new opportunities for Cosprop and a seismic shift in the way film and television are being created and transmitted around the world. A second Golden Age of Television occurred with the US cable network giants HBO and Netflix expanding their remit and programming content to global audiences. To meet these demands, Cosprop continues to evolve and adapt. Jill Harbutt notes that designers no longer have time to sketch their characters, instead they provide mood boards or reference images.

Characters are meticulously created in every room of the costume house. Bright and his dedicated costumiers, makers and milliners hand craft every stitch, dart and button to reflect a character's personality. With film and television production created and filmed on a global level, costume designers use a wide range of resources to meet the demands of the script and to conceive their characters.

***When I begin the task of gathering costumes for a period project, I like to tour the costume rental houses of Europe and the UK to see where the pieces are that are the most suitable for the project. For* Death By Lightning (2025)*, which was set in 1880 and required a nuanced and deep sense of authenticity, by far the most costumes were from Cosprop. The pieces there were richly detailed and full of 'character', which is precisely what a costume designer is looking for. A costume designer knows that when they are using pieces from Cosprop, they were created with both unquestionable artistry and an incomparable amount of knowledge and research. The costumes will represent the period in a manner that is both academically faithful and emotionally expressive – for a costume designer that is gold.*[83] – Michael Wilkinson, Costume Designer**

122. (above) Polly Gray (Helen McCrory) in *Peaky Blinders* (2013–22)

123. (overleaf) Publicity still for *Peaky Blinders* (2013–22)

GARRISON
TAVERN

CHAPTER SIX

RAISING THE CURTAIN

Costume for Stage

'With theatre or opera, productions get revived, so it is an opportunity to develop your designs; with film or television, once its filmed, that's it, you can't redo it but theatre productions sometimes allow you back in and you can try new ideas.'[1] – John Bright

Cosprop has played a central role in the theatre and opera industries, supplying stage costumes for diverse projects. They have to visually communicate information, be seen at a distance, be robust and brilliantly constructed for the continuous 'wear and tear' and rigours of stage performance. To achieve this, costumes from Cosprop's stock must be strengthened to ensure continuous wear can be withstood.

We have to take into consideration quick changes, and the actions of the actor. We have to cut our patterns to consider the movements so that it is not restrictive. Because of the continuous wear-and-tear, we often have to mount fabrics to give them strength; and use fabrics that are up to continuous cleaning and washing.[2] – **Nancy Knapp, Head of the Workroom**

Costumes may be (deliberately) damaged as part of the production and duplicates are required; and particularly for the leading operatic roles, costumes may be needed for multiple performers in the same part. Cosprop's unique collection of original costumes and library has inspired generations of theatre designers. Although producing houses in the UK, such as the National Theatre, Royal Shakespeare Company and the Royal Ballet and Opera have their own costume-making departments, Cosprop's expert range of cutters, dyers and specialists have made costumes for landmark productions.

With a career beginning as an actor and an assistant stage manager, John Bright discovered early in his career the nuances required for costume for stage. Daphne Brooker, Bright's tutor at Southwest Essex Technical College, arranged for him to access the stock at the Players' Theatre near Charing Cross Station in London.

I learnt so much from the clothes at the Players' Theatre; they had been given so much original clothing, which was used in their productions. I would take patterns in the evenings and so alongside the course, I was learning about period clothes and their construction.[3] – **John Bright**

Bright's first theatre position was at Hornchurch Repertory Theatre, London, in 1961. He was engaged as an Assistant Stage Manager, which involved multiple jobs backstage. The first production of the new season was *Jane Eyre* with Annette Crosbie. Jane Howells, the Director, visited his parents' house and together they designed the costumes, with Bright designing and making Jane's wedding dress. They hired some costumes from Oldham Repertory Theatre to complete the number of outfits needed. Bright also worked as a cutter on *Luther* at the Royal Court Theatre, which starred Albert Finney.

At the Queen's Theatre in Hornchurch, Bright made the costumes for *Lady Windemere's Fan* developing his skills on the job.

It was the first time I realised you could get a reaction from the audience just from the way someone dresses. I had made a white dress with black lace and a flamboyant hat. Gillian Martell, who played Lady Windermere, gave it a beat before walking on stage and then came a gasp from the audience.[4] – **John Bright**

Work at Regent's Park Theatre and Chichester Festival Theatre in 1962 provided early commissions to build on the skills learnt at college. Bright realised there was a gap in the market for quality period costuming, and founded Cosprop in 1965, to supply pieces for theatre, film and television. As well as collecting, Bright developed his own costume-making techniques through trial and error, employing other experts to supplement his talents.

Costumes can look very flat and one-dimensional unless the fabric is correct and has depth. John has a special recipe for treating fabric, as it often needs to be washed or manipulated in some way before it can work – in front of a camera – or to be seen by an audience in a theatre.[5] – **Nancy Knapp**

Early major stage productions included the musical *Evita* (1978) starring Elaine Paige, David Essex and Joss Ackland (fig.124). The costumes were designed by husband-and-wife design team Timothy O'Brien and Tazeena Firth.

The museum collection provided a source for one of the most important scenes in the musical, when Eva Perón appears at the balcony of the Casa Rosada and performs the show's signature number, *Don't Cry for Me Argentina*. The scene required Perón to wear a stunning Christian Dior gown.

We provided costumes for the whole musical except the uniforms. We used stock to start it off, some of which went through to the final production, and then we made all of Eva Perón's clothes. We made in total five dresses for **Don't Cry for Me, Argentina,** ***which were a copy of a Dior dress.***[6] – **John Bright**

Not only did we make the outfits for the original cast, but also the understudies and all subsequent casts. One of many dresses made for Elaine Paige was a lovely white ballgown with sequin detail. The skirt was made of many layers or net. The problem came at the first dress rehearsal of the balcony scene, as she had to climb a ladder and go through a door that was too small for the dress, needless to say the set was altered.[7] – **Mary Wing, former Head of the Workroom**

Evita ran for more than 3,000 performances and transferred to Broadway, premiering in 1979. The costume design and its beautiful construction became a template for future revivals of the musical. When preparing for the 1996 film version of *Evita* starring Madonna as Eva, Costume Designer Penny Rose used the Cosprop Museum Collection for her research. She showed an original Dior gown to Madonna for her approval, as Rose wanted to copy it for the 'Rainbow Tour' scene. Madonna declined the offer of wearing the replica and instead wore the original in the film. The circularity of the costume house ensures that clothes are future proofed and can be reimagined for new narratives. A costume that had been worn in the television series *The Pallisers* (1974) by Susan Hampshire was adapted for Eva (Madonna) for the scene when Eva is an aspiring actor.

The end of the 1970s and beginning of the 1980s were productive years for Cosprop. In 1980 the company was 15 years old and by this time every major costume designer was using the Cosprop resources for stock hire, recreation, accessories and advice from Bright. Cosprop moved from its premises in Regent's Park Road to Rochester Place in Camden, North London, where it was located for the next 25 years.

One of the first major theatre productions of the decade was the landmark Royal Shakespeare Company's eight-and-a-half hour stage version of *The Life and Adventures of Nicholas Nickleby* (1980), directed by John Caird and Trevor Nunn and performed over two nights. The costumes were designed by Andreane Neofitou, and the cast featured 150 characters which required the RSC to outsource the majority of the costumes to Cosprop. Bright said they did most of the clothes for *Nicholas Nickleby* from stock. 'We only made [new costumes] when two characters had to look similar, or when Nicholas had to look particularly affluent.'[8]

The production remains one of the RSC's most celebrated shows but is rarely revived due to the large cast. The production was filmed in 1982 by Channel 4 and broadcast in four episodes, with many of the stage actors recreating their roles and Cosprop providing the costumes.

Bright's advice for actors extended across period and genre. Karel Reisz's 1993 revival of Terence Rattigan's 1950s-set *The Deep Blue Sea* starred Penelope Wilton as Hestor Collier, who gives up her privileged life for a dashing RAF pilot, only to find herself living in a squalid London bedsit.

***John is very instinctive about the person you are going to play. For* The Deep Blue Sea, *I went to see him and he found me a Cresta skirt, a nice pink cardigan and some pearls, I put them on and looked in the mirror and there was Hestor Collier staring back at me. Hestor has to look out of place in the world she has found herself in.*[9] – Penelope Wilton**

124. Juan Perón (Joss Ackland) and Eva Perón (Elaine Paige) in *Evita* (1978; Costume Designers Timothy O'Brien and Tazeena Firth)

The Cherry Orchard (1981)

Théâtre des Bouffes du Nord, Paris (1981), Brooklyn Academy of Music, New York (1988)
Director Peter Brook | Costume Designer Chloé Obolensky | Starring Natasha Parry, Niels Arestrup, Michel Piccoli, Claude Evrard

In 1981 director Peter Brook mounted a production of *The Cherry Orchard* in French (*La Cérisaie*) with an international cast including Brook's wife Natasha Parry as Ranevskaya, Niels Arestrup as Lopakhin and Michel Piccoli as Gayev. The production was the beginning of a long collaboration between Chloé Obolensky and John Bright, for film and theatre.

***My first production at Cosprop was* The Cherry Orchard*, it was also the first production I had worked on with Peter Brook. I wanted to get away from Paris to make these costumes. I wanted a different kind of approach, so I phoned my friend David Walker and he told me to visit Cosprop and John Bright. I came to Cosprop and I met John for the first time. I remember we started talking, and I said what I was trying to do, and he showed me to a few things and put them to one side and left me there. So, I thought, this is a wonderful start, because it means that it's somebody who understands that you need to actually find your way around. From then on, we have always worked together.*[10]** – **Chloé Obolensky**

Bright remembers Peter Brook's rehearsal process was very long and very intense:

***We had a long period to create the clothes Peter likes to build through rehearsal. With film, it often has to happen 'now' but with theatre, the process is slower and much more involved. I enjoy building layers and creating new characters. We created all the costumes at Cosprop and then Chris [Prins] and I travelled in Paris to fit the actors at the Bouffes du Nord theatre.*[11]** – **John Bright**

The production was restaged at the Brooklyn Academy of Music in 1988 after touring throughout Africa and the Middle East and is regarded as one of Brook's most significant productions.

125. Gayez (Michel Piccoli) and Madame Ranevskaya (Natasha Parry) in *The Cherry Orchard* (1981)

Eugene Onegin (1991)

Teatro La Fenice, Venice | Director Andrei Serban | Costume Designer John Bright | Set Designer Chloé Obolensky
Starring Dmitri Hvorostovsky, Lucia Mazzaria, Neil Schicoff, Margarita Zimmermann, Gillian Knight, Nucci Condo

Before the 1999 Martha Fiennes film version of *Onegin*, John Bright collaborated with Chloé Obolensky on the Tchaikovsky opera, staged at Teatro La Fenice in Venice. Of the location, Bright said '*A Room with a View* had glorified Italy, so I was welcomed with open arms, but it was a difficult production. The numbers kept going up and up! There were 86 in the chorus.'[12]

As far as costume goes, you have most people thinking in a sort of really one-dimensional way, either carried away by the beauty of the line or something, or the fabrics. But John understands costume. Not just as costume, but the whole thing that lies behind. He has the sensitivity of an actor. He understands it is not as the outside envelope but it is coming from inside. And therefore of all the possibilities that there are, because you hardly ever arrive at a final result until you've tried it out and tried it out in conjunction with other things.[13] **– Chloé Obolensky**

All the costumes were made in London and Christopher Prins did the stock fittings. Bright said, 'For the ballgowns we stylised, I wanted a different feeling for different times of the opera. For the Saint Petersburg scenes, I used silver and pale blue greys in the design.'[14]

Opera Now magazine praised the designs of the opera: 'Obolensky and Bright brought out the social and political significance by shifting the period to that of Tchaikovsky rather than that of Pushkin.'[15]

126. Eugene Onegin (Dmitri Hvorostovsky) and Tatiana (Lucia Mazzaria Scandiuzzi) in *Eugene Onegin* (1991)

The Turn of the Screw (1997)

Barbican Theatre, London (1997), MC 93 Bobigny, Paris (1998), Royal Opera House, Covent Garden, London (2002)
Director Deborah Warner | Costume Designer John Bright | Set Designer Tom Pye
Starring Ian Bostridge, Joan Rodgers, Edward Burrowes, Pippa Woodrow, Jane Henschel, Vivian Tierney

Benjamin Britten's opera *The Turn of the Screw* is based on the Henry James novel, which explores a young inexperienced governess caring for two children, who she is convinced have been corrupted by the ghosts of a previous manservant and governess. How costumes could help create the unsettling atmosphere was crucial for director Deborah Warner.

I showed Deborah the possibilities of the clothes and we explored the movement of the characters and how they could build tension, and this interested her the most. At one point in the opera, the Governess wore a robe that was made out of a very fine linen, and as she shivered in the robe, the tension came through the clothes. Having a clear design vision often goes by the feeling of what's happening on stage, rather than the period that you are recreating.[16] – **John Bright**

I worked closely with the lighting designer Jean Kalman on a concept for a stripped-back, almost empty and derelict, stage for the set design. It wasn't until John's costumes started to inhabit this world that the production really began to work. His costumes were so perfect with their 1860s' detail, form and silhouette, that it really felt like you were watching the stage being haunted by the characters. This juxtaposition was so stark and exciting, and it had a huge influence on me as a designer.[17] – **Tom Pye, Set Designer**

When the production was revived for the Royal Opera House in 2002, Warner wanted to develop the costume design further. For this staging, Bright said that 'Deborah wanted a much more modern look to the clothes. The Governess had to have a skirt which had a different kind of movement, a swirl was required rather than a tension shiver. I dressed the children in the 1860s.'[18]

Bright's extensive collection of children's toys informed a crucial design element of the production.

Deborah wanted Flora to have a 'devil doll'. So, when the child places it at the centre of the Royal Opera House stage – which is huge – it had to show up. I had a doll among the toys I had collected. I created the clothes for the doll in the right period, and when it was placed centre stage it really held its own. The doll is now part of the Cosprop museum in Hastings.[19] – **John Bright**

127. The Governess (Joan Rodgers) and Miles (Edward Burrowes) in *The Turn of the Screw* (1997)

An Enemy of the People (1997)

National Theatre, London | Director Trevor Nunn | Costume Designer John Bright
Starring Ian McKellen, Penny Downie, John Woodvine, Alan Brown, Alan Cox, Murray McArthur, Chris Gillespie

An Enemy of the People was Trevor Nunn's inaugural production as Artistic Director of the National Theatre, with Ian McKellen cast as Dr Thomas Stockmann. Bright had worked with Nunn on *The Life and Adventures of Nicholas Nickleby* (1980) and the film version of *Twelfth Night* (1996). The production featured a large cast of 28 actors and was set contemporaneously with Henrik Ibsen's play in Norway in 1882. For the costume design process, Nunn took an active interest and visited Cosprop for the dressing-up sessions.

***Trevor was keen on an early photographic quality to the production, so I worked in sepias, stripes and checks and applied different surfaces onto the clothes. Trevor came to see the clothes before we moved forward and it's always good when directors come in because they can see the characters in front of their eyes, forming. We made a slight change of one costume, which was a caramel colour – so we dyed it to get it darker.*[20]** – **John Bright**

The Dye Room at Cosprop also contributed to the finish of the costumes: 'For the fishermen and the oil skins, we managed with the help of the Dye Room staff, to create a wet look that covered the hats, smocks, which created a look evocative of the sea.'[21] John Napier's set design encompassed split-level wooden buildings against a backdrop of scudding clouds and dark hills, so the costumes played a huge part in defining this period of history.

In appreciation of Bright's work, Trevor Nunn declared, 'I am in awe of your achievement with the costumes on *Enemy of the People*. With seemingly no fuss or bother, you have created an entire community, replete with the minutest detail of the lives lived, with a thrilling restraint in the palette and with a completeness that means we could start filming it tomorrow.'[22]

The play, which sets environmental and health interests against capitalism, is regularly revived in more contemporary settings, particularly since the COVID-19 pandemic.

128. Thomas Stockman (Ian McKellen) and Aslaksen (John Woodvine) in *An Enemy of the People* (1997)

Fidelio (2001)

Glyndebourne Festival Opera, Sussex (2001, 2006), Théâtre du Châtelet, Paris (2002)
Director Deborah Warner | Costume Designer John Bright
Starring Timothy Robinson, Lisa Milne, Reinhard Hagen, Charlotte Margiono, Mark Holland, Kim Begley, Alan Opie

Bright continued his collaboration with Deborah Warner on a modern-day version of the early nineteenth-century opera *Fidelio*. The opera is inspired by a true story from the French Revolution. Leonore, whose husband has been secretly imprisoned by his political rival, is determined to rescue him and disguises herself as a young man named 'Fidelio' to get a job in the prison where he is being held.

It is an awesome challenge for a director, partly because one has to free it from the shackles of convention, as Beethoven only wrote this one opera, it is a holy one and it deals with these great subjects, matters so big that we feel it is extraordinary. It's both a play and an opera, and staggeringly difficult for the singers and an incredible challenge for the conductor.[23] – **Deborah Warner**

The period is early nineteenth century, but Deborah wanted to set it in a deprived downbeat country in Eastern Europe. There were three different singers playing Fidelio plus the chorus, prisoners and warders, I dressed the warders in blue and the prisoners in khaki. I acquired the uniforms from a company in Saffron Walden.[24] – **John Bright**

The design of the production was unspecific enough to suggest that the events could be happening anywhere, but in a modern-day setting. Warner and Bright's vision highlighted that Beethoven's opera is as painfully relevant as ever.

129. The cast of *Fidelio* (2001)

Cyrano de Bergerac (2004)

National Theatre, London | Director Howard Davies | Costume Designer John Bright
Starring Stephen Rea, Claire Price, Zubin Varla, Malcolm Storry

Edmond Rostand's 1897 romantic melodrama, written as a rebuttal of the theatrical realism of Emile Zola and Henrik Ibsen. The National Theatre revival was set in the late nineteenth century, albeit with a modern verse translation. The play tells of Cyrano's unrequited love for Roxane, who he woos via a young proxy, Christian. With a cast of 28 including several soldiers, most of whom had three costumes, and the arena-style Olivier stage to fill, Bright's initial problem was apparent.

***One of the challenges of costume design is the budget. Every production must be costed and planned, budgets can be opportunities for resourcefulness but challenging for period productions, which tend to cost more to create. Because* Cyrano *was part of the National Theatre's highly successful £10 seat offer, the budgets were more constrained, but we still have to form some sort of spectacle.*[25] – John Bright**

Although the low budget meant the theatre couldn't afford original period costumes, Bright's creativity and problem-solving informed the direction of the show: 'I pointed out that 1880 was quite rigid in look – very perpendicular – very held in and if they went back to 1870 there's more swash and buckle to it and so we decided that's the way forward. I showed the director lots of designs and costumes and he could see what I was on about.'[26]

130. Cyrano (Stephen Rea) and the cast of *Cyrano de Bergerac* (2004)

The Seagull (2001)

Joseph Papp Theater/New York Shakespeare Festival | Director Mike Nichols | Costume Designer Bob Crowley
Starring Meryl Streep, Kevin Kline, Natalie Portman, Marcia Gay Harden, John Goodman, Philip Seymour Hoffman, Christopher Walken

The Seagull was a hotly anticipated production, with the film star cast of Meryl Streep playing ageing actress Arkadina, Kevin Kline her lover Trigorin, and Natalie Portman playing the girl he falls for, Nina ('the seagull'). Streep had not appeared on Broadway for 20 years, and her entrance down a staircase was heralded by audience and critics alike, 'like a scene from *Hello Dolly!*'. Bob Crowley's costume designs set the play when it was written in late nineteenth-century Russia.

We put the clothes together in London and fitted them in New York. Meryl is very precise with her clothes. She had to perform a cartwheel in one of the dresses, and she was wearing a corset, and she had a large voluminous skirt, so we had to make sure that the clothes moved in the correct way for the action that the direction demanded.[27] – **John Bright**

The production was superbly received, with Crowley's costume design and Cosprop's skill in realising them enhancing an atmospheric production that offered, 'more stars than there are in the heavens'.

The United Kingdom's vibrant performance culture of theatre, opera and musicals keep Cosprop busy with regular and diverse commissions ranging from Penelope Wilton's costumes as Queen Elizabeth, The Queen Mother in the comedy *Backstairs Billy* (2023; Costume Designer Tom Rand) to Imelda Staunton's Dolly Levi in the musical revival of *Hello Dolly!* (2024; Costume Designer Rae Smith). Long running plays and musicals also require new costuming and stock for cast changes, doubles and productions that tour.

Cosprop's reach is international; for the 2025 Greek National Opera production of *Turandot*, Chloé Obloensky engaged Cosprop to create several costumes.

131. (left) Irina Arkadina (Meryl Streep) and Boris Trigorin (Kevin Kline) in *The Seagull* (2001)

Death in Venice (2007)

English National Opera, London (2007, 2013), La Monnaie Brussels (2009), La Scala, Italy (2011)
Netherlands Opera, Amsterdam (2013) | Director Deborah Warner | Costume Designer Chloé Obolensky | Set Designer Tom Pye
Starring Ian Bostridge, John Graham-Hall, Peter Coleman-Wright, Eliza Bennett, Benjamin Paul Griffiths, Barbara Bielecka, Raphaelle Burgess-Jones, Joyce Henderson

Deborah Warner's production of Benjamin Britten's opera brought together Chloé Obolensky, Tom Pye (set design) and Jean Kalman (lighting design) as the creative team. Based on the Thomas Mann book, and forever associated with Luchino Visconti's 1971 film, the story tells of an older writer dying of consumption and forming a doomed obsession with an adolescent boy.

Pye said that he and Obolensky 'worked with the director Deborah Warner in quite an organic way. Together we slowly built a concept for the show through a lot of research, closely examining images together, and discussing ideas.'[28] The designers worked closely to create a dreamlike vision of the Venetian lagoon, evocative of William Turner's paintings, through billowing gauze, video projection and atmospheric lighting. In the midst of this were Obolensky's period costumes, made by Cosprop.

I was heavily influenced by my experience of working with John on Turn of The Screw. *I knew the power that could be created through strong period costuming. So, I decided to create a series of portals to frame the costumes, often in silhouette, so that audience could really appreciate the way that the clothing of the period gave a particular shape and form to people's bodies. It was hard not to be influenced by the Visconti film, but theatre is such a different medium and is a different experience for the audience – which invites their imagination to be engaged. For example, in a scene in Act 2 of the opera, there are 12 different locations in a chase across Venice to be covered within ten minutes. So, I knew I had to be economical with the design to evoke many different places.*[29] – Tom Pye

132. (opposite) Gustav von Aschenbach (John Graham-Hall) and the cast of *Death in Venice* (2007)

CHAPTER SEVEN

NEW FRONTIERS

Cosprop in the Twenty-First Century

'John is the bridge between the past and the present worlds of costume design. He is the two worlds put together. John belongs to the world of David Walker, Lila de Nobili and Anthony Powell and to the world of today. John understands both worlds, he is the bridge that connects them with us.'[1] – Chloé Obolensky, Costume Designer

The new century ushered in innovative ways that films and television were created by filmmakers and experienced by audiences. High-definition cameras projected the visual image into homes in a way that was unprecedented. Flat-screen televisions were introduced in the UK in 2005, they were larger and transformed the living space from a small box in the corner of a living room. Size, clarity and detail were amplified.

In global cinema, whilst 3D films were still being released after a Golden Age in the 1950s, their mainstream resurgence took place in the early 2000s. The British Film Institute created Britain's first IMAX cinema; when it was opened in 1999, it was the largest screen in the UK. These developments had an impact on costume design and practice.

The art of costume design has had to change because of the seismic shift from film stock to high-definition digital cameras. With TV screens the size of walls, the audience now has the ability to see tiny details of costume, stitching details, embellishments, jewellery, etc. This has meant that there is even more importance placed on details that previously may not have been seen so clearly. In turn, the use of highly talented craft technicians to support the design process has increased. Although many of us mourn the passing of 35mm and its magical diffused look, in many ways the digital camera now allows for greater story telling in the details, small 'Easter eggs' to be plotted into costumes for viewers to pick up on, should they notice.[2]– **Michele Clapton, Costume Designer**

The advances in screen technology allowed costume designers to marry authentic period shapes with experimental approaches to colour and finishing. *From Hell* (2001; Costume Designer Kym Barrett), which starred Johnny Depp and Ian Holm, was shot through a chocolate-coloured lens, this enabled the makers at Cosprop to experiment with 'lurid hues and man-made fabrics'.[3]

In the early 2000s, UK film production grew in strength and increased studio space, and in 2001 Shepperton Studios was acquired by Pinewood Studios. This renaissance in British-based filmmaking created commissions for Cosprop. *Sleepy Hollow* (1999), *Sweeney Todd: The Demon Barber of Fleet Street* (2007) and *Sherlock Holmes* (2009) were all made at Leavesden Studios, with Cosprop providing stock and making costumes for the principal actors.

Sleepy Hollow continued Tim Burton's fascination with American Gothic. Despite the filmmakers scouting locations in America, the film was primarily shot in England, or 'Sleepy Hollow on the Thames' as it was dubbed by the media. The film introduced Johnny Depp and Costume Designer and frequent collaborator Colleen Atwood to Cosprop.

John Bright welcomed me into the Cosprop family. I am an American designer and he's been a very generous mentor. He really supported me, and suggested things and teamed me with Chris [Prins], who was the key fitter at the time. I don't even know how you would even describe Chris really as a fitter, he was more than that, he could create characters in front of your eyes with clothing ... Chris was so great at capturing not only a period but a character, he really helped me with that film because it was made-up characters but based in reality. And then we had the best of England's character actors in the costumes.[4] – **Colleen Atwood, Costume Designer**

The year 2000 saw Merchant Ivory return to the work of Henry James and an adaptation of *The Golden Bowl*. The film reunited John Bright with the Merchant Ivory team and featured the Edwardian timeframe that he excelled in.

The 2000s were a busy period for Cosprop, which necessitated a move to Holloway Road, London, where the company has been based since 2005.

The post-COVID period was challenging for the creative industries. In 2022 a US writers and actors' strike virtually closed film production in the UK, highlighting the dominance of US funding on UK productions. The shutdown affected all elements of costume design creation, production, and associated staff, from designers to wardrobe assistants to the supply chain. Cosprop continued to work on theatre productions and European film and television productions not affected by the US strike.

In the twenty-first century, Cosprop continues to evolve and expand as streaming services develop to meet global audience demand. With industry changes, costume designers must respond to the demands of the script, the actors and directors, but now also the fast production schedules of the streaming service. United States streaming giant Netflix occupies space at Shepperton Studios to deliver a vast variety of programming to global audiences. Period adaptations continue to be a significant part of this offer.

133. (opposite) Aunt March (Meryl Streep) in *Little Women* (2019)

The Golden Bowl (2000)

Director James Ivory | Costume Designer John Bright
Starring Nick Nolte, Uma Thurman, Kate Beckinsale, Jeremy Northam, Anjelica Huston

The Golden Bowl ***is a film I feel I got the most out of and showcases my best work. It was influenced by my favourite period of 1900 to 1910, Russian ballet clothes, fancy dress costume – all the things I am interested in ... [the film] highlighted what Cosprop does at its very best, taking an original item of clothing, developing it and making it relevant again.***[5] – **John Bright**

An intricately plotted tale of thwarted love and betrayal, the film tells the story of an extravagantly rich American widower Adam Verver (Nick Nolte) and his sheltered daughter Maggie (Kate Beckinsale), both of whom marry only to discover that their respective mates, a beautiful American expatriate, and an impoverished Italian aristocrat (Uma Thurman and Jeremy Northam), are themselves entangled with one another in a romantic intrigue.

The research period for the film involved surveying paintings that captured the Edwardian period as John Bright recalled, 'The impressionists also influenced the design of the film. Painters such as Tissot, Sargent and Boldini were uppermost in my mind because they are Italianate, American and British, Sargent particularly.'[6]

For Assistant Costume Designer Sally Turner, research and the resources at Cosprop were an essential part of the design process:

We looked at photographs from the period and spent time at the National Portrait Gallery archives in London– there was a famous fancy dress ball **[Devonshire House Ball of 1897]** ***– we looked at all of those*** **[photographs]** ***and used them for inspiration. The fancy dress ball scene was a delight to design, as we had Cosprop at our fingertips to draw from*** **(fig.135).**[7] – **Sally Turner**

John Bright's historic costume collection provided a source of inspiration, for the 'Golden Bowl' moment in the film, the scene required something special. Bright describes a dress worn by Kate Beckinsale that had been worn by a Russian duchess in the Cosprop collection, which had been brought out of Russia just before the Revolution around 1916.

I reimagined the dress for Kate Beckinsale – we used the lace, taking it apart. We wanted something slicker than the original with thinner sleeves so that when she is holding the golden bowl it wouldn't distract from the crystal of the bowl. When we put in the new satin, we did it as close to the original as possible and added a very pale green velvet and some expensive jewels **(fig.134).**[8] – **John Bright**

Salvaging the lace from the skirt of the original Russian dress and incorporating it into the new one amongst the tucks and flows was key. I created the shape and pattern for the bodice and built it up from there. The sleeves were silk-net, overlaid with the original lace. I made the bows, John found the brooches, and we made the belt to match. It took around six weeks to make the costume.[9] – **Jill Harbutt, Costume Maker**

134. (right) Maggie Verver (Kate Beckinsale) in *The Golden Bowl* (2000)

135. (opposite, above) Fanny Assingham (Anjelica Huston) and Charlotte Stant (Uma Thurman) in *The Golden Bowl* (2000)

136. (opposite, below) Charlotte Stant (Uma Thurman), Fanny Assingham (Anjelica Huston) and Prince Amerigo (Jeremy Northam) in *The Golden Bowl* (2000)

137. (overleaf, left) Costume for Maggie Verver (Kate Beckinsale) in *The Golden Bowl* (2000)

138. (overleaf, right) Costume for Fanny Assingham (Anjelica Huston) in *The Golden Bowl* (2000)

Gosford Park (2001)

Director Robert Altman | Costume Designer Jenny Beavan
Starring Kristin Scott Thomas, Maggie Smith, Michael Gambon, Helen Mirren, Clive Owen, Derek Jacobi, Eileen Atkins, Richard E. Grant, Emily Watson, Ryan Phillippe, Claudie Blakley, Geraldine Somerville

Narratives such as *Gosford Park* were built from the fascination with English country houses and relationships between aristocrats and their serving staff. Reminiscent of the all-star casts of 1970s' whodunnits *Murder on the Orient Express* (1974) and *Death on the Nile* (1978), *Gosford Park* is a murder mystery set in a classic English stately home over one party weekend in 1932. Jenny Beavan's first challenge was researching some of the people the characters were based on – Ivor Novello (Jeremy Northam) appears as a guest – and then establishing the fictional people.

We talked in detail about every element of the costumes, down to what underwear the maids would be wearing. Robert Altman loves this detail: he wanted everything to be incredibly real without looking stagey or phony. To that end, I did a great deal of research and looked at original clothes from the 1930s that we then remade. We only had one vintage 1930s' gown, in a 'tricky' green colour, as ad-libbed by Maggie Smith.[10] It had to survive 10 weeks of filming. It was glued together daily by Stephen Miles, a genius tailor.[11] **– Jenny Beavan**

The museum and library at Cosprop provided a source of inspiration, as did *Tatler* and *Vogue* magazines (for the British characters) and the Sears Roebuck catalogue for the visiting Americans. Beavan noted, 'American clothing was a bit sharper and brighter then'.[12] Bob Balaban's film producer Morris Weissman wore a brash plaid suit and tweeds; Cosprop supplied a stock overcoat to which they added a woman's fur stole to make an enormous fur collar.

Cosprop's source of original clothing allowed Beavan to copy and amend pieces to suit her colour palette and designs. Lady of the manor, Sylvia McCordle (Kristin Scott Thomas) had a memorable off-white silk satin, bias-cut evening gown, partly from an original dress, which Bright completely rebuilt, incorporating black silk velvet (fig.139). Cosprop also adapted costumes, with Thomas's cream-coloured dress requiring new black trim where it was disintegrating at the top. Cosprop's collection of 1930s' formal wear allowed most of the men's dinner suits to be hired, making new ones to complement, where an actor such as Charles Dance was too tall to fit into the old styles. New shirts were purchased in the 1930s' style from high-end London tailors, before Cosprop treated them to Beavan's specification, 'they're boiled in starch until they're like cardboard, actors hated them'.[13]

The plot is built on the distinction between the gentry and the staff. Unusually, actors playing 'downstairs' characters were as famous as their counterparts, including Derek Jacobi, Helen Mirren and Eileen Atkins.

Whilst there was a lot of inspiration for the upstairs characters, there was less available for the servants. They were not greatly photographed at that time, but we did have some wonderfully written records, by Rosina Harrison, maid to Nancy Astor and by Lady Troubridge **[British aristocrats].[14] – Jenny Beavan**

With its clever mystery, international cast and glamorous costumes, *Gosford Park* was nominated for seven Oscars, including Best Film and Best Costume Design, and Beavan won the BAFTA Award. Julian Fellowes, winning the best Original Screenplay Oscar, developed the 'upstairs / downstairs' narrative in *Downton Abbey* (2010–15; p.158), providing Cosprop with another major project.

139. (opposite, above) Henry Denton (Ryan Phillippe) and Sylvia McCordle (Kristin Scott Thomas) in *Gosford Park* (2001)

140. (opposite, below) Mabel Nesbitt (Claudie Blakley), Louisa Stockbridge (Geraldine Somerville) and Sylvia McCordle (Kristin Scott Thomas) in *Gosford Park* (2001)

'I'm interested in telling stories with clothes. I look at the character, I read the character, I listen to the director. I just try and make it very real. I find that to be the most inspiring.'[15]
– Jenny Beavan

The Others (2001)

Director Alejandro Amenábar | Costume designer Sonia Grande
Starring Nicole Kidman, Fionnula Flanagan, Christopher Eccleston, Alakina Mann, James Bentley

A supernatural psychological horror, *The Others* is set in 1945 post-Nazi occupation Jersey, in a gothic manor house. Filmed in Spain by director Alejandro Amenábar, Costume Designer Sonia Grande used Cosprop to make all the costumes for Grace Stewart (Nicole Kidman). She appears in almost every frame of the movie.

I made all the costumes for Nicole Kidman's character, except for one knitted cardigan. It was unusual to make a complete wardrobe for one character, as usually you make one or two costumes for a project and then the designer unifies it together. A dove-grey outfit was inspired by a dress worn by Catherine Deneuve.[16] **– Susan Hardy, Costume Maker**

The Others *was a very special occasion for me because it was a movie with few characters and I had good support to make it. I wanted to create that atmosphere that goes back in the past to the 1940s with ghosts. I had to design and construct everything. The costumes were made in England, and it was one of the few times that I could make a movie completely designed by me.*[17] – Sonia Grande

One important plot strand is that the lead children have Xeroderma pigmentosum – a photosensitive inability to block out light. In the story, curtains are mostly kept shut, and so the costumes are often seen only under candlelight.

Grande was inspired by 1940s' British clothing (fig.141), adding subtle Catholic references to reflect the conventional lead character. The costume palette is mostly monochrome, either in dark tones (black, aubergine) or white night-dresses, so the exquisite detailing is everything.

***I loved working with Nicole Kidman in* The Others. *I had to hold myself back when designing the clothes for her. Nicole was really too pretty for the character, an extremely Catholic woman. I had to play with her body, her height, her physiognomy, her light eyes, her blond hair, and take her to a fainter and hieratic concept.*[18]– Sonia Grande**

The Others was an international box-office success and was nominated for 15 Goya Awards in Spain, including for Sonia Grande's costumes. It won eight and was the first English language film to win a prestigious Best Film award.

The first few years of the twenty-first century experienced several film genre revivals that made an immediate impact on popular culture – work that expanded Cosprop's making remit.

141. Anne Stewart (Alakina Mann), Grace Stewart (Nicole Kidman), Nicholas Stewart (James Bentley) in *The Others* (2001)

Harry Potter and the Chamber of Secrets (2002)

Director Chris Columbus | Costume Designer Lindy Hemming
Starring Daniel Radcliffe, Emma Watson, Rupert Grint, Kenneth Branagh, Richard Harris, Maggie Smith, Alan Rickman, Fiona Shaw

In 2001 Leavesden Studios had been acquired by Warner Bros., who would begin to film the *Harry Potter* book franchise. All eight films (from seven books) were shot in the UK, which harnessed the skills of many costume designers and makers. Cosprop became involved with one of the most popular film franchises of the decade.

The franchise's template had been established by Judianna Makovsky for the first film; for the second film, Lindy Hemming took over the costume design and created several new iconic characters in the process, which took her to Cosprop.

It was Tom Rand who really filled me in on the phenomenon that is John Bright and how his knowledge and design ethos and rigorous eye had moulded not only the whole business that he founded but influenced the quality and standard of every garment that left the building.[19] – **Lindy Hemming**

For one significant character, Hemming required the specialist quality that Cosprop offered: 'For the second Harry Potter film, Kenneth Branagh was to play Gilderoy Lockhart, a famous author and villain. In his story, he required quite a few costume changes. He was vain, pompous, narcissistic, and found it hard to pass a mirror without liking what he saw. A kind of wizard Prince Charming meets Errol Flynn.'[20]

Hemming devised a colour scheme for the wizard in collaboration with the actor and used pastels and lilac. The fabrics chosen were luxurious silks, cashmeres and brocades.

Hemming designed a series of 'sweeping and swooshing' academic gowns, frock coats, waistcoats and an embroidered velvet dressing gown. The cloak was designed to be 'flourished during a Zorro-like wand fencing battle', with an individually monogrammed fencing costume.

Kenneth Branagh was very familiar with everyone at Cosprop, who had made so many costumes for him and John Bright; and the wonderful costumier Chris Prins knew Kenneth well, [it] made it a perfect match and a lovely experience.[21] – **Lindy Hemming**

'We wanted to create a hybrid between a period dandy and someone who looked as if they could fit in at Hogwarts. Lockhart struts like a peacock, wears a different costume in every scene.'[22] – Kenneth Branagh

142. Gilderoy Lockhart (Kenneth Branagh), Ron Weasley (Rupert Grint) and Harry Potter (Daniel Radcliffe) in *Harry Potter and the Chamber of Secrets* (2002)

The White Countess (2005)

Director James Ivory | Costume Designer John Bright
Starring Natasha Richardson, Ralph Fiennes, Vanessa Redgrave, Madeleine Potter

Set in Shanghai in 1936, Natasha Richardson plays Sofia, a Russian Countess who, with the remaining members of her family, has been left stateless by the Revolution. Forced by reduced circumstances to support herself and her family as a bar girl and hostess, Sofia forms a relationship with Todd Jackson (Ralph Fiennes), a blind former diplomat who opens an elegant bar, The White Countess.

Merchant Ivory was reunited with author Kazuo Ishiguro and a familiar group of actors, including Vanessa Redgrave and Madeleine Potter. Bright was intrigued by the 'very specific and interesting time in Shanghai, the mid-1930s. When you have a melting pot of different nations coming together for various reasons, you always get an interesting sartorial mix'.

For Natasha Richardson's Sofia, Bright designed a wardrobe that reflected her perilous existence alongside her role in the nightclub.

There were so many influences. The Russians had been forced out in 1917, and so all that had to be explored through the clothes. She also has a job to do as a hostess so she has several evening dresses, one of which is almost falling apart, so she has to bargain in the market.[23] – **John Bright**

For Natasha Richardson, the period had a brittle elegance which evoked the golden age of Hollywood, as she said, 'I especially liked the green coat with matching hat that John designed for me. Carol Hemming styled my hair to reflect Greta Garbo's influence on fashions at the time and I was lit beautifully by Christopher Doyle. I had never felt so glamorous.'[24]

***For Natasha's signature dress, John found some original panels, very beautiful, with wisps of silver threadwork running from the centre outwards, thought to have come from a 1930s' wedding dress train. I created a simple evening gown with added centred tiny, glass antique buttons, worn with a white fox-fur stole. I adored working on the dress and that period for a wonderful actress* (fig.144).**[25] – **Jill Harbutt, Costume Maker**

For the role of Todd Jackson, Ralph Fiennes's wardrobe had to distill his life experience, which is slowly revealed to the audience in a series of flashbacks.

We needed to get the contrast on [Jackson's] earlier life to him now. In his later life, I wanted him to have a spectral, an apparitional feeling about him. You have to get the idea of this character and then see what happens to him, with the bombings and the loss of his family and that's something that has affected him profoundly. It was so shocking for someone who is an idealist and we had to reflect that in the clothes. When we were fitting him, there were certain colours that gave us that quality.[26] – **John Bright**

Bright was nominated for a Satellite Award for Best Costume Design for his work. *The White Countess* marked the end of an era of filmmaking for the Merchant Ivory Company as Ismail Merchant died before the film was released.

143. (left) Countess Sofia Belinskya (Natasha Richardson) in *The White Countess* (2005)

144. (opposite) Costume for Sofia Belinskya (Natasha Richardson) in *The White Countess* (2005)

Pirates of the Caribbean: The Curse of the Black Pearl (2003 + sequels)

Director Gore Verbinski | Costume Designer Penny Rose
Starring Johnny Depp, Keira Knightley, Orlando Bloom, Geoffrey Rush

Other film genres also enjoyed a revival in the early 2000s. *Gladiator* (2001; Costume Designer Janty Yates) was inspired by the sword and sandal epics of the 1950s. *Pirates of the Caribbean* ignited another genre long dormant – the world of swashbuckling pirates.

When Johnny Depp came into Cosprop for his first costume fittings, we discussed everything about this pirate. We wanted him to be a bit of a rogue, slightly hopeless, threadbare, so everything he attempts goes wrong.[27] – **Penny Rose**

At the costume fitting, Rose and Christopher Prins witnessed an iconic character being created. Depp tried on several frock coats and breeches and 'within about half an hour Jack Sparrow was born'. Rose recalls, 'as an actor, he is acutely aware of his clothes. We put eight hats on the floor and he picked up the leather one and said 'that's the one'.[28]

There's a lot of fantasy in the story, but not in the costumes. We want these clothes to look like they've been slept in and worn forever. Ageing and dyeing for a period film are absolutely vital. I don't like people to look as if they've just walked out of a shop. It's a really specialised field and very underestimated and undervalued and the people who do it are geniuses because it's very subtle. All the shoes go into a cement mixer with a few rocks and by the time they come out they've aged five years.[29] – **Penny Rose**

I made 12 coats for Captain Jack, all the same, there's one for the stunt double, the flying double and the wet double, etc.[30] – **Susan Hardy, Costume Maker**

Depp's charismatic performance combined with Rose's design was a global box-office success and the film spawned several sequels. As the franchise progressed, Rose made very few changes to the iconic costume, only adding some trinkets over time and creating a new waistcoat.

'I design real clothes, they're dirty, creased and broken down if it's appropriate ... that's what I strive for, whether it is a wedding dress or a ragamuffin's hand-me-downs.'[31]
– Penny Rose

145. (left) Costume design sketch for the *Pirates of the Caribbean* franchise

146. (opposite) Captain Jack Sparrow (Johnny Depp) in *Pirates of the Caribbean* (2003)

‘Pirates were rock-and-rollers, I based Captain Jack on Keith Richards and others, including the cartoon character Pepé Le Pew.’[32] – Johnny Depp

The Duchess (2008)

Director Saul Dibb | Costume Designer Michael O'Connor
Starring Keira Knightley, Ralph Fiennes, Hayley Atwell, Dominic Cooper

The Duchess is based on the life of Georgiana Cavendish, Duchess of Devonshire, an important figure in the eighteenth century, famous for her charisma, political influence and unusual marital arrangements. The role gave Keira Knightley an opportunity to portray one of the most celebrated women of the era, whose influence continues into the modern day.

For costume designer Michael O'Connor, research began with period paintings, in particular the Thomas Gainsborough portrait of Georgiana, explaining 'she was the typical Gainsborough lady' (fig.148). Georgiana used her clothing to make public statements, dressing in political colours of the period or in a military fashion.

Eighteenth-century clothes were really quite extraordinary, but in a film the characters are speaking dialogue that needs to be paid attention to. You can take inspiration from the past, but you have to play down large patterns and bright colours. You don't want the clothes to distract, though in reality they were probably extremely distracting. I looked at portraits of Georgiana to get an idea of her character. I always aim to sketch and have reference material and I always use Cosprop's Museum Collection for ideas and inspiration.[33] **– Michael O'Connor**

Georgiana begins the film in pale blue **(fig.147, above).** ***When we meet Lady Bess Foster (Hayley Atwell) she is wearing dark brown, as they grow closer, and when they are at their most sisterly, they're both wearing white; at the end Bess is in pale blue and Georgiana is in chocolate brown.***[34] **– Michael O'Connor**

Jill Harbutt created some of the costumes for the film, which delighted O'Connor, 'Jill takes her time with costume and it's a different product. That's the Cosprop identity, there's a discipline that Cosprop maintains'.[35]

For Keira Knightley, I created a very delicate blue and faun striped dress which was worn with a straw hat, made by the millinery department **(fig.147, below).** ***The period is an absolute favourite of mine and Keira can wear the clothes beautifully with absolute poise and grace, like Georgiana.***[36] **– Jill Harbutt, Costume Maker**

Keira was wonderful to fit because everything looked stunning on her. Ralph [Fiennes] was exacting with his clothes and can stand for hours while you fit him, everything has to come together until he has found his character. All that happens in the fitting room. I had worked at legendary costume house Bermans but Cosprop was completely different. John has created an extraordinary space for designers and his encouragement and support is always right. John has given me some of the best advice of my career, he will say 'stop and pause, think about it'.[37] **– Michael O'Connor**

Michael O'Connor won both a BAFTA and an Oscar for Best Costume Design for the film.

147. (opposite, above and below) Georgiana Cavendish, Duchess of Devonshire (Keira Knightley) in *The Duchess* (2008)

148. (right) Georgiana Cavendish, Duchess of Devonshire by Thomas Gainsborough (1785–7), Chatsworth House, Derbyshire

Tulip Fever (2017)

Director Justin Chadwick | Costume Designer Michael O'Connor
Starring Alicia Vikander, Dane DeHaan, Christoph Waltz, Jack O'Connell, Holliday Grainger, Judi Dench

Based on Deborah Moggagh's popular 1999 novel of the same name, *Tulip Fever*, is set in seventeenth-century Amsterdam. The plot follows the affair of an unhappy young wife with the artist commissioned to paint her portrait.

Paintings were a huge source of inspiration; Moggach was inspired to write the book based on a Dutch painting she had bought at Christie's. Domestic paintings by Pieter de Hooch and Gabriel Metsu inspired the darker interiors of the set design. O'Connor's costuming of 1630s' Amsterdam recreated the Golden Age of portraiture commissioned to depict merchants and wives by artists such as Frans Hals (fig.149) and Anthony van Dyck; Vermeer also painted servants. O'Connor required around 50 principal costumes, 25 nun costumes (led by Judi Dench's Abbess) and 35 orphan girl costumes; with another 500 costumes for the extras.

Cornelis (Christoph Waltz) and Sophia Sandvoort (Alicia Vikander) are rich Protestant merchants and that meant including the colour black and big ruffs. You'd think he was wearing plain black, but it was black silk with textures, and often the fabric was even cut through to show a pink lining underneath. There was a class to the fabric, because to dye a fabric black showed a sign of wealth because it took a difficult three-step process to make.[38] – **Michael O'Connor**

Sophia's emotional journey from rich merchant's wife, through her extra-marital affair to her becoming a nun was reflected in the costuming.

The idea for Sophia was strong looks done in typical Dutch fashion because Cornelis and his family are dressing her **(fig.150)*****. As the affair progresses, the clothes become more revealing: her collars and caps start going, and her dresses become less strict and robust. At the end, she's in a bodice with a simple more demure costume.***[39] – **Michael O'Connor**

Embroidery was an important feature of early seventeenth-century elite dress and O'Connor used Cosprop's expertise to enhance the costumes.

There's a scene where Cornelis and Sophia are together wearing these linen nightshirts with tulip embroidery. It was important to do because that was a form of embroidery people used on their linens called blackwork. If you look closely at old portraits, you'll see linen creeping out for a dress or a doublet with this specific embroidery. I was also interested in pinks and oranges. They seemed to compliment all the black quite well.[40] – **Michael O'Connor**

The 1630s is not a period we know very well. The bodice was very complex to create, it was very highly boned, the clothes of that time were very sculptural. Michael provided an image reference and the fabric. We built the bodice for the first fitting and then moved forward once we had more knowledge.[41] – **Jill Harbutt, Costume Maker**

149. (left) *Portrait of Aletta Hannemans* (1625) by Frans Hals

150. (opposite) Sophia Sandvoort (Alicia Vikander) in *Tulip Fever* (2017)

'Doing historical things is part of the pleasure – you're reliving history a little.'[42]
– Michael O'Connor

My Cousin Rachel (2017)

Director Roger Michell | Costume Designer Dinah Collin
Starring Rachel Weisz, Sam Claflin, Iain Glen, Holliday Grainger

Director Roger Michell and Dinah Collin have collaborated on several television and film projects. In 2017 they revisited *My Cousin Rachel*, based on the classic Daphne Du Maurier novel based in Cornwall and Florence. The novel is set in the 1830s, but director and designer looked for visual reference outside this time frame. In her research for the period, Collin found an Italian portrait, made much later around 1900, which was showed to Roger Michell who liked the image for Rachel, a woman wearing simple black but which emphasised her pale hands and face.

One of the first things to come up in discussions was that we thought Rachel* [*Rachel Weisz*] *should look like something from outer space compared to the Cornish locals. We wanted her to look really elegant and also classic so we set her in the 1840s. Rachel was established as an alien creature in the English countryside, before railways changed the landscape forever.[43] – **Dinah Collin**

For the ambiguous title character, whose motives the viewer is always questioning, getting the right costume was essential.

John discovered a black silk dress in stock, which was sadly disintegrating so he brilliantly made a new one for Rachel when she came for her first fitting. There is a wealth of lovely stock items which we used, the hires are an important source of income for Cosprop and as a designer it's important to know this. The making being rather longer term as it eventually goes into stock after screening.[44] – **Dinah Collin**

Rachel's veil played a strong role in the narrative and to Weisz's interpretation.

Mystery is something that comes with many things colliding in the narrative. To me, the veil reminds me of a Spanish painting, like an El Greco or a Goya painting. Very high fashion, in a fabulous way – and respectful of my dead husband, obviously'.[45] – **Rachel Weisz**

To create the look, the underwear and corset also had to be correct to the period.

Wearing a corset, you can't put it on yourself, someone has to lace you in. So it takes time and once you're in it, you're very restrained and it immediately makes you more formal, more poised. You feel less modern, it's kind of like a cage of femininity strapped onto you. It's quite intense, wearing a corset. You can't breathe. I understand why women used to say, you can only shallow breathe. It's a whole other feeling, than if I was in jeans and T-shirt. There's a certain oppression of the time that is expressed through the clothes, and also beauty, there's great beauty in them as well.[46] – **Rachel Weisz**

In contrast to the other worldliness of Rachel, Louise (Holliday Grainger) was described by Collin as 'scented like roses so we printed two dresses for her at Cosprop'. Collin printed her own fabrics based on two original printed dresses she found in the Bath Fashion Museum's reference collection, 'which had a real sense of the English countryside'.[47]

We realised when we fitted her even before we had the hair done, it was a winner. Emma Burke* [Costume Maker] *made a lovely evening dress, that was furnishing silk, so it has a wider pattern, obviously because it was going into a piece of furniture but John cleverly found a way of making the distance between the stripes less and the colour was beautiful.[48] – **Dinah Collin**

Sometimes with silks, the weight is exactly right, between a furnishing silk and one that's made for clothes. In the workroom, we try and make the clothes as close to the original as possible. If it is technical things, then it is up to Cosprop to suggest ways that we can make something work that maybe doesn't quite, because it is over scale or some other reason. The technical things are done by us, and we can suggest solutions to a designer.[49] – **John Bright**

For the character of Philip (Sam Claflin), Du Maurier's narrator, it was important that Philip looked as though he was a farmer. Collin said, 'Bright had the workroom make large bottomed breeches, a source of query from US producers. We did lots of breaking down so the clothes looked lived in and had been worn outside in the weather.'[50]

Collin was nominated for a British Independent Film Award for her costuming of the film.

151. (opposite) Page from continuity workbook for *My Cousin Rachel* (2017)

Character: RACHEL	Artist: RW
Change Number: #34A	Scene Numbers: 231 - 237

- WHITE CORSET w/ L/UP BACK + SILVER BUSK OPENING @ CF "COSPROP"
- WHITE/IVORY PLAIN RIDING PETTICOAT w/ PLEATS @ HEM.
- WHITE THIN COTTON PETTICOAT w/ PLEATS @ HEM + 2x BUTTONS @ CB.
- BLACK WOOLEN TIGHTS "WOLFORD"
- TEAL SILK U/S DRESS w/ PLEATING @ CF + COVERED BUTTONS @ CF + @ CUFFS.
- DEEP RICH RED VELVET RIDING JACKET w/ OPENING @ CF + FANNED SKIRT OF DRESS + 2x LONG FRONT PIECES / HOOK + BARS FASTENING
- CREAM SILK STOCK w/ HAND EMBROIDERY IN 'GRAPE' SHAPES
- AUBERGINE RED/PURPLE LEATHER GLOVES w/ STITCH LINES @ TOP OF PALM
- BROWN LEATHER L/UP ANKLE BOOTS 'CROCKETT + JONES'
- THIN GOLD WEDDING BAND

Peterloo (2018)

Director Mike Leigh | Costume Designer Jacqueline Durran
Starring Rory Kinnear, Maxine Peake, Pearce Quigley

Jacqueline Durran has had a long collaboration with director Mike Leigh and his working method of writing the screenplay is only after a long period of improvisation with the actors.

Peterloo, set from 1815 to 1819, told the story of a horrific massacre in Manchester at a hitherto peaceful meeting after the Napoleonic War. Whilst not having a script in advance challenges the costume designer, *Peterloo* was based on a number of real people supplemented with fictional characters. Some lead characters were working class for which limited historical material is available – neither reference images, nor existing costumes.

At least half of the cast were playing historical characters, but for Rory Kinnear [who played Henry Hunt], we had a picture of his character on the hustings and other pictures from other moments. We know from historical research and costume history the sort of clothes that Hunt would wear. Then we made a stab at that based on our knowledge, on Rory's interpretations, and the images we had of Hunt.[51] – **Jacqueline Durran**

Cosprop's extensive collection was used, as stock items could be hired for some of the aristocracy, such as for the magistrates and politicians. Without knowing which characters would be foregrounded (due to the improvised nature), Durran hired a large stock of appropriate costumes of the period. A lot had to be created to clothe many of the 300 working-class characters. Whilst she used the makers' expertise to differentiate costumes with details, Durran wanted them all to appear first as an indistinguishable mass. 'All the costume houses collaborated with us and made a batch of costumes to augment their own stock, which we then hired for the crowd.'[52]

The most difficult thing, unique to Leigh's films, was not knowing which characters would be injured or killed in the massacre, and which costumes would need to show damage.

Even when we knew which people were wounded, we didn't know where they were wounded, or how they were wounded, or any of those things that you know in a normal film. We had to just make a guess at what we were going to do. We tripled the costumes of the people we knew were going to be injured, but we couldn't afford to do more than three each because we didn't know which ones were going to be prioritised.[53] – **Jaqueline Durran**

With its large cast and powerful story, the film brought to light an infamous incident in British history that many had forgotten. To commemorate the 200th anniversary, the exhibition *Disrupt? Peterloo and Protest* ran at the People's History Museum in Manchester (2019).

152. Scene from *Peterloo* (2018)

'We found some original working-class images of clothes. John made some of those in bulk. Some clothing items are missing in costume houses, so these clothes – once returned – would then build up the stock of costume for the future.'[54] – Jacqueline Durran

Little Women (2019)

Director Greta Gerwig | Costume Designer Jacqueline Durran
Starring Saoirse Ronan, Emma Watson, Florence Pugh, Eliza Scanlan, Meryl Streep, Timothée Chalamet, Laura Dern, James Norton

Louisa May Alcott's coming-of-age 1868 novel has been adapted several times for stage and screen since publication, but Greta Gerwig's 2019 film used a Hollywood cast for a new generation. A much-loved novel, many readers have their favourite March sister, or one they identify with, so a challenge for Jacqueline Durran was individualising the sisters, whilst making them a family. 'If you start from the roots of the character each time, for each individual, then that's the touchstone of it. You make design choices for each person as you go along, and you say, well, 'That's so Jo,' or 'That's very Meg.'[55]

Durran and Gerwig spent the research period at Cosprop exploring the collection as Gerwig wanted 'them to feel like they weren't costumes, but that they were just the people's clothes. Because that for me is what makes it feel modern'.[56] As well as researching at Cosprop, Durran and Gerwig were inspired by the girls in the paintings of Winslow Homer, such as *Eagle Head* (1870).

Key costume moments included discreet sharing of costumes between Jo (Saoirse Ronan) and Laurie (Timothée Chalamet). A red and gold waistcoat worn by Laurie when Jo hands him a ring, is later donned by Jo for the mirrored scene where he proposes to her, and she turns him down.

What we were trying to achieve was to emphasise a back and forth of fluidity between the two of them in a way that they were just best friends, and they identified with each other, and they wanted to be the other person, and they shared clothes. The mutual wardrobe also showed how Jo's boyish side was part of her friendship with Laurie.[57] – **Jacqueline Durran**

With two time frames, Durran also cleverly threaded visual links between the older and younger characters, particularly in relation to a colour palette that was developed for each sister – this was inspired by the coloured notebooks their mother gives them one Christmas. Once established, it could be subverted: Beth's clothing was worn by Jo after Beth dies to emphasise their closeness and how much Jo misses her; it adds to the realism of a house of sisters where clothing was likely to be shared or repurposed.

John Bright was once again able to work with Meryl Streep playing Aunt March, the stern, wealthy aunt representing the previous generation to the more colourfully attired girls. Durran remembers the process fondly, 'I had a lovely experience with John on *Little Women*, it was a joy to work with him. Meryl is very precise in her costumes. John is up to the challenge, we reached a very high level of costuming in the room, when we did the fittings in New York.'[58]

Where there was fluidity and flexibility in designing for the girls, Durran cleverly contrasted this for their grumpy, conventional aunt. With Bright's unparalleled eye for period detail, Cosprop made all four outfits, all dark and in silk. Cosprop supplied the material down to the lace she wears in her hair.

Some actors are really influenced by the clothes, they can be revelatory, John found lace and trim, it was a great experience for me. He always suggests what might work, he never dictates. John delegates to the maker who he thinks would be best at that job, I respect his judgement on that.[59] – **Jacqueline Durran**

The film was nominated for six Oscars including Best Picture, winning Durran her second Oscar. Gerwig and Durran went on to collaborate on *Barbie* (2023), the first solo female-directed picture to gross more than a billion dollars.

153. (opposite, above) John Brooke (James Norton) in *Little Women* (2019)

154. (opposite, below) Aunt March (Meryl Streep) in *Little Women* (2019)

'With the girls, we tried to capture a sense of freedom and fight against the Victorian rules as we know them. With Aunt March, we recreated the Victorian style as accurately as possible down to the slightest detail.'[60] – Jacqueline Durran

Carmilla (2019)

Director Emily Harris | Costume Designer John Bright
Starring Jessica Raine, Greg Wise, Hannah Rae, Tobias Menzies, Devrin Limgnau

For film director and writer Emily Harris, Bright's insight informed the direction of an adaptation of *Carmilla* (2019), a coming-of-age story based on Sheridan Le Fanu's novella of the same name. Lara lives with her father and strict governess in isolation. When a carriage crash near their home brings a young girl into the family home to recuperate, Lara becomes enchanted by the eponymous Carmilla.

John boarding the project early served as reassurance for everyone who followed. It was a big endorsement having John part of it from the beginning, especially for a low-budget independent film. Casting directors felt confident that any actor they put forward would be in good hands being dressed by John.[61] – **Emily Harris**

Through conversations between Bright and Harris, the creative direction of the project began to take a different approach. 'It was clear to John that the vision I was expressing for how I wanted the film to look and feel didn't align to the time period I had set it, in terms of the lines and silhouettes for the clothing of that era. John pointed out that the soft lines I was imagining and describing would be more suited for the styles and cuts of 1790s. So I rewrote the script to shift the time frame from the 1800s to the late 1700s. Shifting the timeframe also opened up other opportunities to connect the narrative to some nice details of that era to do with both the natural world as well as the supernatural. For example, superstition around reflections in water of the time became a useful motif for the story.'[62]

Bright's costume design process informed the visual storytelling.

For this project, the colour palette and textures of the costume design came first. These design decisions carried through to inform cinematography and production design choices as well. All three departments worked symbiotically to create a full, rich and unified look that put nature at the heart of the aesthetic. We used natural tones, greens, earth tones – colours outside this palette were used sparingly, for effect. For example, no reds were used in fabrics at all, the only red that appears in the film are ladybirds and blood, so it makes a big impact when the audience sees the colour red.[63]– **Emily Harris**

For the costume design process, the resources at Cosprop were utilised for a range of storytelling devices: 'John had an original unmade waistcoat, which he used in the film's costume design, this was something I wasn't aware of: that waistcoats were assembled – Ikea style – in the eighteenth century and John had an original, still 'flat-packed' and unassembled, which he decided to bring to life for the film.'[64]

Working with Bright was a wonderfully collaborative experience for Harris: 'John is very perceptive and can read what an actor is feeling in the fitting room, this is a very rare quality – he works from inside out so that he's tapping into that same well the actor is drawing from. It's a beautiful thing to observe. John finds the energy of the character and builds on that and brings it into that process. John has an ability to knit the past and the present together fearlessly.'[65]

155. Carmilla (Devrin Limgnau) and Lara (Hannah Rae) in *Carmilla* (2019)

'Cosprop is a tapestry, each object has a history, and this history becomes the future when an object of clothing is reused for a different production. The actor feels this history whenever they try something on, so the clothes become part of them.'[66] – Emily Harris

Mrs. Harris Goes to Paris (2022)

Director Anthony Fabian | Costume Designer Jenny Beavan
Starring Lesley Manville, Isabelle Huppert, Lucas Bravo

As the world emerged from the COVID-19 crisis and a global lockdown, the film industry began to reignite its production schedules. *Mrs. Harris Goes to Paris* is a story of a 1950s' working-class woman (Lesley Manville) who cleans houses to earn a living. In post-war austerity Britain, she sees a Christian Dior dress in one of the homes she works in and she dreams of owning her own. She plans a trip to Paris to secure one, navigating the Parisian couturier system with a Blitz-spirit attitude.

Jenny Beavan spent time in the Dior archives in Paris, however, Dior were unable to loan any clothing for the film or recreate clothing from the 1950s. One of the scenes called for a catwalk of classic Dior designs from the late 1950s.

While the staff at Dior were extremely helpful with the archives from the 1950s, they didn't have any of the dresses as fashion houses didn't see the importance of keeping them back then. They made a collection, sold it, and then moved onto the next collection.[68] – **Jenny Beavan**

At Cosprop, John Bright owned several original Christian Dior dresses, which became the template for the costume design. Beavan found it nerve-wracking recreating Dior

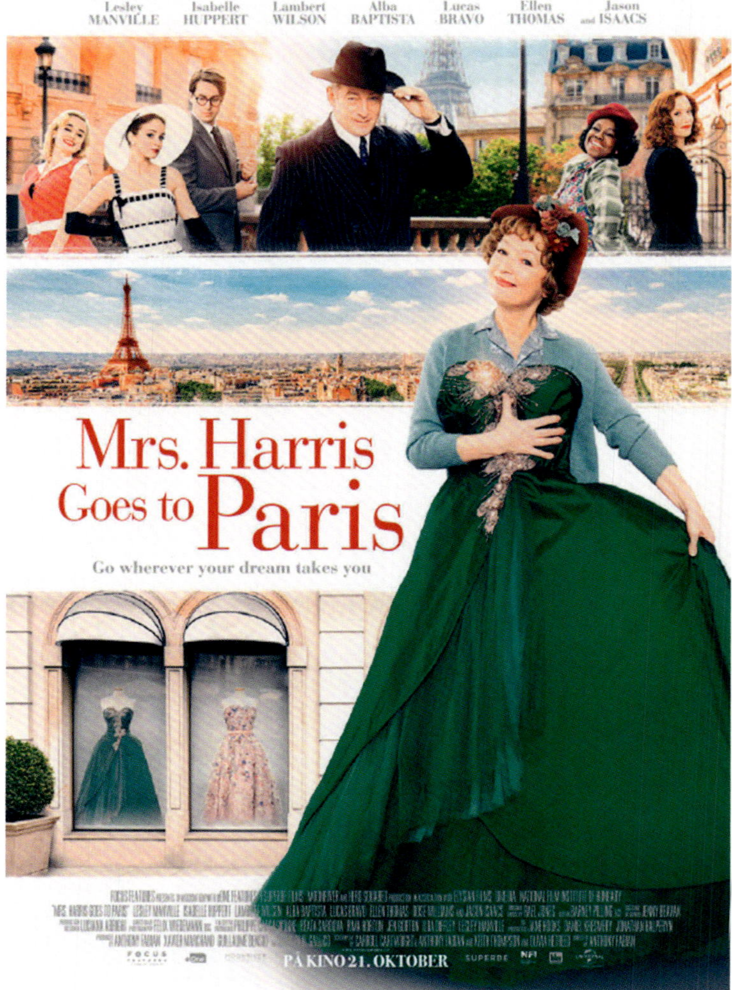

'No one really thinks about who makes the clothes, but the green dress that she holds in the poster is a proud moment. I don't have a favourite, every costume I've made is equal, but when I see my work on screen, on a poster, or on the side of a bus, it's a lovely moment.'[67]
– Emma Burke, Costume Maker

because she is 'not a fashion person',[69] but was fascinated when she saw the Dior dresses.

The fabric was an essential element of the reconstructions and Beavan 'was very reliant on what John and Jane [Law] had in their fabric stocks'.[70] The makers at Cosprop studied and echoed Dior's classic features, mirroring the brand's archetypal interior underpinnings to give the work the appropriate shape.

As Design Assistant on the production, Sally Turner sourced fabric options for the Dior gowns, noting that, 'London was emerging from the COVID lock-down, so many fabric shops hadn't quite reopened for business so it was a challenge finding the right fabrics needed to recreate the gowns'.[71] Costume Maker Emma Burke created the green Dior gown, which is depicted in virtually all the marketing that promoted the film.

The dress wasn't a direct copy but was a composite of two Dior dresses for that moment in the story. I had to make two and a half of them, one for the model in the fashion show, then one for Mrs Harris. There had to be a half-done dress because you see her having a fitting.[72] – **Emma Burke**

Mrs. Harris Goes to Paris captured the zeitgeist, giving audiences a positive and uplifting story after the COVID era. Beavan was nominated for an Oscar and a BAFTA.

156. (opposite, left) Costume for Mrs Harris (Lesley Manville) in construction, Cosprop workroom

157. (opposite, right) Publicity poster for *Mrs. Harris Goes to Paris* (2022)

158. (below) Mrs Harris (Lesley Manville) in *Mrs. Harris Goes to Paris* (2022)

Napoleon (2023)

Director Ridley Scott | Costume Designers Janty Yates, David Crossman
Starring Joaquin Phoenix, Vanessa Kirby, Tahar Rahim Ian McNeice, Paul Rhys

Ridley Scott's epic retelling of Napoleon Bonaparte, his rise to power and being crowned Emperor in 1804, was a project long in the making. Napoleon has long fascinated filmmakers across a century of cinema. Writer David Scarpa drew inspiration from Scott's *The Duellists* (p.28), costumes for which had been created at Cosprop in 1977, designed by Tom Rand. Costume Designer Janty Yates is a regular collaborator with Ridley Scott, and with co-designer David Crossman, she used the Cosprop resources for her research process and costume making.

I first worked with Cosprop on Charlotte Gray *(2001) and they made a beautiful coat for Cate Blanchett. On any project I always defer to John as his knowledge is so enormous and his fabric selections so perfect. I used Cosprop comprehensively on* Napoleon. *They made several wonderful costumes for Tahar Rahim, who portrayed Paul Barras. For Ian McNeice, playing King Louis XVIII, they created two amazing, embroidered outfits and three costumes for Paul Rhys (Charles Talleyrand).*[73] – Janty Yates

Cosprop makers dedicate their time and resources to understanding and researching the clothes from an era they are recreating. When Cosprop Tailor Dan Ashworth began making the costumes for *Napoleon*, he used the reference books *Citizens and Kings* and *The Age of Napoleon: Costume from Revolution to Empire 1789–1815*.

Napoleon was a real person and his clothing has survived, so it was possible to scrutinise the cut and shape of his clothes for interpretation. There is a 1790s' coat in the Museum Collection, a striped coat. The fabric was sourced and I made an exact copy for Tahar Rahim ... We have a personal connection with the costume, because we've made it, you've found the right reference, the right fabric, practised the right technique, found the right buttons, and the designer is pleased with the outcome, we are here to do the best for one costume – by putting character into it.[74] – Dan Ashworth

For Vanessa Kirby's Josephine, some of the design process was informed by the choice of fabric.

Janty gave us some references; for this particular dress, the design was created around the fabric. Janty found a piece of heavily beaded and embroidered net. It came as a rectangle piece, all the intricate shapes were in a block going widthwise. For the dress we needed the motifs going lengthwise and to be concentrated around the hem and becoming lighter toward the bodice. After deciding with John which motif should go where, I started cutting carefully apart each motif and, like a jigsaw, placing it on the front of the dress. It took a very long time to make as each piece had to be stitched back on and sometimes re-beaded. The front itself took three weeks, I then had to make the rest of the dress around it.[75] – Thaïs Demontrond, Costume Maker

159. (opposite) Costume for Paul Barras (Tahar Rahim) in *Napoleon* (2023)

160. (right) Napoleon Bonaparte (Joaquin Phoenix) and Paul Barras (Tahar Rahim) in *Napoleon* (2023)

COSPROP: INFLUENCE AND LEGACY

John Bright and the staff at Cosprop have, for more than sixty years, been part of a movement. This work ethic, ethos and practice has been sewn into every character created at Cosprop. Despite the changes in technology, audience taste, and international global streaming platforms, Cosprop stays close to its original founding mission, to create clothes for actors that are a truthful interpretation of a period in time and place. This practice has informed the visual identity of some of the most beloved characters in film and television history, which in turn has shaped popular perception. Cosprop's influence is global. For Bright, 'The work at Cosprop comes from the truth, the truth of a period. Certain details may need to be emphasised for theatrical effect. If that work creates a house style, but does not superimpose itself, then that's our house style.'

Costume designer Lindy Hemming states the impact of Cosprop on the design industry, 'John and Cosprop have raised the standard of period costumes and how we view and perceive them from the distance of our times. He was one of a small number of designers who believed that the period clothing worn by the actors should reflect the character and class they were playing and be sociologically correct, rather than look pretty and slavishly follow costume illustrations. It was quite revolutionary in our small world.'

Cosprop is more than a costume house, it is the place for research, development and teaching. Actor Greta Scacchi says, 'What John Bright has contributed to, in terms of training, is a vast array of skills and the expertise of makers, of millinery, many of these skills have [elsewhere] become obsolete, but Cosprop trains new generations of makers, to ensure in this niche world, that skills are retained.'

John Bright has also been a mentor to several generations of costume designers as Cosprop has come to be known as the best place for the highest level of period costume recreation. Costume Designer Jenny Beavan recognises that, 'What John offers all costume designers and actors, is a feeling of confidence combined with a formidable knowledge and skill with clothes and history which he shares freely with us all. The museum room at Cosprop preserves some of the amazing clothes that have come his way to offer to designers as a resource, to inspire and understand how clothes were made and to be able to feel the real fabrics.' For Costume Designer Joanna Johnston, Cosprop is the first port of call for historical and period dress: 'At Cosprop, you have someone with extraordinary knowledge. John can look at a piece of lace and tell you it is from the 1760s, but he also knows where you could put something from the 1870s, and what will work with the 1760s. The business of Cosprop is wrapped into the craft of the organisation and that is unique. John gives designers enormous confidence as soon as we enter the building.' For Bright, *The Leopard* (1963), which inspired him as a young designer, was reimagined by Netflix in 2025 (Costume Designers Carlo Poggioli, Edoardo Russo). Bright was delighted that Cosprop was commissioned to create several new pieces and provide items from stock, introducing this classic text to new audiences.

Whilst its costume work often recreates the past, future stories are always on the horizon, requiring the skills of a new generation of makers and designers. Cosprop offer a range of opportunities for students beginning their career path and works with leading costume design courses across the UK and Europe to help facilitate this training. Deputy Manager Mia Walldén says that Cosprop works with art schools such as Wimbledon School of Art, London College of Fashion, Bristol Old Vic Theatre School and London Screen Academy – to name but a few. 'We offer two-week placements and work experience so that the next generation of designers and makers can see at first hand how a costume house operates and what role it plays in the film, theatre and television industry. Students have the opportunity to work across the organisation in all the different workrooms, so they can get a taste of each department and understand more about what is takes to realise costumes from a designer's vision. Future proofing our industry by offering work placement is both an easy and important way for us to give back.'

In the evolution of Cosprop, a new approach merged and has come to shape, influence and inspire. At its heart, Cosprop is about recreating the truth of a period and time, and this ethos has informed its reputation. Bright's collection of historic clothing has been the foundation for a vast array of creative projects. In his generosity of spirit, John Bright is not only preparing young designers for the future, but also investing in the future of children and young adults with the same objects which inspired him. His collection of children's toys, games, railway sets, dolls houses and other ephemera has become the cornerstone of a new project, The Bright Foundation.

Keith Lodwick

THE BRIGHT FOUNDATION

Since working with John Bright and Cosprop from 2013, I have made it my mission to steer Cosprop into the modern world, always keeping a firm eye on preserving the intimate 'Cosprop factor' that is so welcomed by designers and actors. As original Cosprop staff members have retired over the years, we have recruited a new team of young creatives, who respect the culture and the history of the place. We have never lost our enthusiasm to continue moving forward as a company, and to meet all the challenges of the new world of online streaming and the decline of cinema head on. Our skill lies in our ability and willingness to adapt, while continuing to play to our strengths of superb-quality costume making and period truthfulness.

Alongside the growth of the company has been the formation of The Bright Foundation, who will eventually inherit, from John, the ownership of Cosprop and a portfolio of property. The Bright Foundation is John's generous final gift to the creative world. It is an arts and education charity for children and young adults based in two beautiful locations near Hastings, East Sussex. I established the charity in 2018 together with Christine Hill, a former Manager at Cosprop. The purchase and renovation of the buildings will be entirely funded by John Bright and Cosprop. For the foreseeable future the operational costs will be supported by way of an extensive annual grant from Cosprop. The first building, Rodgers Farm, was officially opened in 2022 and the second venue, The Benbow Arts Space, was launched in 2024.

The Foundation now employs an enthusiastic team, managed by a Chief Executive. The achievement of providing rich arts- and film-based experiences and learning for thousands of children and young people has been impressive and very well received locally. John continues to work with the Trustees and the team of staff to enhance the facilities even further and ensure the long-term future of the charity. Cosprop's creative connection and ongoing annual grants to The Bright Foundation, enriches it still further.

Chris Garlick, Company Manager, Cosprop

EPILOGUE

The beginnings of Cosprop were tentative and started with my work with amateur dramatic societies at our local church and then at Cripplegate Theatre in the of City of London. My initial making area was in the family dining room and the first costumes were made on my mother's hand-cranked sewing machine from the 1920s, which had had a motor added. I had struck up a friendship with the owner of a fabric store called Lucille at Gants Hill, Ilford, near to where my family lived in Holcombe Road by Valentine's Park.

By the time I had finished college in 1961, I had built up my theatre and costume experience. My Lecturer, Daphne Brooker, introduced me to the Players' Theatre in Charing Cross, London and to Stratford Upon Avon where she had connections. Visits to the Paris fashion shows, Dior, Givenchy and Chanel were also informative. Another important moment was meeting Doris Langley Moore, who was incredibly useful when I set up Cosprop in Gloucester Avenue, as she lived nearby and was starting her Fashion Museum in Bath.

From 1961 I worked in repertory in Hornchurch where we had to produce a new show every two weeks. I then did a two-year acting course at the newly formed E15 acting school and then in 1964 went back to Hornchurch for a year doing designing and acting – including Jim Hawkins in *Treasure Island* and Hopcroft Minor in *The Happiest Days of Your Life*. All those early influences were crucial in the foundation of what would become Cosprop.

Everyone who has worked at Cosprop during the last 60 years has contributed, but certain key people have given so much of themselves. I'd like to mention some names who have made a long term impact and have worked closely with me: May Koenraads, Christopher Prins, Susie De Broë-Ferguson-Hanbury, Stuart Belton, Christine Hill, Mary Wing, Jill Harbutt, Janet Ingafield, Sandy Ireland, Bernie Chapman, Dany Everett, Sally Turner, Dena Barber, Jane Smith, Gina Ferri, Susan Hardy, Katharine Swailes, Nancy Knapp, Dani Webb, Claire Ramsell, Ross Braganza, Hannah Monkley, Dan Ashworth, Gary Lachman, Maggie Lachman, Elizabeth Owen and Chris Garlick.

Cosprop has been my life's work and many of the people I worked alongside have been my friends and some were like family to me. As well as those who have stayed with me on this extraordinary journey, I have been heartened by how many young people have moved on from Cosprop into the industry and have had extraordinary careers of their own. I am so pleased by what we have all achieved.

Despite the continuing development and change in the film and television industries, Cosprop stays true to its core values and will continue to develop and flourish. Our legacy is The Bright Foundation now realised in Hastings and St Leonards, inspiring young people especially those from disadvantaged backgrounds. A lifetime of collecting is helping to stimulate the next generation – and will continue to be the basis for creativity and design.

John Bright, Cosprop

NOTES

Title page: Author interview with Helena Bonham Carter, Victoria and Albert Museum, London, 22 February 2024

HISTORY OF A COSTUME HOUSE
60 YEARS OF COSPROP

1 Author interview with John Bright, 25 June 2023
2 A costume designer is responsible for communicating the narrative through what the actors wear. A costumier is the bridge between the costume house stock and the making and alternations department, they ensure that the costume designer's vision is realised.
3 John Bright interview with Rosa Weber, 2020
4 Ibid.
5 Ibid.
6 Ibid.
7 Author interview with John Bright, 25 June 2023
8 Ibid.
9 Ibid.
10 Ibid.
11 Ibid.
12 Author correspondence with Anthony Powell, 2016
13 Author interview with John Bright, 25 June 2023
14 John Bright interview with Rosa Weber, 2020
15 Author interview with John Bright, 25 June 2023
16 Email to author from Christine Hill, 25 November 2024
17 Author interview with Chris Garlick, 16 April 2024
18 Email correspondence from Elizabeth Waller to Tom Rand, 2024
19 Author interview with Jacqueline Durran, 29 August 2023
20 James Acheson in 'The History Man', *Sunday Telegraph Magazine*, 29 January 1996
21 Author interview with Nancy Knapp, 3 August 2023
22 Susie de Broë-Ferguson-Hanbury, 6 July 2024
23 Author interview with Tom Rand, 4 August 2023
24 Author interview with Helena Bonham Carter, Victoria and Albert Museum, London, 22 February 2024

THE REDESIGN OF THE COSTUME DRAMA 1965–1999

1 Obituary, *Guardian*, 15 August 2019
2 Ibid.
3 Author interview with John Bright, 25 June 2023
4 Ibid.
5 Tony Richardson, *The Long-Distance Runner: A Memoir*, Faber and Faber (1993)
6 Author interview with John Bright, 25 June 2023
7 Ibid.
8 Vincent Canby, 'Howard Thompson, The Charge of the Light Brigade', *New York Times*, 7 October 1968, https://www.nytimes.com/1968/10/07/archives/screen-charge-of-the-light-brigadevanessa-redgrave-and-john-gielgud.html [accessed 8 February 2025]
9 John Bright interview with Rosa Weber, 2020
10 Author interview with Tom Rand, 4 August 2023
11 Ibid.
12 Ibid.
13 Ibid.
14 Ibid.
15 Ibid.
16 Anthony Powell, *Tess* (1979), BFI Blu-ray Special Edition, DVD notes, 2012
17 Email to author from Joanna Johnston, 19 November 2024
18 Author interview with John Bright, 25 June 2023
19 Ibid.
20 Anthony Powell, *Tess* (1979), BFI Blu-ray Special Edition, DVD notes, 2012
21 Email to author from Jill Harbutt, 17 May 2024
22 Author email with Joanna Johnston, 19 November 2024
23 Letter to author from Tom Rand, 4 August 2023
24 Ibid.
25 Ibid.
26 Meryl Streep, transcript from the *Hollywood Costume* exhibition, Victoria and Albert Museum, London, 2012
27 Email to author from Susan Hardy, 5 September 2024
28 Letter to author from Tom Rand, 4 August 2023
29 Ibid.
30 Milena Canonero in *Screen Craft: Costume Design* by Deborah Nadoolman Landis, Focal Press (2003)
31 Email to author from Susan Hardy, 5 September 2024
32 Author interview with John Bright, 25 June 2024
33 Milena Canonero in *Screen Craft: Costume Design* by Deborah Nadoolman Landis, Focal Press (2003)
34 Meryl Streep, transcript from the *Hollywood Costume* exhibition, Victoria and Albert Museum, London, 2012
35 James Acheson in *Screen Craft: Costume Design* by Deborah Nadoolman Landis, Focal Press (2003)
36 James Acheson in 'The History Man', *Sunday Telegraph Magazine*, 1996
37 James Acheson in 'Designing Liaisons', *The Sunday Times Magazine*, March 1989
38 Email to author from Susan Hardy, 5 September 2024
39 James Acheson in 'The History Man', *Sunday Telegraph Magazine*, 29 January 1996
40 Email to author from Susan Hardy, 5 September 2024
41 Jane Campion, *The Portrait of a Lady* (1996), DVD notes, 2001
42 Author interview with Sally Turner, 7 September 2023
43 Jane Campion, *The Portrait of a Lady* (1996), DVD notes, 2001
44 Author interview with Jill Harbutt, 17 May 2024
45 Author interview with Diana Thomas, 4 August 2023
46 Author interview with Jill Harbutt, 17 May 2024
47 Author interview with Nancy Knapp, 3 August 2023
48 Author interview with Jill Harbutt, 17 May 2024
49 Author interview with Sally Turner, 7 September 2023
50 Ibid.
51 Trevor Nunn in 'The History Man', *Sunday Telegraph Magazine*, 29 January 1996
52 Author interview with John Bright, 25 June 2023
53 Imogen Stubbs in 'The History Man', *Sunday Telegraph Magazine*, 29 January 1996
54 Author interview with Helena Bonham Carter, Victoria and Albert Museum, London, 22 February 2024
55 Author interview with John Bright, 25 June 2023
56 Email to author from Susan Hardy, 5 September 2024
57 Author interview with Alexandra Byrne, 23 April 2023
58 Ibid.
59 Ibid.
60 Ibid.
61 Author interview with Lindy Hemming, 12 November 2023
62 Ibid.
63 Email to author from Lindy Hemming, 10 September 2024
64 Ibid.
65 Author interview with Michael O'Connor, 21 May 2024
66 Ibid.
67 Xan Brooks, 'Topsy-Turvy', *Guardian*, 8 February 2000
68 Email to author from Lindy Hemming, 27 February 2025
69 Author interview with Chloé Obolensky, 16 November 2023
70 Martha Fiennes in 'Shooting for the Heart', *Sunday Times Magazine*, 31 October 1999
71 Ibid.

72 Author interview with John Bright, 25 June 2023
73 Author interview with Chloé Obolensky, 16 November 2023
74 Ibid.
75 Ralph Fiennes in 'Shooting for the Heart', *Sunday Times Magazine*, 31 October 1999
76 Ibid.
77 Derek Malcolm, 'Onegin', *Guardian*, 1999
78 Derek Elley, 'Onegin', *Variety*, 27 September 1999, www.variety/film/reviews/onegin [accessed 3 March 2025]
79 Author interview with John Bright, 25 June 2023

MERCHANT IVORY
THE RENAISSANCE OF THE COSTUME DRAMA

1 James Ivory in 'The History Man', *Sunday Telegraph Magazine*, 29 January 1996
2 Ismail Merchant in 'The History Man', *Sunday Telegraph Magazine*, 29 January 1996
3 Author interview with Helena Bonham Carter, Victoria and Albert Museum, London, 22 February 2024
4 Ibid.
5 Author interview with Jenny Beavan, 3 August 2023
6 Author interview with John Bright, 3 August 2023
7 Author interview with John Bright, 3 August 2023
8 James Ivory in *The Films of Merchant Ivory*, by Robert Emmet Long, Harry N. Abrams Publishers (1997), p.102
9 Author interview with John Bright, 25 June 2023
10 Author interview with Jenny Beavan, 3 August 2023
11 James Ivory in *James Ivory On the Bostonians*, Cohen Media Collection, Blu-ray, 2018
12 Vincent Canby, 'The Bostonians: A Proper Jamesian Adaptation', *New York Times*, 5 August 1984, https://www.nytimes.com/1984/08/c5/movies/film-bostonians-a-proper-jamesian-adaptation.html [accessed 8 February 2025]
13 James Ivory in *The Films of Merchant Ivory*, by Robert Emmet Long, Harry N. Abrams Publishers (1997), p.139
14 Author interview with John Bright, 25 June 2023
15 Ibid.
16 Ibid.
17 Author interview with Jenny Beavan, 3 August 2023
18 Author interview with John Bright, 25 June 2023
19 Julian Sands, *A Room with a View* (1985), The Criterion Collection Special Edition Blu-ray, 2015
20 Author interview with Jenny Beavan, 3 August 2023
21 Author interview with John Bright, 16 May 2023
22 Ibid.
23 Author interview with Sally Turner, 7 September 2023
24 Ibid.
25 Ibid.
26 Ibid
27 Author interview with John Bright, 3 August 2023
28 Author interview with Jenny Beavan, 3 August 2023
29 Author interview with John Bright, 16 May 2024
30 Helena Bonham Carter, *A Room with a View* (1985), The Criterion Collection Special Edition Blu-ray, 2015
31 Author interview with Anthony Powell, 2016
32 Author interview with John Bright, 3 August 2023
33 Author interview with Jenny Beavan, 3 August 2023
34 Author interview with Susan Hardy, 5 September 2024
35 James Ivory in James Ivory *In Conversation: How Merchant Ivory Makes Its Movies* by Robert Emmet Long, University of California Press (2005)
36 Author interview with John Bright, 16 May 2023
37 Author interview with Jenny Beavan, 3 August 2023
38 James Ivory in *The Films of Merchant Ivory* by Robert Emmet Long, Harry N. Abrams Publishers (1997), p.151
39 Luciana Arrighi, *Howards End* (1992), Cohen Media Blu-ray Special Edition, 2016
40 Author interview with John Bright, 16 May 2023
41 Author interview with Jenny Beavan, 3 August 2023
42 Author interview with John Bright, 16 May 2023
43 Author interview with Jenny Beavan, 3 August 2023
44 Author interview with John Bright, 3 August 2023
45 Author interview with Jill Harbutt, 17 May 2024
46 Author interview with John Bright, 12 December 2024
47 *New York Times* review published in *The Films of Merchant Ivory* by Robert Emmet Long, Harry N. Abrams Publishers (1997), p.194
48 Author interview with Jenny Beavan, 3 August 2023
49 Author interview with John Bright, 16 May 2023
50 Ibid.
51 Author interview with Jenny Beavan, 3 August 2023
52 Ibid.
53 Ibid.
54 Author interview with Jenny Beavan, 3 August 2023
55 Author interview with John Bright, 3 August 2023
56 Ibid.
57 Mary Blume, 'Merchant Ivory on Growing Up in France', *New York Times*, 1 November 1997, www.newyorktimes.com/merchantivoryongrowingupinfrance [accessed 3 March 2025]
58 Author interview with Greta Scacchi, 16 September 2024

THE WORLD OF JANE AUSTEN
DESIGNING FOR THE REGENCY ERA

1 Author interview with John Bright, 16 May 2024
2 Email to author from Michele Clapton, 16 September 2024
3 Rosemary Harden in *Jane Austen: Film and Fashion*, Bath Fashion Museum, 2004, p.10
4 Author email with Alexandra Byrne, 1 September 2024
5 Anna Massey in *Jane Austen: Film and Fashion*, Bath Fashion Museum, 2004, p.24
6 Author interview with Alexandra Byrne, 23 April 2023
7 Author interview with John Bright, 6 May 2024
8 John Bright in *Jane Austen: Film and Fashion*, Bath Fashion Museum, 2004, p.10
9 Author interview with John Bright, 6 May 2024
10 Author interview with Jill Harbutt, 17 May 2024
11 Greg Wise, *Jane Austen: Film and Fashion*, Bath Fashion Museum, 2004, p.15
12 Ibid.
13 Ibid., p.14
14 Ibid.
15 Ibid.
16 Email to author from Katharine Swailes, 17 November 2024
17 Author interview with Dinah Collin, 24 June 2023
18 Andrew Davies in *The Making of Pride and Prejudice* (1995), DVD Special Edition, 2015
19 Simon Langton in *The Making of Pride and Prejudice* (1995), BBC Books, p.47
20 Andrew Davies in *The Making of Pride and Prejudice* (1995), DVD Special Edition (2015)
21 Ibid.
22 Author interview with Dinah Collin, 24 June 2023
23 Ibid.
24 Author interview with Dinah Collin, 16 August 2024
25 Ibid.
26 Author interview with John Bright, 24 June 2023

27 Email to author from Dinah Collin, 16 August 2024
28 Ibid.
29 Jennifer Ehle, *The Making of Pride and Prejudice* (1995), DVD Special Edition, 2015
30 Email to author from Dinah Collin, 16 August 2024
31 Ibid.
32 Ibid.
33 Christopher Prins in *Jane Austen: Film and Fashion*, Bath Fashion Museum, 2004, p.22
34 Email to author from Dinah Collin, 16 August 2024
35 Christopher Prins in *Jane Austen: Film and Fashion*, Bath Fashion Museum, 2004, p.22
36 Greg Wise in *Jane Austen: Film and Fashion*, Bath Fashion Museum, 2004, p.23
37 Christopher Prins in *Jane Austen: Film and Fashion*, Bath Fashion Museum, 2004, p.22
38 Author interview with Jenny Ireland, 26 June 2024
39 Author interview with Emma Burke, 24 January 2024
40 Author interview with Ross Braganza, 26 June 2023
41 Joe Wright's Enduring *Pride & Prejudice*: A Fan Favourite for Focus Features' 20th Anniversary, focusfeatures.com, https://www.focusfeatures.com/article/focus-features-20th-anniversary_prideprejudice [accessed 3 March 2025]
42 Ibid.
43 Ibid.
44 Author interview with Jacqueline Durran, 29 August 2023
45 Ibid.
46 Ibid.
47 Ibid.
48 Email to author from Michele Clapton, 16 September 2024
49 Ibid.
50 Ibid.
51 Author interview with John Bright, 24 June 2023
52 David Morrissey in 'Austen's Powers', *Liverpool Echo*, 21 December 2007
53 Author correspondence with Michele Clapton, 16 September 2024
54 Email to author from Alexandra Byrne, 1 September 2024
55 Ibid.
56 Author interview with Alexandra Byrne, 23 April 2024
57 Author interview with Jill Harbutt, 17 May 2024
58 Author interview with Julia Buckmiller, 11 September 2024
59 Author interview with John Bright, 24 June 2023
60 Anya Taylor-Joy in 'Meet the Stars of the Sumptuous New Emma', *Vogue*, 2020 https://www.vogue.com/article/anya-taylor-joy-johnny-flynn-emma-adaptation [accessed 8 February 2025]

INSIDE THE COSTUME HOUSE
THE WORKROOMS

All quotations by John Bright, Cosprop staff, costume designers and actors from interviews and emails with the author during the research process, July 2023–January 2025

MAKING A GOLDEN AGE
TELEVISION COSTUME DRAMA

1 Author interview with Elizabeth Waller, 15 July 2024
2 Author interview with John Bright, 24 June 2023
3 Author interview with Susannah Buxton, 7 August 2024
4 Author interview with John Bright, 24 June 2023
5 Author interview with John Bloomfield, 12 August 2024
6 Author interview with Elizabeth Waller, 15 July 2024
7 Author interview with Vanessa Hopkins, 19 October 2023
8 Author interview with Christine Rawlins, 18 October 2024
9 Author interview with John Bright, 24 June 2023
10 Charles Knode in 'War and Peace', *Radio Times* Souvenir Special Edition, BBC, 1972, p.15
11 Author interview with John Bloomfield, 12 August 2024
12 Ibid.
13 Author interview with Elizabeth Waller, 15 July 2024
14 Author interview with John Bloomfield, 12 August 2024
15 Author interview with Elizabeth Waller, 15 July 2024
16 Author interview with John Bloomfield, 12 August 2024
17 Author interview with Vanessa Hopkins, 19 October 2023
18 Author interview with Phoebe de Gaye, 18 September 2024
19 Author interview with John Bloomfield, 12 August 2024
20 Author interview with Jill Harbutt, 12 September 2024
21 Sarah Cardwell, *Adaptation Revisited: Television and the Classic Novel*, Manchester University Press (2002), p.125
22 Author interview with Jane Robinson, 19 September 2024
23 Editorial, *Harpers & Queen* Magazine, December 1981
24 Ibid.
25 John Mortimer, *Out on Tuesday*, Channel 4, 1990
26 David Suchet in *Being Poirot* (2013)
27 Ibid.
28 Ibid.
29 Ibid.
30 Ibid.
31 Ibid.
32 Author interview with John Bright, 24 June 2023
33 Author interview with Susannah Buxton, 7 August 2024
34 Ibid.
35 Author interview with Phoebe de Gaye, 18 September 2024
36 Ibid.
37 Ibid.
38 Author interview with Susannah Buxton, 7 August 2024
39 Ibid.
40 Jessica Fellowes, *The World of Downton Abbey*, Collins (2001), p.8
41 Author interview with Susannah Buxton, 7 August 2024
42 Ibid.
43 Author interview with John Bright, 24 June 2023
44 Author interview with Susannah Buxton, 7 August 2024
45 Ibid.
46 Michelle Dockery in 'Dressing Downton', *Vogue* magazine, 2010
47 Author interview with Susannah Buxton, 7 August 2024
48 Email to author, 31 January 2025
49 Email to author from Michele Clapton, 16 September 2024
50 Ibid.
51 Ibid.
52 Author interview with John Bright, 24 June 2023
53 Ibid.
54 Email to author from Michele Clapton, 16 September 2024
55 Author interview with Michele Clapton, 28 November 2024
56 Email to author from Susan Hardy, 5 September 2024
57 Michele Clapton, with Gina McIntyre, *Game of Thrones: The Costumes*, Harper Voyager (2019)
58 Author interview with Susannah Buxton, 7 August 2024
59 Author interview with Rosalind Ebbutt, 16 October 2024
60 Ibid.
61 Author interview with Emma Burke, 24 January 2024
62 Author interview with Dan Ashworth, 24 January 2024
63 Ibid.
64 Ibid.
65 Author interview with Nancy Knapp, 3 August 2023
66 Tom Pye in 'Interview with Gentleman Jack Costume Designer Tom Pye', Frockflicks.com https://frockflicks.com/interview-with-gentleman-jack-costume-designer-tom-pye/ [accessed 8 February 2025]

67 Ibid.
68 Ibid.
69 Author interview with Dan Ashworth, 23 January 2024
70 Author interview with Ross Braganza, 26 June 2023
71 Tom Pye in 'Interview with Gentleman Jack Costume Designer Tom Pye', Frockflicks.com https://frockflicks.com/interview-with-gentleman-jack-costume-designer-tom-pye/ [accessed 8 February 2025]
72 Ibid.
73 Ibid.
74 Suranne Jones in 'Catching Up with Gentleman Jack', willowandthatch.com, https://www.willowandthatch.com/hbo-gentleman-jack-period-drama-series/ [accessed 8 February 2025]
75 Stephanie Collie in 'The Period Drama for People Who Hate Period Dramas: An Oral History of *Peaky Blinders*', Esquire.com, https://www.esquire.com/uk/culture/a39071635/peaky-blinders-oral-history/ [accessed 8 February 2025]
76 Ibid.
77 Ibid.
78 Alison McCosh in 'The Period Drama for People Who Hate Period Dramas: An Oral History of *Peaky Blinders*', Esquire.com, https://www.esquire.com/uk/culture/a39071635/peaky-blinders-oral-history/ [accessed 8 February 2025]
79 Ibid.
80 Author interview with Ross Braganza, 26 June 2023
81 Stephanie Collie in 'The Period Drama for People Who Hate Period Dramas: An Oral History of *Peaky Blinders*', Esquire.com, https://www.esquire.com/uk/culture/a39071635/peaky-blinders-oral-history/ [accessed 8 February 2025]
82 Ibid.
83 Author interview with Michael Wilkinson, 15 September 2024

RAISING THE CURTAIN
COSTUME FOR STAGE

1 Author interview with John Bright, 25 June 2024
2 Author interview with Nancy Knapp, 25 June 2024
3 Author interview with John Bright, 25 June 2024
4 Ibid.
5 Author interview with Nancy Knapp, 25 June 2024
6 Author interview with John Bright, 25 June 2024
7 Email correspondence with Mary Wing, 4 November 2024
8 Author interview with John Bright, 25 June 2024
9 Author interview with Penelope Wilton, 13 December 2024
10 Author interview with Chloé Obolensky, 16 November 2023
11 Author interview with John Bright, 25 June 2024
12 Ibid.
13 Author interview with Chloé Obolensky, 16 November 2023
14 Author interview with John Bright, 25 June 2024
15 David Hirst, 'Eugene Onegin', *Opera Now*, 24 February 1991, www.oceanexacteditions.com/issues/page.33 [accessed March 2025]
16 Author interview with John Bright, 20 August 2024
17 Author interview with Tom Pye, 15 October 2024
18 Author interview with John Bright, 20 August 2024
19 Ibid.
20 Author interview with John Bright, 25 June 2024
21 Ibid.
22 Letter to John Bright from Trevor Nunn, John Bright Archive
23 Deborah Warner in 'How I Learnt to Love Opera', *Independent*, 2006, https://www.independent.co.uk/arts-entertainment/music/features/deborah-warner-how-i-learnt-to-love-opera [accessed 3 March 2025]
24 Author interview with John Bright, 20 August 2024
25 Ibid.
26 Ibid.
27 Author interview with John Bright, 20 August 2024
28 Author interview with Tom Pye, 15 October 2024
29 Ibid.

NEW FRONTIERS
COSPROP IN THE TWENTY-FIRST CENTURY

1 Author interview with Chloé Obolensky, 16 November 2023
2 Author interview with Michele Clapton, 16 September 2024
3 'The Art of the Costume Drama', *Empire* magazine, November 2000
4 Author interview with Colleen Atwood, 7 August 2023
5 Author interview with John Bright, 25 June 2023
6 Ibid.
7 Author interview with Sally Turner, 7 September 2023
8 Author interview with John Bright, 25 June 2023
9 Author interview with Jill Harbutt, 17 May 2024
10 One of the witty lines in *Gosford Park* (2001) was unscripted and delivered by Maggie Smith. When Claudie Blakley as Mabel Nesbitt arrived on set in a green dress, Smith said, 'Difficult colour, green ... very tricky' at which the screenplay writer, Julian Fellowes, burst out laughing and the line was kept in.
11 Email to author from Jenny Beavan, 22 November 2024
12 Ibid.
13 Ibid.
14 Ibid.
15 Ibid.
16 Author interview with Susan Hardy, 9 August 2024
17 Sonia Grande in 'Interview with Sonia Grande, Costume Designer of *The Others*', StyleLovely.com, https://stylelovely.com/stylemeifyoucan/2012/12/05/interview-with-sonia-grande-costume-designer-of-midnight-in-paris-the-others-vicky-cristina-barcelona/ [accessed 8 February 2025]
18 Ibid.
19 Author interview with Lindy Hemming, 30 August 2024
20 Ibid.
21 Ibid.
22 Kenneth Branagh in 'Kenneth Branagh as Gilderoy Lockhart in *Harry Potter and the Chamber of Secrets*', Branaghcompendium.com, https://www.branaghcompendium.com/gilderoy_ken.html [accessed 8 February 2025]
23 Author interview with John Bright, 25 June 2023
24 Natasha Richardson in *The White Countess* (2005), DVD Special Features, 2008
25 Author interview with Jill Harbutt, 17 May 2024
26 John Bright in *The White Countess* (2005), DVD Special Features, 2008
27 Penny Rose in *50 Designers/50 Costumes: Concept to Character*, edited by Deborah Nadoolman Landis, AMPAS (2004), p.92
28 Ibid.
29 Ibid.
30 Author interview with Susan Hardy, 22 August 2024
31 Penny Rose in *50 Designers/50 Costumes: Concept to Character*, edited by Deborah Nadoolman Landis, AMPAS (2004), p.92
32 Johnny Depp, interview with Patti Smith, *Vanity Fair*, January 2011, p.98
33 Author interview with Michael O'Connor, 11 September 2024
34 Ibid.
35 Ibid.
36 Author interview with Jill Harbutt, 12 September 2024
37 Author interview with Michael O'Connor, 11 September 2024
38 Ibid.
39 Ibid.
40 Ibid.
41 Author interview with Jill Harbutt, 12 September 2024

42 Author interview with Michael O'Connor, 11 September 2024
43 Author interview with Dinah Collin, 16 August 2024
44 Ibid.
45 Rachel Weisz in 'Interview with Rachel Weisz and Roger Michell: *My Cousin Rachel*', Scriptmag.com, https://scriptmag.com/features/interview-rachel-weisz-roger-michell-cousin-rachel [accessed 8 February 2025]
46 Ibid.
47 Author interview with Dinah Collin, 16 August 2024
48 Ibid.
49 Author interview with John Bright, 26 June 2024
50 Author interview with Dinah Collin, 16 August 2024
51 Orla Smith, 'Jacqueline Durran on why period costumes can never be "pure"', Seventh-row.com, https://seventh-row.com/2019/04/28/jacqueline-durran-peterloo/ [accessed 8 February 2025]
52 Ibid.
53 Ibid.
54 Author interview with Jacqueline Durran, 29 August 2023
55 Jacqueline Durran in 'Dressing *Little Women*: Costume Designer Jacqueline Durran on Color, Character and Breaking the Rules', *Vogue*, 2019, https://www.vogue.com/article/little-women-movie-costume-designer-jacqueline-durran-interview [accessed 8 February 2025]
56 Ibid.
57 Ibid.
58 Author interview with Jacqueline Durran, 29 August 2023
59 Ibid.
60 Ibid.
61 Author interview with Emily Harris, 23 July 2024
62 Ibid.
63 Ibid.
64 Ibid.
65 Ibid.
66 Ibid.
67 Author interview with Emma Burke, 24 January 2024
68 Author interview with Jenny Beavan, 22 October 2024
69 Ibid.
70 Ibid.
71 Author interview with Sally Turner, 7 September 2023
72 Author interview with Emma Burke, 24 January 2024
73 Author interview with Janty Yates, 9 August 2024
74 Author interview with Dan Ashworth, 25 June 2024
75 Author interview with Thaïs Demontrond, 5 September 2024

SELECT PRODUCTIONS BY JOHN BRIGHT

FILMMAKER

Costume Design (1977), *The Puppet Maker* (1977), *Say Beau* (1982), *Moon Princess* (2002), *Mr. Punch's Nightmare* (2022), *The Silent Movie Star* (2025), *Boudoir Dolls* (in progress), *The Fat Lady* (in progress), *Underwater* (in progress)

COSTUME DESIGN

The Bostonians (1984) | Directed by James Ivory
Co-design with Jenny Beavan
Oscar and BAFTA nomination Best Costume Design

A Room with a View (1985) | Directed by James Ivory
Co-design with Jenny Beavan
Oscar and BAFTA Award Best Costume Design

Maurice (1987) | Directed by James Ivory
Co-design with Jenny Beavan
Oscar nomination Best Costume Design

The Deceivers (1988) | Directed by James Ivory
Co-design with Jenny Beavan

The Mountains of the Moon (1990) | Directed by Bob Rafelson
Co-design with Jenny Beavan

White Fang (1991) | Directed by Randal Kleiser
Co-design with Jenny Beavan

Howards End (1992) | Directed by James Ivory
Co-design with Jenny Beavan
Oscar and BAFTA nomination Best Costume Design

The Remains of the Day (1993) | Directed by James Ivory
Co-design with Jenny Beavan
Oscar nomination Best Costume Design

Jefferson in Paris (1995) | Directed by James Ivory
Co-design with Jenny Beavan

Sense and Sensibility (1995) | Directed by Ang Lee
Co-design with Jenny Beavan
Oscar and BAFTA nomination Best Costume Design

Twelfth Night (1996) | Directed by Trevor Nunn

Onegin (1999) | Directed by Martha Fiennes

The Last September (1999) | Directed by Deborah Warner

The Golden Bowl (2000) | Directed by James Ivory

The Magnificent Ambersons (2001) | Directed by Alfonso Arau

The White Countess (2005) | Directed by James Ivory
Satellite Award nomination, Outstanding Costume Design

Carmilla (2019) | Directed by Emily Harris

THEATRE, OPERA AND OTHER COMMISSIONS

The Women (1986) | Directed by Keith Hack
Old Vic Theatre, London

Eugene Onegin (1991) | Directed by Andrei Serban
Teatro La Fenice, Italy

La Bohème (1996) | Directed by Michael Hunt
Royal Albert Hall, London

A Month in the Country (1997) | Directed by Marco Sciaccaluga
Teatro di Genova, Italy

Les Fausses Confidences (1997) | Directed by Marco Sciaccaluga
Comédie Française Production
Teatro di Genova, Italy and National Theatre, London

Lady Windermere's Fan (1998) | Directed by Marco Sciaccaluga
Teatro di Genova, Italy

An Enemy of the People (1997) | Directed by Trevor Nunn
National Theatre, London

The Turn of the Screw (1997) | Directed by Deborah Warner
Barbican Theatre, London MC 93 Bobigny, Paris, Royal Opera House, London

After October (1997) | Directed by Keith Baxter
Minerva Theatre, Chichester, England

Easy Virtue (1999) | Directed by Maria Aitken
Chichester Festival Theatre, England

Three Sisters (2003) | Directed by Michael Blakemore
Playhouse Theatre, London

Cyrano de Bergerac (2004) | Directed by Howard Davies
National Theatre, London

Fidelio (2001) |Directed by Deborah Warner
Glyndebourne Festival Opera, England, Théâtre du Châtelet, Paris

Pains of Youth (2009) | Directed by Katie Mitchell
National Theatre, London

Clemency (2011) | Directed by Katie Mitchell
Linbury Studio, Royal Opera House, London

A House Taken Over (2013) | Directed by Katie Mitchell
Aix-en-Provence, France and European Tour

The Silver Tassie (2014) | Directed by Howard Davies
National Theatre, London

FURTHER COMMISSIONS

The Angel Project (1999–2003) | Directed by Deborah Warner
London International Festival of Theatre in Euston Tower, London
Perth International Arts Festival, Australia and Lincoln Center Festival, New York

Dress for HRH Diana, Princess of Wales (1983) Canadian Tour

A recreation of Cornelia Vanderbilt's Wedding Dress (2014), Biltmore Estate, North Carolina (USA)

John Bright OBE

As one of the world's leading costume designers and costumiers, John Bright has captured the imaginations of audiences around the globe over the past six decades. The attention to detail in the costumes he has created have brought people, places and moments in time vividly and authentically to life on both stage and screen.

In 1965 his personal costume collection formed the beginnings of Cosprop, now one of the world's leading period costume houses. Over these years, John and his team at Cosprop have collaborated and made costumes for several generations of designers for productions ranging from *Pirates of the Caribbean* to *Downton Abbey*. For his own distinguished creative career he was awarded an Oscar and BAFTA in 1987 for Best Costume Design for *A Room with a View*. In 2024 he was awarded an OBE for Services to Costume Design and Heritage.

Keith Lodwick

Keith Lodwick is a writer, curator and theatre and film historian. He is the former Curator of Theatre and Screen Arts at the Victoria and Albert Museum, London. At the V&A, Keith was the assistant curator for the major exhibition *Hollywood Costume* (2012). He curated the exhibition *Vivien Leigh: Public Faces, Private Lives,* which toured the UK and co-curated *Censored: Stage, Screen, Society* (2019) for the Theatre & Performance galleries. Keith has contributed to a wide range of publications, including *The Bloomsbury Encyclopedia of Film and Television Costume Design* (2025), *George Hoyningen-Huene* (Thames & Hudson, 2024), *DIVA* (V&A, 2023), *Studies in Costume and Performance* (Bloomsbury, 2021), *Shoe Reels: The History and Philosophy of Footwear in Film* (Edinburgh University Press, 2021), *Hollywood Costume* (V&A, 2012) and *Oliver Messel: In the Theatre of Design* (Rizzoli, 2010).

Acknowledgements

This book would not have been possible without the dedication and commitment of Chris Garlick and Christine Hill. Your vision of a book to celebrate John Bright and Cosprop has been talked about for decades and it is through your passionate enthusiasm that this publication exists.

As it takes a small army to create a film, television or theatre project, this book would not have been possible without the support, generosity and kindness of the staff at Cosprop – past and present. The staff welcomed me into their world and offered time, expertise and knowledge. Retired Cosprop staff also shared their creative process and opened their archives for visual references. I'd like to thank all of them, including Kate Anderson, Dan Ashworth, Ross Braganza, Susie de Broë-Ferguson-Hanbury, Julia Buckmiller, Emma Burke, Peter Costen, Annalise Clark, Pippa Cleator, Hannah Curtis, Thaïs Demontrond, Clara Drumez, Julia Fallon, Sage Foley, Kat Goodall, Clemmi Greeley, Nicolina Griffiths, Charlotte Hald, Jill Harbutt, Susan Hardy, Janet Ingafield, Barbara Kloss, Nancy Knapp, Gary Lachman, Stacey Liddall, Annie Lloyd, David Lothian, Eva Mallet, Guila Manto, Hannah Monkley, Elizabeth Owen, Donna Simmons, Christine Stallard, Diana Thomas, Max Yeomans, Mia Walldén, Mary Wing and Heather Wood.

Many leading industry figures have generously given their time and expertise and shared archival material for inclusion, and I am hugely grateful to Colleen Atwood, Jenny Beavan, John Bloomfield, Helena Bonham Carter, Hugh Bonneville, Susannah Buxton, Alexandra Byrne, Melissa Chung, Michele Clapton, Dinah Collin, Jacqueline Durran, Rosalind Ebbutt, Dany Everitt, Phoebe De Gaye, Jane Greenwood, Emily Harris, Carol Hemming, Lindy Hemming, Tom Hollander, Alan Hopkins, Vanessa Hopkins, Joanna Johnston, Lynette Mauro, Michael O'Connor, Chloé Obolensky, Tony Pierce-Roberts, Madeline Potter, Tom Pye, Sarah Quill, Tom Rand, Christine Rawlins, Jane Robinson, Greta Scacchi, Meryl Streep, David Suchet, Sally Turner, Elizabeth Waller, Michael Wilkinson, Dame Penelope Wilton, Robert Worley and Janty Yates.

Anthony Powell (1935–2021) spoke to me at length about John and Cosprop, long before I became involved with this book. I am fortunate I recorded those conversations so that his voice is part of the story as Anthony's career paralleled the development of Cosprop.

Special thanks to Tom Rand for his appreciation of Christopher Prins (1949–2005), integral to the Cosprop story. Tom's dedication to Christopher highlights the creative and vital work that takes place in the costume house – the role of the costumier.

I am very grateful to Dame Judi Dench for writing the gracious foreword.

Many thanks to the following individuals who provided support and expertise to the project: Susanna Brown, Anne Coco (AMPAS), DHA Designs, Aine Duffy, Jo Elsworth (Bristol Theatre Collections), Rosemary Fernandez-Day, Joana Granero, Dr Veronica Isaac, Sarah Law (BFI), Dr Reina Lewis, Professor Lesley Miller, Nathalie Morris (AMPAS), Dennis Nothdruft and the staff at the Fashion and Textile Museum London, Ciara Pedrotta-Parsons, Polly Risbridger (The Bright Foundation), Claire Smith (BFI), Patzi Stevenson, Dr Phil Wickham and the staff at the Bill Douglas Cinema Museum, University of Exeter.

Rosa Weber conducted interviews and early research for the project and I am grateful for her input.

Special thanks to the freelance book project team: Commissioning Editor Anjali Bulley for seeing the vision, guiding the project and bringing all parts of the jigsaw puzzle together, Lizzie Ballantyne for the beautiful and elegant design and Marina Asenjo for able production support. Thanks go to Axelle Russo-Smith for providing vital image research, Jon Stokes and Paul Bulley for their evocative photographs. I am grateful to Mark Eastment at Yale University Press for support and guidance.

I could not have produced this work without the love and continual support of David Robertson.

As a teenager living in rural Shropshire in 1986, I went to my local cinema and watched *A Room with a View*. I was immediately swept into the glorious past of Edwardian Florence and England, a world more appealing to me than 1980s' Britain, such is the power of film. Never in my wildest dreams would I be writing about the designer who created, along with Jenny Beavan, the impeccable clothes. John and Jenny's beautiful work on this film has not only inspired me but a generation of film enthusiasts.

John has created, built, shaped and steered Cosprop from 1965 into the twenty-first century, and his work is celebrated around the world. This book is dedicated to your vision, creativity and spirit. Thank you for trusting me to write the history of Cosprop.

John holds a unique place in film, television and theatre, a costumier and a costume designer, the two roles are different yet overlap and inform one another. John has had some level of input to hundreds of film, television and theatre projects across sixty years of creativity. John's generous philanthropy will continue to inspire young people, designers and makers for decades to come through the work of The Bright Foundation, just as *A Room with a View* inspired me.

Keith Lodwick

Image credits

Academy Awards show photographs, Margaret Herrick Library, Academy of Motion Picture Arts and Sciences: p.69

AJ Pics / Alamy Stock Photo: pp.164, 206 (above)

Album / Alamy Stock Photo: pp.28, 105 (right), 144, 159, 163, 173 (right), 176–177, 195 (above)

BBC Archive: pp.13, 97 (below), 103, 156

Courtesy of BBC Archive / © Mammoth Screen Limited: p.166

BFA / Cinecom / Alamy Stock Photo: p.64

Courtesy of the BFI National Archive: pp.34, 151

Courtesy of the Biltmore Museum / Photography Martyn Goddard: p.141

Photography © Paul Bulley: back cover, pp.9, 10, 17 (above and below), 106, 108, 109, 110, 111, 112, 114–115, 120, 121, 122 (above and below), 126, 127, 129 (above and below), 130–131, 132, 133, 134, 135, 136, 137, 138–139

Cinematic / Alamy Stock Photo: pp.29, 49, 77, 91 (above), 97 (above), 162, 206 (below)

Collection Christophel / Alamy Stock Photo: 218 (right)

Courtesy of Michele Clapton: p.102

Courtesy of Dinah Collin: p.95 (above and below)

© Donald Cooper / Photostage: pp.181, 184, 185, 186, 187, 189

Cosprop Archive: p.218 (left)

Cosprop Archive / Archive Photography Paul Bulley: pp.14 (above), 16, 18, 26, 27, 46, 50, 52, 61 (above and below), 73, 74 (left), 76, 128, 146 (left and right), 149, 154, 188, 204, 211

Cosprop Archive / Archive Photography Paul Bulley / Courtesy of Dan Ashworth: p.169 (below)

Cosprop Archive / Archive Photography Paul Bulley / Reproduced with the kind permission of Hugh Bonneville: p.21 (middle left)

Cosprop Archive / Archive Photography Paul Bulley / Sean Connery: p.21 (top right)

Cosprop Archive / Archive Photography Paul Bulley / Reproduced with the kind permission of Mackenzie Crook, Jack Davenport, Johnny Depp, Tom Hollander, Kevin McNally: p.19

Cosprop Archive / Archive Photography Paul Bulley / Tom Cruise: p.21 (top left)

Cosprop Archive / Archive Photography Paul Bulley / Jennifer Ehle: p.96

Cosprop Archive / Archive Photography Paul Bulley / Reproduced with the kind permission of Ralph Fiennes: p.21 (bottom right)

Cosprop Archive / Archive Photography Paul Bulley / Estate of Albert Finney: p.21 (bottom left)

Cosprop Archive / Archive Photography Paul Bulley / Seth Gilliam: p.82

Cosprop Archive / Archive Photography Paul Bulley / Estate of Robert Hardy: p.15

Cosprop Archive / Archive Photography Paul Bulley / Suranne Jones: p.172 (right)

Cosprop Archive / Archive Photography Paul Bulley / Courtesy of Janet Patterson and Jill Harbutt: p.42 (left and right)

Cosprop Archive / Archive Photography Paul Bulley / © Radio Times: p.168

Cosprop Archive / Archive Photography Paul Bulley / Estate of Christopher Reeve: p.21 (middle right)

Cosprop Archive / Archive Photography Paul Bulley / Courtesy of Jane Robinson: p.152

Cosprop Archive / Archive Photography Paul Bulley / Reproduced with the kind permission of Toby Stephens: p.19

Cosprop Archive / Photograph courtesy Christine Hill: p.12

Cosprop Archive / Lindy Hemming: p.48

Cosprop Collection / Photography Jon Stokes: front cover, pp.4, 22, 31, 33, 35, 39, 43, 44, 45 (right), 53, 54, 59, 62, 63, 70, 71, 78, 79, 84, 85, 86, 93, 99, 116, 119, 124, 142, 147, 171, 178, 190, 196, 197, 203, 220

The Devonshire Collections, Chatsworth Reproduced by permission of Chatsworth Settlement Trustees / Bridgeman Images: p.207

Entertainment Pictures / Alamy Stock Photo: pp. 200, 209

Everett Collection Inc. / Alamy Stock Photo: pp.37, 38, 88, 157, 160–161, 169 (above), 202

FlixPix / Alamy Stock Photo: p.205

Fondazione Teatro La Fenice: p.183

ITV / Shutterstock: p.155

Courtesy of Joanna Johnston: pp.30 (left and right), 32

Kerry Taylor Auction Ltd: 233, 239

Kerry Taylor Auction Ltd / Photography George Mavrikos: p.167

LANDMARK MEDIA / Alamy Stock Photo: pp.92, 101 (above), 175, 192, 215 (above and below), 219, 221

Lookout Point Limited: p.170

Mauritshuis, The Hague: p.208

Maximum Film / Alamy Stock Photo: p.165

Maximum Film / Alamy Stock Photo: pp.40, 101 (below), 199 (below)

© Angelo Mellili / Roger-Viollet: p.182

Merchant Ivory / Kobal / Shutterstock: p.74 (right)

© Merchant Ivory; Photographs courtesy Sarah Quill: pp.2, 6, 7, 65, 67, 68

Merchant Ivory Productions / RGR Collection / Alamy Stock Photo: p.75

Moviestore Collection Ltd / Alamy Stock Photo: pp.47, 51, 72, 81 (above), 153, 194

CCo Paris Musées / Palais Galliera, musée de la Mode de la Ville de Paris: p.105 (left)

Photo 12 / Alamy Stock Photo: 24, 41, 56, 91 (below), 195 (below), 199 (above)

Pictorial Press Ltd / Alamy Stock Photo: pp.25, 36, 212–213

PictureLux / The Hollywood Archive / Alamy Stock Photo: pp.81 (below), 83

Courtesy of Tom Pye: p.172

RGR Collection / Alamy Stock Photo: p.58

TCD / Prod.DB / Alamy Stock Photo: p.201

Courtesy of the Sally Turner Archive: p.66

United Archives GmbH / Alamy Stock Photo: p.45 (left)

COSPROP
D. SCOTT

COSPROP
C. BLANCHETT

COSPROP
JOHNNY DEPP

COSPROP
H. LEDGER

COSPROP
SIENNA MILLER

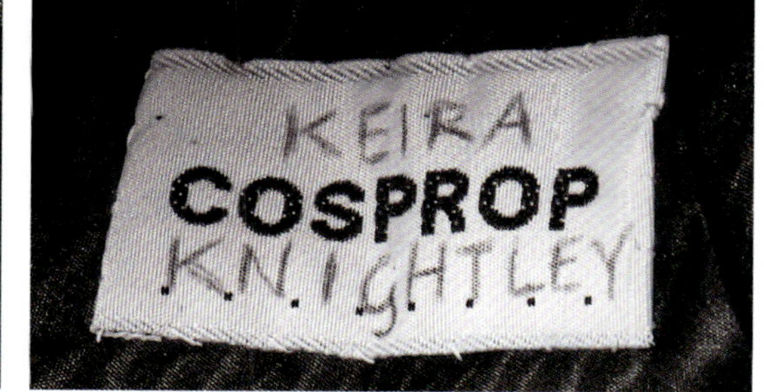
KEIRA
COSPROP
KNIGHTLEY

COSPROP
R. FIENNES

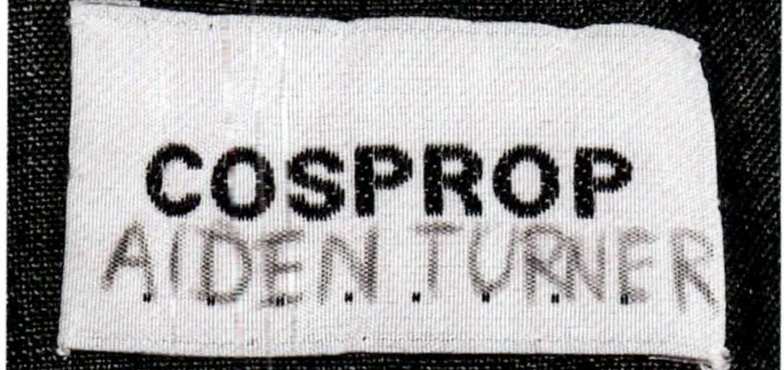
COSPROP
AIDEN TURNER

COSPROP
JULIE ANDREWS

COSPROP
G. PALTROW

COSPROP
COLIN FIRTH

ALAN RICKMAN
COSPROP
F.C.0.0.0.2.3A

MERYL STREEP
COSPROP
.HZ.0.0.0.0.1.

SCARLETT
COSPROP
JOHANSSON

CAREY
COSPROP
MULLIGAN

COSPROP
NICOLE KIDMAN

ELIZABETH
COSPROP
TAYLOR

COSPROP
R.ZELLWEGER

COSPROP
EMILY BLUNT

HELENA
COSPROP
BONHAM-CARTER

COSPROP
U.THURMAN

Index

Page numbers in *italic* refer to the illustrations

ABC Television 145
Abigail's Party 48
Academy Awards *see* Oscars
Acheson, James 16, 38, *38–9*, 145, 150
Ackland, Joss 180, 181
Addy, Mark 164
Addy, Wesley 58
Adley, Ian 89
Adrian 89, 145
After October 229
Agatha Christie's Poirot 20, 155, *155*
The Age of Innocence 82
Agertoft, Marianne 167
Alcott, Louisa May 214
Alexander, John 102
Alinari, Fratelli 64, 67
Altman, Robert 198
Amateur Dramatics Society 11
Amenábar, Alejandro 200
Amhurst, John Francis 140
Anderson, Gillian 113
Anderson, Kate 136
Anderson, Paul 174
Andrews, Anthony 152, 153
The Angel Project 229
Annis, Francesca 13, 150
Anonymous 16, 46
Antony and Cleopatra 13
Arbeid, Murray 36
Arestrup, Niels 182
Aris, Jonathan 48
Armstrong, Joe 170
Arnold, Janet 46, 148
Arrighi, Luciana 75, 77
Ashworth, Dan 128, 131, 168, *169*, 170–2, 221
Astor, Nancy 198
Atkins, Eileen 198
Attenborough, Sir Richard 140
ATV 150
Atwell, Hayley 207
Atwood, Colleen 193
Audley, Maxine 13, *13*
Austen, Jane 18, 87–105

Bacall, Lauren 69, *69*
Backstairs Billy 135, 189
BAFTAs 8, 16, 27, 28, 38, 40, 47, 58, 60, 69, 74, 77, 80, 90, 100, 135, 146, 150, 155, 163, 165, 198, 207, 219
Bailey, Jonathan 98
Bakst, Léon 118, *119*
Balaban, Bob 198
Bale, Christian 40
Ballets Russes 118, 140
Banton, Travis 145
Barbican Theatre, London 184, 229
Barbie 214
Barrett, Kym 193
Bartholomew Fair 12
Barton, Lucy 46
Batarda, Beatriz 157
Bates, Ralph 150
Bathurst, Otto 174
Baxter, Lynsey 34, 36
Bazalgette, Ed 167
BBC 8, 13, 15, 27, 28, 38, 46, 65, 89, 90, 94, 98, 102, 104, 113, 145, 146, 148, 150, 156, 157, 167, 174
Bean, Sean 164, 165, *165*
Beaton, Cecil 30
Beavan, Jenny 17, 19, 57, 58, 60, *61–2*, 64–9, *64–79*, 72–7, 80, *81*, 82–3, *82–5*, 90–2, *90–3*, 198, *218–19*, 218–19, 222
Beckham, David 174
Beckinsale, Kate 194, *194*, 196
Beethoven, Ludwig van 186
Begley, Kim 186
Bel Ami 148
Belfast Film Festival 15
Belgravia 157
Benioff, David 164
Bennett, Eliza 189
Bennett, Jill 26
Bennett, Joseph 75, 77
Benois, Alexandre 118
Bentley, James *200*
Bermans 36, 145, 148, 207
Bertolucci, Bernardo 38
Bielecka, Barbara 189
Biltmore Museum 140
Blake, Yvonne 5
Blakley, Claudie *199*
Blanchett, Cate 46–7, *47*, 221
Bleak House 113
Blethyn, Brenda 100
Blixen, Karen 37
Bloom, Claire 152
Bloom, Orlando 204
Bloomfield, Ann 145
Bloomfield, John 145, 148–50
Blundell, Christine 48, 49
La Bohème 229
Boldini, Giovanni 194
Bolger, Jordan 174
Bolt, Ben 158
Bombay Talkie 57
Bonham Carter, Helena 1, 2, 17, 45, *45*, *56*, 57, 64, *68*, 69, *71*, 75, 82, 117, 125
Bonneville, Hugh *21*, 158, 163, *163*
Booker Prize 80
The Bostonians *21*, 60, *61–3*, 117, 140, 229
Bostridge, Ian 184, 189
Boudoir Dolls 229
Bowles, Peter 168
Braganza, Ross 100, 111, 118, 125, 172, 174
Branagh, Kenneth 201, *201*
Brandauer, Klaus Maria 37
Bravo, Lucas 218
Brazil 38
Brideshead Revisited 113, 152–3, *152–3*
The Bridge of San Luis Rey 5
Bridgerton 9, 98
The Bright Foundation 9, 118, 222, 223
Bright Foundation Museum and Barn Theatre, Hastings 118
Bristol Old Vic Theatre School 222
British Film Institute 140, 193
British Film Year 140
The British Film Year Roadshow (1985) 140
British Heritage Cinema 117
British Independent Film Awards 210
Britten, Benjamin 184, 189
Broadbent, Jim 48
Brody, Adrien 174
Brook, Peter 182
Brooker, Daphne 12, 180
Brooklyn Academy of Music, New York 182
Brown, Alan 185
Buckle, Richard 140
Buckmiller, Julia 104
Bullmore, Amelia 170
Burden, Howard 167
Burgess-Jones, Raphaelle 189
Burke, Emma 98, 125, 128, 131, 168, 210, 218–19
Burrill, Timothy 30
Burrowes, Edward 184, *184*
Burton, Tim 193
Buxton, Susannah 117, 145, 156, *156*, 158–63, 167
Byrne, Alexandra 16, 46–7, *47*, 89, 104, *105*, 131

Cadbury family 117
Caird, John 181
Callow, Simon 64, *65*, 82
Campion, Jane 40
Canby, Vincent 27
Cannes Film Festival 28, 58
Canonero, Milena 37
Cards on the Table 155
Carmichael, Laura 158
Carmilla 216, *217*, 229
Carradine, Keith 28–9, *29*
Cartlidge, Katrin *49*
Casino Royale 48
Carter, Jim 158
Caswell, Amy 96
Caswell, Ruth 98
Caulfield, Alexandra 174
Chadwick, Justin 208
Chalamet, Timothée 214
Chancellor, Anna 156
Chanel, Coco 12, 118
Channel 4 Television 181
Chaplin, Charlie 140
The Charge of the Light Brigade 15, 26–7, *26–7*
Charlotte Gray 221
Cherry, Helen 26
The Cherry Orchard 182, *182*
Chichester Festival Theatre 12, 19, 180, 229
Chips with Everything 13
Chirico, Giorgio de 118
Christie, Agatha 155
Christie, Julie 50
Christl, Lisy 16
A Christmas Carol 12
Claflin, Sam 210
Clapton, Michele 16, 89, 102–3, *102–3*, 125, 164–5, *164–5*, 193
Clarissa 113
Clark, Annalise 133
Clarke, Emilia 164
Clay, Jim 52
Cleator, Pippa 128
Clemency 229
Clift, Montgomery 12
Close, Glenn 38, 60
Cocteau, Jean 118
Colchester Repertory Theatre 13

Cole, Finn 174
Cole, Joe 174
Coleman, Jenna 168, *168–9*
Coleman-Wright, Peter 189
Collie, Stephanie 174
Collin, Dinah 94–6, *95–9*, 98, 100, 104, 145, 150, 210, *211*
Collin, John 30
Columbus, Chris 201
Comedie Francaise Productions 229
A Company of Wolves 140
Condo, Nucci 183
Connery, Sean *21*
Cook, Ron 48, *49*
Cooper, Dominic 102, 207
Corduner, Allan 48, *49*
Costen, Peter 133
Coster-Waldau, Nikolaj 164
Costume 15
Costume Design 229
Costume Designers Guild Awards 103, 165
Costumi d'Arte 28
Courtenay, Margaret 148
Cox, Alan 185
Cranford 113
Cripps, Andrea 48
Cripplegate Theatre, London 11
Crook, Mackenzie *21*
Crosbie, Annette 12, 150, 180
Crossman, David 48, *220*, 221
Crowley, Bob 188, *188*
Cruise, Tom *21*
Curran, Paul 150
Curtis, Hannah 133
Cyrano de Bergerac 187, *187*, 229

Dance, Charles 198
Dangerous Liaisons 38, *38–9*, 113, 140
Daniel Deronda 21
Davenport, Jack 21
David, Eleanor 48, *48*, *49*
David, Joanna 117, 146
Davies, Andrew 94, 102, 156
Davies, John 146
Davies, Howard 187, 229
Davies, Rupert 146
Day-Lewis, Daniel 64, 67
de Broë-Ferguson-Hanbury, Susie 17, 18
de Gaye, Phoebe 150, 157, *157*
De Nobili, Lila 25, 26, 50, 193
de Wilde, Autumn 104
Dear Octopus 11
Death by Lightning 175
Death in Venice 18, 25, 69, 189, *189*
Death on the Nile 155, 198
The Deceivers 229
The Deep Blue Sea 181
DeHaan, Dane 208
Demontrond, Thaïs 110, 125, 128, 131, 221
Denby-Ashe, Daniela 113
Dench, Judi 6, *6*, 7, 64, 65, 68, 168, 208
Deneuve, Catherine 200
Depp, Johnny 17, 21, 193, 204–5, *205*
Dern, Laura 214
Diaghilev, Sergei 118
Diana, Princess of Wales 36, 229
Dibb, Saul 207
Dickens, Charles 8, 18
Dickman, Cyril 80
Dietrich, Marlene 174
Dinesen, Isak 37
Dinklage, Peter 164, *164*, 165
Dior, Christian 12, 180, 181, 218–19
Dobie, Alan 146
Dockery, Michelle 113, 158, *158*, 162, *162*
Doctor Who 38, 150
Doctor Zhivago 50
Doran, Lindsay 90
Down, Angela 146
Downie, Penny 185
Downton Abbey 8, 17, 118, 135, 140, *144*, 148, 157, 158–63, *159–63*, 165, 167, 198
Doyle, Christopher 202
Dracula 15
Du Maurier, Daphne 210
The Duchess 117, 135, *206–7*, 207
The Duellists 28, *28–9*, 221
Durran, Jacqueline 15, 48, 100, *101*, 117, 124–5, 212–13, *212–13*, 214, *215*

Easy Virtue 229
Ebbutt, Rosalind 104, 158, 168, *168–9*
Eccleston, Christopher 46, 200
Edward the Seventh 150
Ehle, Jennifer 94, 96, *96*, *97*, *99*
Eichhorn, Lisa 58
Elizabeth 16, 46–7, *46–7*, 140
Elizabeth, The Queen Mother 189
Elizabeth II, Queen 80
Elizabeth R 145
Ellacott, Joan 15, 94, 157
Elliott, Denholm 64, *65*
Ellis, Robin 58, *58*, 148, 150, 167
Emma (2020) 98, 104, *105*, 131
EMMYs 98, 163, 165
An Enemy of the People 185, *185*, 229
English National Opera 189
Essex, David 180
Eugene Onegin 183, *183*, 229
The Europeans 19, 57, 58, *58–9*, 60
Evita (1978) 180–1
Evita (1996) 148, 181, 181
Evrard, Claude 182

Fabian, Anthony 218
Fairley, Michelle 164
Fallon, Julia 1[illegible]3
Far and Away 21
Farthing, Jack 167
Fashion in Film (2004–7) 140
Fashion Museum Bath 13, 89, 94, 98, 104, 210
Fashionable Romance, Biltmore Estate (2014) 140
The Fat Lady 229
Les Fausses Confidences 229
Fellowes, Julian 158, 198
Fidelio 186, *186*, 229
Fiennes, Joseph 26
Fiennes, Martha 50–2, 183
Fiennes, Ralph 21, 50–2, *50*, *52*, 117, 202, 207
Findlay, Jessica Brown 158, *158*
Fingersmith 156
Finney, Albert 21, 26, 155, 180
Firbank, Heather 158
Firth, Colin 17, 94, 96–8, *97*
Firth, Peter 30
Firth, Tazeena 180, *181*
Flanagan, Fionnula 200
Fleet, James 90
Fleming, Catherine 168
Flynn, Johnny 98, 104
Foale, Marion 11
Foley, Sage 117–18
Fonteyn, Dame Margot 117
Fordham, Alex 102
Forster, E.M. 8, 64, 67, 72, 75
The Forsyte Saga (1967) 15, 145, 146, 153, 157, 174
The Forsyte Sage (2002–3) 157, *157*, 174
Foster, Jodie 60
Four Weddings and a Funeral 48
Fowles, John 34
Fox, Edward 13, 18, 28
Fox, James 80
Fox's 13
Francis, Jan 15
Fraser, Hugh 155
Fraser-Paye, Robin 145, 155
Frears, Stephen 38
The French Lieutenant's Woman 34–6, *34–6*, 140
From Hell 193
Furtwangler, Wilhelm 19

Gainsborough, Thomas 207, *207*
Gainsborough Studios 15
Galer, Andrea 155
Galsworthy, John 157
Gambon, Michael 198
Game of Thrones 16, 163, 164–5, *164–5*
Garai, Romola 104
Garbo, Greta 202
Garlick, Chris 8–9, 15, 109–10, 116, 126
The Gathering Storm 21
Gentleman Jack 117, 170–3, *170–3*
Gerwig, Greta 214
Gielgud, John 18, 26, 152
Gilbert and Sullivan 48
Gillespie, Chris 185
Gilliam, Seth 82, *82*
Gilliam, Terry 38
Givenchy 12
Gladiator 204
Glen, Iain 164, 165, 210
Glyndebourne Festival Opera 186, 229
Goddard, Andy 158
Godfrey, Patrick 65
The Golden Bowl 193, 194, *194–7*, 229
Goldeneye 48
Golden Globes 77
Golden Satellite Awards 47, 202
Goncharova, Natalia 118
Goodall, Kat 134–5
Goodman, John 188
Goodwin, Daisy 168

Gosford Park 158, 198, *199*
Goth, Mia 104
Goya Awards 200
Graham, Winston 148
Graham-Hall, John *189*
Grainger, Holliday 208, 210
Granada 150
The Grand 157
Grande, Sonia 200, *200*
Grant, Hugh 72, *72*, 80, 90
Grant, Richard E. 198
Graves, Rupert 64, 72, 74, 82, 157
Great Expectations 13, *13*, 145
Greek National Opera 189

Griffiths, Benjamin Paul 189
Griffiths, Nicolina 123
Grint, Rupert 201, *201*
Guard, Christopher *13*

Hagen, Reinhard 186
Hale, Elvi 148
Hall, Dinny 96
Hals, Frans 208, *208*
Hammond, Joyce 13
Hampshire, Susan 148, 181
The Happiest Days of Your Life 13
Harbutt, Jill 32, 40, 76, 90, 104, 128, 152, 175, 194, 202, 207, 208
Harden, Marcia Gay 188
Harden, Rosemary 89
Harding, Sarah 170
Hardy, Richard *15*
Hardy, Susan 36, 37, 38, 46, 70, 165, 200, 204
Hardy, Tom 174
Harker, Susannah 94
Harper, Tom 174
Harpers & Queen 153
Harington, Kit 164
Harris, Emily 216
Harris, Richard 201
Harrison, Rosina 198
Harry Potter and the Chamber of Secrets 201, *201*
Hart, Avril 94
Hart, Miranda 104
Harwood, Ronald 19
Hawes, Keeley 156, *156*
Head, Edith 145
Headey, Lena 164
Heat and Dust 64, 113
Hello Dolly! 189
Hemming, Carol 82, 83, 202
Hemming, Lindy 48–9, *48–9*, 201, 222
Hemmings, David 26
Henderson, Joyce 189
Henderson, Shirley 48
Henry V 13
Henschel, Jane *184*
Henson, Basil 147
Heritage Lottery 116
Hershey, Barbara 40, 42
Hill, Christine *12*, 15, 140
Hitchcock, Alfred 140
Hoffman, Philip Seymour 188
Holdich, Charlotte 155
Holland, Mark 186
Hollander, Tom *21*
Hollywood 15, 25, 60, 89, 145, 155, 202 , 214
Hollywood Costume, London (2012) 140
Holm, Ian 193
Home Box Office (HBO) 156, 175
Homer, Winslow 214
Hooch, Pieter de 208
Hopkins, Alan 75–6, 90, 128, 150
Hopkins, Anthony 75, 80, *81*, 146
Hopkins, Vanessa 75–6, 90, 128, 145, 150
The Hopkins Collection 76, 128, 145, 150
Hornchurch Repertory Theatre 13, 180
The House of Eliott 157
A House Taken Over 229
Howard, Trevor 26
Howards End 15, 17, 57, 75–7, *75–9*, 90, 229
Howells, Jane 12, 180
Hoyle, Winifred 11

Hudson, June 148
Hughes, Raymond 145, 148, *149*
Hughes, Tom 168, *168–9*
Huppert, Isabelle 218
Huston, Anjelica 194, *195*, *197*
Hvorostovsky, Dmitri 183, *183*

Ibsen, Henrik 185, 187
Indiana Jones and The Temple of Doom 139
Ingafield, Janet 52
Ingres, Jean-Auguste- Dominique 28
Ireland, Jenny 98, 117, 136, 139
Irons, Jeremy 34, 36, 152, *153*
Ishiguro, Kazuo 80, 202
ITV 8, 148, 150, 152, 157, 167, 168, 174
Ivory, James 57, 194, 202
see also Merchant Ivory

Jackson, Glenda 46, 47
Jackson, Philip 155
Jackson, Sheila 148
Jacobi, Sir Derek 198
James, Adam 157
James, Geraldine 118
James, Henry 40, 57, 58, 60, 64, 184, 193
Jameson, Louise 150
Jane Eyre 12, 180
Jeeves and Wooster 155
Jefferson in Paris 82–3, *82–5*, 229
Jhabvala, Ruth Prawer 57, 58, 60, 64, 67, 75, 77
John Bright Collection 116–17, 170, *171*
Johnston, Joanna 30, 32, 222
Jones, Gemma 170
Jones, Suranne 117, 170–3, *170*, *173*
Joseph Papp Theater, New York 188

Kalman, Jean 189
Kapur, Shekhar 46–7
Karan, Donna 37
Keast, James 168, *168–9*
Keitel, Harvey 28–9, *29*
Kelly, Brian 158
Kempson, Rachel 26
Kendall, Jo 15
Kidman, Nicole 40, *40–1*, *43*, 139, 200, *200*
Kinnear, Rory 212
Kinski, Nastassja *24*, 30, *31–3*
Kirby, Vanessa 221
Kline, Kevin 188, *188*
Kloos, Barbara 117
Knapp, Nancy 16, 40, 126, 128, 131, 169, 180
Knight, Gillian 183
Knightley, Keira 100, 117, 135, 204, *206*, 207
Knode, Charles 145, 146, *146–7*
Koenraads, May *16*
Kors, Michael 37
Kronig, Barbara 155
Kurtz, Swoosie 38, *38*

La Monnaie, Brussels 189
La Scala, Milan 189
Lady Windermere's Fan 180, 229
Langley Moore, Doris 12, 117, 157
Langton, Simon 94
The Last Emperor 38
The Last September 229
Latham, Philip 148
Lauren, Ralph 37
Laurie, Hugh 155

Law, Jane 219
Lawley, Kevin 18
Lawson, Leigh 30
Le Fanu, Sheridan 216
Le Touzel, Sylvestra 89
Leach, Rosemary 64
The League of Extraordinary Gentlemen 21
Lean, David 60
Leavesden Studios 193, 201
Lee, Ang 90, 229
Leigh, Mike 48, 100, 212
Leigh, Vivien 140
The Leopard 25, *25*
Lewis, Damian 157
Lewis, Sharon 155
Lhomme, Pierre 74
Liddall, Stacey 120, 123
The Life and Adventures of Nicholas Nickleby 45, 181, 185
Lillie 150
Limgnau, Devrin 216, *216*
Linbury Studio, Royal Opera House, London 229
Lincoln Center Festival, New York 229
Lindsay-Hogg, Michael 152
Little, Ros 167
Little Women *192*, 214, *215*
Lodwick, Keith *17*
Logan, Phyllis 158
London College of Fashion 222
London International Festival of Theatre 229
London Screen Academy 222
Lonsdale, Michael 82
Look Back in Anger 26
Lothian, David 132
Love's Labour's Lost 12
Lowe, Penny 148
Ludwig 25
Luther 26, 180
LWT (London Weekend Television) 150

Maberly, Polly 94, *99*
McArthur, Murray 185
McCall, Caroline 158
McCarthy, Tom 164
McCormack, Daryl 174
McCosh, Alison 174
McCrory, Helen 174, *175*
Macfadyen, Matthew 100, *101*
McGovern, Elizabeth 157, 158
McGregor, William 167
McKee, Gina 157, *157*
McKellen, Ian 185
McKern, Leo 34
McNally, Kevin *21*
McNeice, Ian 221
McRae, Hilton 34
McTeer, Janet 102
Madonna 148, 180
The Magnificent Ambersons 229
Makovsky, Judianna 201
Malcolm, Derek 52
Malkovich, John 38, 40, 42, 139
Mann, Alakina *200*
Mann, Thomas 189
Mansfield Park 89
Manville, Lesley 48, 218–19, *218–19*
Marchand, Nancy 60, *63*
Margiono, Charlotte 186

Marsh, Joanna 117
Martell, Gillian 180
Martin, George R.R. 164
Mary, Queen 118
Massey, Anna 89, 148
Massey, Daniel 19
Mattock, Linda 155
Maurice 57, 72–4, *72–4*, 229
May, Jodhi 156
Mazzaria, Lucia 183, *183*
The Meaning of Life 38
Menaul, Christopher 157
Menzies, Tobias 216
Merchant, Ismail 57, 202
Merchant Ivory 8, 16, 19, 55–85, 193, 202
Mesguich, Daniel 82, 85
Messel, Oliver 30
MGM 89, 98
Michell, Helena 72
Michell, Roger 210
The Mikado 48
Miles, Ben 157, *157*
Miles, Stephen 198
Milne, Lisa 186
Minerva Theatre, Chichester 229
Mirren, Helen 13, 198
Mishima, Yukio 229
Miss Potter 32
Missoni 36
Mr. Punch's Nightmare 229
Mrs Brown 168
Mrs Dalloway 157
Mrs. Harris Goes to Paris 218–19, *218–19*
Moggach, Deborah 100, 208
Mogil, Eddie 19, 36
Mollo, John 26
Monkley, Hannah 110, 111–13, 125
A Month in the Country 229
Monty Python 38
Moon Princess 229
Moorcroft, Judy 58, *58–9*, 60, 117, 140
Moore, David 157
Morahan, Hattie 102, *103*
Moran, Pauline 155
Morrissey, David 102
Mortimer, John 153
The Mountains of the Moon 229
Mugan, Lorna Marie 174
Mugler, Thierry 37
Murder on the Orient Express 155, 198
Murphy, Cillian 17, 174
Museum of the Moving Image, London 140
My Beautiful Laundrette 48
My Cousin Rachel 210, *211*
Myers, Ruth 104

Napier, John 185
Napier, Sheena 155
Napoleon *220*, 221
Nathan's 26, 145, 148
National Portrait Gallery, London 194
National Society of Film Critics 60
National Theatre, London 180, 185, 187, 229
National Youth Theatre 13
Natwick, Mildred 38, *39*
Neofitou, Andreane 181
Netflix 175, 193
Neville, John 12
New York Shakespeare Festival 188
New York Times 27, 60, 77, 82
Newton, Thandiwe 82
Nicol, Lesley 158, *159–60*
Nichols, Mike 188
Nighy, Bill 104
Nolte, Nick 82, *83*, 194
Norris, Luke 167
North and South 113
Northam, Jeremy 194, *195*, 198
Nunn, Trevor 45, 181, 185, 229

Obolensky, Chloé 50–2, *50–3*, 182, *182*, 183, *183*, 189, *189*, 193
O'Brien, Timothy 180, *181*
The Observer Film Exhibition, London (1956) 140
O'Connell, Jack 208
O'Connor, Michael 48, 49, 110, 111, 117, 135, *206–7*, 207, 208–9, *209*
Old Vic Theatre, London 229
Oldham Repertory Theatre 12, 180
Olivier, Laurence 12, 152
Oman, Julia Trevelyan 26
The Onedin Line 148
Onegin 21, 50–2, *50–3*, 117, 140, 183
Opera Now magazine 183
Opie, Alan 185
The Orchid House 113
Oscars (Academy Awards) 8, 16, *16*, 26, 30, 32, 38, 47, 48, 49, 58, 60, 69, *69*, 74, 75, 77, 78, 80, 90, 104, 135, 198, 207, 214, 219
The Other Boleyn Girl 16
The Others 200, *200*
Out of Africa 37, *37*, 140
Owen, Clive 198
Owen, Elizabeth 117

Paige, Elaine 180–1, *181*
Pains of Youth 229
The Pallisers 148, *149*, 181
Paltrow, Gwyneth 104
Parry, Natasha 182, *182*
A Passage to India 60, 64, 140
Patterson, Janet 40–2, 139
PBS 174
Peake, Maxine 212
Peaky Blinders 9, 17, 135, 140, 174–5, *175–7*
Pentax Gallery, London 15
People's History Museum, Manchester 212
Percival, Brian 158
Perrot, Jennifer 170
Persuasion 89, 104
Perth International Arts Festival 229
Peruzzi 82, 96
Peruzzi, Ruggero 28
Peterloo 212, *212–13*
Pfeiffer, Michelle 38
Phillippe, Ryan 198, *199*
Phillips, Sian 65
Phoenix, Joaquin 221, *221*
The Piano 40
Picasso, Pablo 18
Piccoli, Michel 82, *82*
Pierce, William 67
Pierce-Roberts, Tony 75
Pignotti, Angelo 28
Pike, Rosamund 100
Pinewood Studios 193
Pinter, Harold 19
Pirates of the Caribbean: The Curse of the Black Pearl 17, 21, 204, *204–5*
The Players' Theatre, London 12, 180
Playhouse Theatre, London 229
Plowright, Joan 12
Poirot, Paul 118
Polanski, Roman 30
Poldark 135, 140, 148–50, *151*, *166–7*, 167
Pollack, Sydney 37
Portman, Natalie 188
The Portrait of a Lady 16, 40–2, *40–3*, 139, 140
Potter, Madeleine 60, 202
Powell, Anthony 13, 30–2, *30–1*, 69, 116, 139, 146, 193
Powell, Sandy 16
Pre-Raphaelites 34
Price, Claire 187
Pride and Prejudice (1940) 89
Pride and Prejudice (1995) 17, 90, 94–8, *95–9*, 102, 104
Pride & Prejudice (2005) 100, *101*
Princess Ida 48
Prins, Christopher 15, *15*, 18–20, *18*, *19*, 21, 36, 42, 48, 49, 52, 58, 60, 65, 72, 80, 82, 96–8, 100, 150, 156, 183, 193, 201, 204
Proud, Trefor 48, 49
Pugh, Florence 214
Puliti, Elena 67
The Puppet Maker *14*, 15, 229
Pushkin, Alexander 50, 183
Pye, Tom 170–3, *170–3*, 184, 189

The Queen's Theatre, Hornchurch 13, 180
Quick, Diana 28, 152, *153*
Quigley, Pearce 212

RADA 11
Radcliffe, Daniel 201, *201*
Radio Times 118, 168, *168*
Rae, Hannah 216
Rahim, Tahar *220–1*, 221
Raine, Jessica 216
Rand, Tom 17, 18–20, 28–9, *29*, 34, 36, 125, 135, 140, 189, 201, 221
Rattigan, Terence 64, 181
Rawlins, Christine 146
Ray, Stuart 12
Rea, Stephen 187, *187*
Redford, Robert 37, 60
Redgrave, Corin 157
Redgrave, Jemma 75, *77*
Redgrave, Vanessa 17, 26, 60, *61–2*, 75, 76, *77–8*, 117, 202
Reed, Heida 167
Reeve, Christopher *21*, 60, 80
Regent's Park Theatre, London 12, 180
Reilly, Kelly 100, *101*
Reisz, Karel 34, 181
The Remains of the Day 15, 57, 80, *81*, 229
Remick, Lee 58, *58–9*
Rhys, Paul 221
Richardson, Joely 26
Richardson, Natasha 26, 202, *202–3*
Richardson, Tony 15, 26–7
Rickman, Alan 90, *92*, 201
Robinson, Jane 152–3, *152–3*
Robinson, Timothy 186
Rodgers, Joan 184, *184*
Roeg, Nicolas 27
Ronan, Saoirse 214

A Room with a View 7, 8, *14*, *16*, 17, 57, 64–9, *64–71*, 72, 74, 140, 158, 183, 229
Root, Amanda 157
Rose, Penny 148, 180, 204, *204–5*
Rostand, Edmond 187
Royal Albert Hall, London 229
Royal Ballet 180
Royal Cornwall Museum 148
Royal Court Theatre, London 26, 180
Royal Opera House, London 180, 184, 229
Royal Shakespeare Company 38, 180, 181
Runacre, Jenny 28, *29*
Rundle, Sophie 170, *170*, 174
Rush, Geoffrey 46, 204
Russell, Ken 11, 27
Russell, Shirley 11, 116, 118

Saint Laurent, Yves 37
Sallis, Peter 148
Samuel's 13
Sandberg, Mathilde 36
Sands, Julian 64, *64*, 65
Sargent, John Singer 194
Sawalha, Julia *94*, 98
Sax, Geoffrey 156
Say Beau 15, 229
Scacchi, Greta 82–3, *83–4*, 113, 222
Scanlan, Eliza 214
Scarpa, David 221
Schéhérazade *119*
Schlesinger, John 152
Scorsese, Martin 82
Scott, Lil 32
Scott, Ridley 27, 28, 221
Scott Robbins, Anna Mary 158
Scott Thomas, Kristin 198, *199*
The Seagull 188, *188*
Sears Roebuck 198
Secret Army 15
Sense and Sensibility (1995) *15*, 89, *89*, 90–2, *90–3*, 98, 229
Sense and Sensibility (2008) 89, 102–3, *102–3*, 104
Serban, Andrei 183
The Servant of Two Masters 12
Shakespeare, William 45
Shakespeare Wallah 57
Shaw, Fiona 201
Shepperton Studios 193
Sherlock Holmes 193
Shicoff, Neil 183
The Shooting Party 140
Shoulder to Shoulder 65, 148
Siddig, Alexander 174
The Silver Tassie 229
Simmons, B.J. & Co. 11, 13
Sky 156
Sleepy Hollow 193
Smith, Dodie 11
Smith, Jane 18
Smith, Maggie 7, 17, 30, 64, 65, *68*, *70*, 109, 135, *144*, 158, 198, 201
Smith, Rae 189
The Sorceror 48
Somerville, Geraldine 198, *199*
Southwest Essex Technical College and School of Art 11–12, 180
Spall, Timothy 48
Spielberg, Steven 139
The Stage magazine *12*
Starstruck in the Cathedral, Worcester (2009) 140
Staunton, Imelda 45, 189
Steadman, Alison 48, 94, *94*
Steidelman, Frances 117
Stephens, Toby 45, 50
Stevens, Dan 102, 158
Stewart, Eve 48
Stirling, Rachael 156, *156*
Storry, Malcolm 187
Streep, Meryl 34–6, *34–6*, 37, *37*, 188, *188*, *192*, 214, *215*
Strong, James 158
Stubbs, Imogen 45, *45*
Sturridge, Charles 82, 152
Suchet, David 20, 155, *155*
Sutherland, Donald 100
Swailes, Katharine 90, 92, *92*
Swan Theatre, Worcester 13
Sweeney Todd 193
Swift, David 146

Taking Sides 19
A Taste of Honey 26
Tatler 198
Taylor-Joy, Anya 104, *105*
Tchaikovsky, Pyotr Ilych 183
Teatro di Genova 229
Teatro La Fenice, Venice 183, 229
Tess *24*, 30–2, *30–3*, 140
Thackeray, William Makepeace 18
The Sorceror 48
Theatre du Chatelet, Paris 186, 229
Theatre Royal Stratford East 12
Theatre Workshop 12
Theatrical Ladies' Guild 118
Thomas, Diana 40, 128
Thompson, Emma 75, 76–7, 79, 80, *81*, 90, *91*
Thomson, Sue (Susi) 155
Three Sisters 229
Thurman, Uma 38, 194, *195*
Tierney, Vivien 184
Time Bandits 38
Tipping the Velvet 156, *156*
Tiramani, Jenny 117
Tissot, James 194
Tom Jones 26
Tomlinson, Eleanor 167
Topsy-Turvy 48–9, *48–9*
Tosi, Piero 18, 25, *25*
Travels with My Aunt 30
Trollope, Anthony 18
Troubridge, Lady 198
Tuffin, Sally 11
Tulip Fever 208, *208–9*
Turandot 189
The Turn of the Screw 184, *184*, 189, 229
Turner, Aidan 135, *166*, 167
Turner, Sally 40, 42, 65, 67, 194, 219
Turner, Sophie 164
Twelfth Night *44–5*, 45, 185, 229
Tyler, Liv 50, 52, *51–3*

Underwater Film 229
Upstairs, Downstairs 148, 152, 158
Ustinov, Peter 155

Van Dyck, Anthony 208
Vanderbilt, Cornelia 140, *141*, 229
Vanderbilt family 140
Varla, Zubin 187
Verbinski, Gore 204
Vermeer, Johannes 208
Victoria 117, 168–9, *168–9*
Victoria and Albert Museum, London 17, 48, 94, 110, 117, 140, 158
Vikander, Alicia 208, *209*
Visconti, Luchino 18, 25, 189
Vogue 168, 198

Wainwright, Sally 170
Wakefield, Charity 102, *103*
Walken, Christopher 188
Walker, David 12, 15, 26–7, *26–7*, 50, 146, 182, 193
Wallace, Dorothea 148
Walldén, Mia 222
Waller, Elizabeth 15, 145, 148, 150, 155
Waltham Forest College 11
Waltz, Christoph 208
Wanamaker, Zoë 155
War and Peace 146, *146–7*
Warner, David 34
Warner, Deborah 184, 186, 189
Warner Bros. 201
Waters, Sarah 156
Watson, Emily 198
Watson, Emma 201, 214
Waugh, Norah 168
Wedge, James 12
Weiss, D.B. 164
Weisz, Rachel 210, *210*
West, Samuel 75, *77*
West, Timothy 150, 170
Wharton, Edith 82
Whelan, Gemma 170
Where Angels Fear to Tread 82
The White Countess 19, 202, *202–3*, 229
White Fang 229
Whitelaw, Billie 72
Whitrow, Benjamin 94, *97*
Wickham, Saskia 113
Wicks, Margaret 117
Wilby, James 72, *72*, *74*, 75, *77*
Wilkinson, Michael 131, 175
Wilson, Andy 157
Wilton, Penelope 34, 135, 158, 181, 189
Wimbledon School of Art 222
Wimbush, Mary 150
Wing, Mary 36, 180–1
Winslet, Kate *88*, 90–2, *91–3*
Wise, Greg *88*, 90, *91*, 98, 216
Woad, Heather 128
A Woman of No Importance 11
The Women 229
Woodrow, Pippa 184
Woodvine, John 185, *185*
Woodward, Tim 58
Wright, Joe 98, 100
Wright, George *18*

Yates, Janty 204, *220*, 221, *221*

Zeffirelli, Franco 26
Zimmermann, Margarita 183
Zinkeisen, Doris 26, 146
Zola, Emile 187

COSPROP
AMY ADAMS

COSPROP
KATE WINSLET

COSPROP
EMMA THOMPSON

V. REDGRAVE
COSPROP

COSPROP
D. RADCLIFFE

COSPROP
E. HALL

EVITA
COSPROP
MADONNA

MAGGIE SMITH
COSPROP
KL00161

HUGH
COSPROP
BONNEVILLE

COSPROP
MARION COTILLARD

COSPROP
DAN STEVENS

SHIRLEY
COSPROP
MACLAINE

PENELOPE
COSPROP
WILTON

ELIZABETH
COSPROP
McGOVERN

LILY JAMES
COSPROP
KN00558

COSPROP
DANIEL CRAIG

COSPROP
E. REDMAYNE

COSPROP
M. ROBBIE

HELEN
COSPROP
MC CRORY

COSPROP
TOM HARDY

COSPROP
JUDI DENCH

First published by Cosprop
469 - 475 Holloway Road
London N7 6LE

Distributed by Yale University Press
302 Temple Street, P.O. Box 209040, New Haven CT 06520-9040
47 Bedford Square, London WC1B 3DP
yalebooks.com | yalebooks.co.uk

To accompany the exhibition
Costume Couture: 60 Years of Cosprop
at the Fashion and Textiles Museum, London
26 September 2025–8 March 2026

ISBN 978-1-3999-9400-2
Library of Congress Control Number: 2025933349
A catalogue record for this book is available from the British Library.
Authorized Representative in the EU: Easy Access System Europe, Mustamäe tee 50, 10621 Tallinn, Estonia, gpsr.requests@easproject.com

10 9 8 7 6 5 4 3 2 1
2027 2026 2025

Facilitated and managed at Cosprop by Christopher Garlick and Christine Hill

Project management and editorial by Anjali Bulley
Design by Lizzie Ballantyne
Picture research by Axelle Russo-Heath
Production by Marina Asenjo, BookLabs
Photography by Paul Bulley and Jon Stokes

All proceeds from this book go to The Bright Foundation

Printed in China

Front cover: Concept by John Bright
Costume worn by Maggie Verver (Kate Beckinsale) in *The Golden Bowl* (2000)
Photograph by Jon Stokes

Back cover: Pattens, ice skates with boots attached, hat with candles worn by Stellan Skarsgärd in *Goya's Ghosts* (2006; Costume Designer Yvonne Blake), hat worn by Drosos Skotis in *The Durrells* (2016–10; Costume Designer Charlotte Holdich)
Photograph by Paul Bulley

Endpapers: Silk brocade, designed by Anna-Maria Garthwaite, 1740s. Museum Collection, Cosprop

page 2: Lucy Honeychurch (Helena Bonham Carter) in *A Room with a View* (1985)

page 5: Costume for *The Bridge of San Luis Rey* (2004; Costume Designer Yvonne Blake)